Praise for Emotional S

"What Peter Dunne's *Emotional Structure* achie
many other scriptwriting manuals–not to mention scr
sis of the emotional and the intellectual, the practical and the creative,
leading, most importantly, to that perfect synthesis of what you want to say
and what others want to see."

—Paula Quigley, head of the Masters and Doctoral Programs in
Film Studies at Trinity College Dublin, Ireland

"Peter Dunne's *Emotional Structure* is a must read. He not only delivers
clear explanations of the key elements of the craft of screenwriting but he uses
the same gentle care that supports the title of the book to teach writers how
story is the emotional needs of characters."

—Steve Duncan, co-creator of *Tour of Duty*; screenwriter and
producer of *A Man Called Hawk* and *The Court-Martial of Jackie
Robinson*

"It's as if Peter Dunne is writing this book by flashlight, at your elbow
on a very dark night, whispering a steady stream of the most necessary,
seldom-mentioned cautions, directions, encouragements, as he accompanies
you through that dangerous tanglewood he knows so well, the writing of a
screenplay. Your heart grows quiet as you go along together, dark shadows
begin to assume familiar shapes and you know you can do what he asks."

—Stewart Stern, *Rebel Without A Cause, The Ugly American, Rachel,
Rachel, Summer Wishes, Winter Dreams,* and *Sybil*

"All too often you see 'The last book you will ever need to read on writing.'
Peter Dunne's book is the first book all aspiring writers should read. I will use this
information for the rest of my career as a professor and as a director."

—Chip Chalmers, Director's Guild of America's Filmmaker in
Residence for the College of Motion Picture, Television, and Record-
ing Arts, Florida State University

"For all of us who have doubts that we can really write well, Peter
Dunne provides a smart, very readable, hands-on guidebook to success. He
offers a wealth of Practical Wisdom. Every writer–whether novice or seasoned
pro–can gain truly important insights from Mr. Dunne."

—Kenneth Johnson, Emmy Award winning director/writer/producer,
The Bionic Woman, The Incredible Hulk, The Original Mini-Series *V, Alien
Nation, Short Circuit 2,* and *Steel*

EMOTIONAL STRUCTURE

EMOTIONAL STRUCTURE

CREATING THE STORY BENEATH THE PLOT

—A GUIDE FOR— SCREENWRITERS

PETER DUNNE

Fresno, California

Published by Quill Driver Books
an imprint of Linden Publishing
2006 S. Mary, Fresno, CA 93721
559-233-6633 • 1-800-345-4447 • FAX 559-233-6933
QuillDriverBooks.com
Info@QuillDriverBooks.com

Quill Driver Books and Colophon are trademarks of Linden Publishing, Inc.

Quill Driver Books project cadre:
Doris Hall, Kenneth Lee, Linda Kay Hardie, Stephen Blake Mettee

ISBN: 1-884956-53-X • 978-1884956-53-9

Third printing August 2009

Printed in the United States of America

To order another copy of this book, please call
1-800-345-4447

Illustrations by Peter Dunne

For my children Patrick, Michael, and Alexandra, and for Ben Masselink, the gentlest writer there ever was.

Library of Congress Cataloging-in-Publication Data

Dunne, Peter, 1943-
Emotional structure: creating the story beneath the plot : a guide for
screenwriters / by Peter Dunne
p. cm.
ISBN 1-884956-53-X
1. Motion picture authorship. I. Title.
PN1996.D847 2006
808.2´--dc22   2006020052

Contents

Part 4
Building Blocks: Step-by-Step Construction

Part 5
Writing the Script

Part 1

What Writers Write About and Why

The Writer's Rulebook

Rule No. 1 — Write
Rule No. 2 — See Rule No. 1

Writers must make choices. The first choice you will have to make as a writer is to choose to be a writer. This means you will choose to write. Every day for the rest of your life. Because you can only be a writer on the days you write. On the other days, the days you decide not to write, you will be something else. However, there is a caveat. On the days you decide to be a writer and you write, even if it's for only an hour, you get to be a writer for the other twenty-three hours, too. Pretty good, huh?

You can see, then, that it's possible to be a writer no matter what your day job is. Notice, too, there's nothing in the writer's rulebook that says you have to write about certain things. You just have to write. Anything. And it doesn't say anywhere in the rulebook that you have to sell what you write. You just have to write. Whatever you want to write. Especially write what's important to you. Write what's on your mind. It wouldn't be important to you if it weren't on your mind. When you have so much on your mind you don't know where to begin, begin with that, that there's too much on your damn mind. By the time you get that off your chest, there won't be so much on your mind. And you'll know what to write next.

Sometimes this can seem like an impossible undertaking. Sometimes we fail. For which we are forgiven. Sometimes we don't try. For which forgiveness comes harder.

Because trying is the key.

And trying is hard work. Turn what's inside of you into entertainment for a mass audience, and you'll see what I mean. It can be torturous. It is not the same as baking a cake. People will eat cake even if it's not good cake.

People will laugh at stupid jokes. And even more will bob and weave to idiotic songs. But the people sitting in a theater watching your movie are far less gregarious. And far less generous. They came for what *they* thought the movie should be. They are unforgiving, self-appointed critics more concerned with their dates, and their popcorn, and their parking meters and babysitters. So naturally, a lot of writers don't want to open themselves up to people who don't give a crap. Some writers, scared and bitter about this reality, actually write the crap they think those people deserve. But creating crap is a dumb way to go through life. And creating crap on purpose is not officially writing.

You must never give in to the fear of others' responses to your writing. If you do, you will be trying to write what you think someone else will like. And that is not officially writing, either. Writing to please someone else will destroy the true writer in you. Writing what's important to you will make you an important writer.

It takes time to develop as a writer. A lifetime. And yet time is the one thing we are guilty of not giving it. I would imagine that a great majority of all people, not just writers and artists, are guilty of the same thing. And the sad truth is that more people than not wind up immobile in a rest home angry with themselves and the world for not having done the things they most wanted to do in their lives. Who is to blame? Are we lazy? Are we stupid? I don't think so.

I think we are human. We have doubts. We have fears that if we try to live out our dreams and we fail, we will have to live the rest of our lives without a dream and with self-loathing. What a risk, we say. It is too great a risk for any individual who doesn't have a cheerleading section behind him or her, or a way out. So we try to lessen or eliminate the risk. A common approach to lessening the risk is to wait for the right moment. The moment when the risk is lowest. And that moment never comes. Because the paradox is that that moment has to be made by taking the risk.

So we choose to take the risk by dropping the argument that we don't have the time to write. We all have the time. How do I know that? I know that because that is *Peter Dunne's Secret to Writing*:

The time you spend writing must never be thought of as time not spent doing something else.

Some things are, because they are. "Beauty is its own reason for being," according to Shakespeare. And I believe writing is its own reason for being. It is not something you should ever think of as a thing to get to when you're not doing something else.

You give your body food and drink, and air to breathe. You give your mind nutrition, too, by remaining inquisitive and teachable. But most important of all, you must feed your soul. Praying can feed your soul. Meditation certainly does. Acts of kindness and selflessness are at the top of that list, too. And right up there with them, because often they are vehicles for the others, is artistic expression. Art is born in the soul. It is actually the expression of the soul. So if we don't make time for that, we are not making time for the most important thing a human can do: express himself.

So we must find time to express ourselves.

Knock fifteen minutes off lunch and dinner, and put that half hour aside for writing. Knock another fifteen minutes off the time you spend zoned out in front of the television and bank it with the other minutes. Knock fifteen minutes off your cell phone obsession, and take at least fifteen minutes from browsing the web. Put those minutes in the bank, too. Now take all that time, that hour or hour and a half, light an aromatherapy candle, grab your Calgon, a pad, a pen, and turn on the hot water. Slip into the soapy mix and rest your mind and body in the best part of the day… your writing part. Wiggle your toes, take a deep, relaxing breath, and be a writer.

Okay, you're in bubbles up to your eyeballs and you're committed to being a writer. All you have to do now is to decide what to write about. Another choice. And amazingly, this is a very difficult choice to make. It seems that we have so much to write about that we can't wait to get started, but we have so much trouble starting. We know we have a hundred good ideas, better ideas than the ones we see made into films day in and day out, but when it comes to putting those ideas down on paper, more often than not, we are stumped. We can't get started. It's frustrating and humiliating. And the more frustrated and humiliated we become, the harder it is to start. So how do we break that cycle? How do we start?

With *one* idea.

We have to learn to stop tossing around two or three or more ideas at a time. When we do that we just go back and forth forever. There is no "better" idea to start with. All your ideas are good. Well, almost all of them. Remember, we said in the beginning that writers have to make choices. The first choice is to be a writer. The second choice is to choose one, and only one, idea to develop into your screenplay. You will have plenty of time to develop the other ones in the future.

This act of choosing your first idea is a giant step. And, once you make the choice you must stick with it. Just because the idea may prove difficult to develop into a screenplay does not give you the right to abandon it. Every idea is difficult to develop into a screenplay. And most times, the better the idea the more difficult it will be to get down right. That's the way it goes. I'm almost willing to say that if it's too easy, something's wrong. And the "something wrong" is almost always a symptom of an undeveloped Emotional Structure. And that is because most of us feel we should develop the broad strokes of the plot first, and fill in the emotional layer later on. Big mistake. It is precisely this big mistake that ruins script, after script, after script.

The emotional through line, that is to say the Emotional Structure, is the first story to be developed deeply. Only then can the plot be developed to serve it. Never vice versa.

Now, this is about the time, if you were in my writing class and I were standing in front you and your fellow students that I would be getting...The Deadly Stare.

What is it that you and they are feeling, I wonder. Expectation? Self-doubt? Judgment of me or of each other? Buyer's remorse? Because, really, they just sit there and stare.

So I stare back. I sit on my desk and give nothing. Time passes. They shift. They look at me. They look at each other. Back and forth, back and forth. Then a hand goes up, and I win because I know what the hand will ask.

"Mr. Dunne," the hand says. "What the hell is emotional structure, anyway?"

They all nod. The same question on every mind. Every class. And these are people who have already paid for the course.

To most people, maybe you too, Emotional structure certainly sounds like an oxymoron. After all, aren't our emotions those mutinous little rats that jump us when we least expect them? Shocking us? Angering us? Confusing us, and embarrassing us, and depressing us?

And in fact, isn't the secret of their power in their ability to surprise us? And isn't the surprise element the thing we dread most about them? We don't so much fear the emotion, as we do the emotion's unpredictability. That's why we "fight our emotions." That's why we say we "hate surprises."

If you're like me, you don't know when your anger is going to flare up. And you don't like it when it does. You don't know either, when or why anxiety will grab you by the throat and turn you into a shivering mass. But it will attack whenever it damn pleases, and when it does, like some hysterical preschooler off his medication howling in that startled hollow between your ears, you just have to deal with it. Right then. Right there. That's the nature of emotions, and of our relationship with them.

So then, how the heck *do* we discipline them?

How do we *structure* them?

First, let's consider a screenplay's "structure."

While I am not a structure fanatic, I do bow to the necessity of it and teach it, and acknowledge that without an understanding of it no writer will succeed in creating a logical work. However, having said that, and having sat through a few hundred painfully unsuccessful movies, I do not subscribe to the theory that understanding structure is the same as understanding writing. To understand writing we must understand emotion and capture it. And we do that by learning emotional triggers and responses, and tricking them to show up in the script where and when we want them.

Now you're probably asking yourself if all this tricking and triggering is really necessary? You don't want to be a psychiatrist; you want to be a scriptwriter for crying-out-loud. Well, yes, it is necessary, and here's why. Without understanding Emotional Structure, the beginning, the middle, and the end of your script have a 100 percent chance of becoming the beginning, the *muddle*, and the end. Because emotions rule the central, most misunderstood and most feared element of a screenplay: that of the story's underlying meaning. And only by understanding Emotional Structure can we bring solid, creative solutions to the writing process, and meaning to your story. It is the only sure way to turn your script's problems into your script's power.

So now we consider "emotions."

Knowing your idea for a screenplay is a start. Knowing who you are as the writer of that idea is equally vital. Who you are emotionally, that is. If you're like me, you probably had a father and a mother. Let's see a show of hands. Good.

Some of you had, as I did, siblings. Hands? Good.

Others of you were, as I was, raised in a fun-loving, balanced, nurturing, peaceful, sober, non-judgmental, spiritual home. Hands? Anyone?

Okay, so here's the point. I may never actually start out to write about my family and my upbringing, but I can't write anything *with meaning* without allowing those influences to inform what I'm writing about. There is proof aplenty of failure to do so.

Earlier in my career as a "Development Executive" I read scripts by the pounds, week in and week out, year after year. Where did they come from? They were breeding out there. Inbreeding. These were "spec" scripts mostly, written not on assignment, but on a wing and a prayer, in the hopes of selling it to a studio for a sack full of gold.

All across town, dozens of other development executives at agencies, studios, and networks were doing the same thing I was. Often we'd be reading the same scripts. We'd compare notes, shake our heads and wonder, "where are the good scripts?" How can so many people—many of them professional writers—turn out so many mediocre scripts? Are the ideas that bad? Are the writers that bad?

No. And, no. But, getting the best out of the idea, and getting the best out of the writer were the great, unmet goals.

Turning a good idea into a good screenplay is not child's play. It is work not meant for the faint of heart. Sometimes writing is euphoric, and sometimes it is sadistic. It can be extremely rewarding one day, and it can be a complete waste of time the next. It can be like having a good cry. Or having great sex. Or both at the same time. Or nary a bit of either ever.

Sometimes writing can seem magical. But the truth is, writing is not magic. You are the magic. And it is this magic that turns the hard work into art.

The hard work of writing a screenplay is not, as some would have you believe, analogous to climbing Mount Everest. It's more like taking a long hike. A very, very long hike where you may risk losing your footing, but never your life. Parts of the hike are uphill. Parts sweep gently downward. There are beautiful glades now and then. Just as there are surprise encounters with bears and bad guys. There are valleys, of course, but they are not the famous valleys of death. Even when they feel like it. There are difficulties in the emotional landscape, and they are there for a reason even when you don't know why. There are fields of wildflowers. There are lakes of rainbows. And the longer you are on this screenwriter's hike, the more elevation you will gain until your reach the point of rare atmosphere where only writers and writing breathe. To the home of meaning, and the triumph of ideas. To emotional gratification.

In the end, it won't matter if you write about dog sleds in the Klondike, or gay monks in Greece. What will matter is your ability to touch me with your story. To move me with your movie. To inspire me. To validate me. To encourage me. Those are the things you will have to do to get me into the theater. Not an easy task, but not impossible either, considering all you have to do to reach *my* emotions is to use *yours*.

Know Your Story, Know Your Plot, Know the Difference

When we think about great stories, about great movies, we remember first and foremost about whom the story is told. More than the twists and turns of the plot and the grand scale of the action and the stunts, we recall the character around whom all of the action swirls. Who is the good guy? Who is the bad guy? Who falls in love with whom? With whom did we fall in love? Who was most memorable? Who? Who? Who?

The answer to the question, What is your film about? is nothing if it's not about Who.

And that is the difference between story and plot. The plot is *what* happens in the film. The story is what it does to the *who* it happens to. And, of the who and what of it, the who is far more important than the what. The what would be worthless without the who. But, to be fair, the who wouldn't be much without the what, either.

We can also look at it this way. The plot provides the action: the film's motion. And the story provides the *re*action: the film's *e*motion.

Inside the story, where the emotions play out, the portraits of your characters are subtly sketched. The portrait is sketched by revealing the character's emotions through his behavior. This behavior can be as exaggerated as provoking a barroom brawl, or as delicate as a seductive glance. Your character's behavior is most telling when it is in reaction to some unexpected event. His or her emotional reaction can bring unpredicted results, and more importantly, unwanted revelations. Truth arrives on the coattails of surprise—truth that up until this point in your plot has escaped your hero's consciousness.

Suddenly the truth is out in the open. And the reasons for your hero not wanting to let you see his truths are the gist of his or her mystery. Your hero's truths—like everyone else's—are buried deep down inside. And often they are buried unknowingly. Subconsciously. When they are uncovered and examined through the story's arc, the reason they were buried provides the story with "meaning." As each of these epiphanies takes place, the hero becomes stronger for it. This is a new strength that he uses to forge ahead, and eventually, to forge a victory. His victory is usually the climax to the plot. Afterwards, his understanding of the changes that took place within him creates the film's resolution.

The story is the journey for truth.
The plot is the road it takes to get there.

We use the plot—the action—to push the story along to its logical conclusion. The plot comes from external, uncontrollable sources. Something "happens" to your protagonist that she has no control over. It could be an Act of Fate, or an Act of God—a natural disaster could take a loved one away in an earthquake or flood. It could be the sudden onset of an incurable disease, or a heart attack. It could be a husband leaving his wife. It could be losing a job, watching your house burn down, or the miscarriage of a child.

Plot happens to your protagonist. We see plot first, well before story—but the seeds of story are there if we know to look for them... if we recognize them. As the writer, you have to plant them where they are needed. Sometimes you will think of them while you are there. Sometimes you go back to a point earlier in your screenplay and plant them after you've noticed the need for them.

What are the seeds of your story?

Everything we do in life, everything we experience, makes an imprint in our subconscious, and contributes to the formation of our core person. We become that accumulation of major and miniscule events; events of unimaginable heartache, and events of unexpected elevation and joy. We become complex. And there is no limit to our complexity. The more we take in our experience, that is to say the more we make ourselves available to them and learn from them the more complex our personal nature becomes. This personal nature, which is the combination of a deep and meaningful union of intellect and emotion, is our true spiritual self. When we know and trust our spiritual self we become learned. Which is not at all the same as becoming educated. It is our complex subconscious nature, our spiritually charged emotional self, which makes each of us unique. The difference between your story and my story is the difference in these seeds of our unique nature. I cannot live your story. You cannot live mine. Your protagonist and your antagonist have their own stories, too—each unique, each complex and dramatic. It is up to you to mine these stories if you are to create a truly rich and emotionally variegated film.

We use plot to help us see patterns in your protagonist's life.

And patterns are emotional footprints. If we take the plot of a man leaving a woman, for example, we may discover during the story a pattern in the woman's life regarding other relationships that haven't lasted. Or perhaps she wrestles with issues of abandonment. Friends of hers may have said they could see the break-up coming for a long time. Why? What did they see that the woman could not or would not? Was denial involved out of desperation that any relationship is better than none? Sometimes we see the woman blame herself, feeling she wasn't worthy of him in the first place. How often have we heard stories of a jilted lover moving to a different city to start over, only to relive the same experience? What's that about?

Well, "that," my friends, is your story. It is not a story of events. It is a story of emotional contradiction. It is the journey of discovery and growth. Of loneliness even in the middle of a crowded life. Of isolation from feelings we cannot trust. Of building and tearing down the walls that protect us.

Let's assume your hero has survived in life so far by using practical ways in an unwavering manner to avoid pain and loneliness. She depends on these habits of response to protect her heart. Her life would be too uncomfortable, too risky, without them. Now, at the start of your screenplay, something happens—the plot happens—and this time her practiced, habitual, dependable defenses don't work. Oh, my God. She is forced to take a new path—a risk—in order to survive long enough to get back to normal—to safety—to where her defenses still work. She is pushed outside her walls.

Then another event occurs, and the risky journey is extended beyond her initial plan. Further, her tools for survival are not working very well under these new circumstances. Anger and fear substitute for confidence. Her protective walls show signs of cracking. Her strengths are diminished and her weaknesses are exposed. Weaknesses of which even she was unaware. Suddenly she finds herself at the mercy of events and people completely unknown to her. She must put aside her old strengths, which are now useless. This does not make her weak, however. This makes her brave. As she takes this risk, this leap of faith, she leaves behind the moment of fear. And in this new moment she becomes vulnerable. This is not inconsequential. This is huge. This is life changing. Though plot-wise it may seem to be a small event, story-wise it is enormously important. Because at this moment she discovers the great value in all vulnerability: She becomes teachable.

And what you must teach her at this point is her hidden history. Her hidden history is that which caused her to build the walls in the first place. It is very often a history so deeply buried that it is painful to ever face again. But she must face it in order to free herself from the fear it created.

Events and new people challenge the *basis* of her defenses rather than the defenses themselves. Physical survival is now directly linked to psychological and emotional stability. And she discovers that a seriously underdeveloped emotional life lay useless under her defense system. She faces an impoverished core, devoid of self-esteem. This is the grand epiphany and the mid-point of your film, and the point at which emotional war must be declared.

She comes to realize that by having created a defensive shell around her feelings (lest she risk having those feelings hurt) she has kept those emotions from ever maturing. Now, in your film, she must learn to use those emotional tools in order to survive. She is clumsy at it, and frustrated. And she is scared because all of this is boiling down to one thing: She has to grow up. And she has to grow up fast.

The more challenging the story is in terms of emotional complexity, the deeper the seeds of discontent are buried, the harder your heroine has to dig to find the answers. Until finally she reaches the unthinkable place where pain and suffering have been hidden in shame for so long. She must confront this shame in order to get to the answer she needs to survive the plot.

If you are clever enough, we will all identify with your heroine's dilemma. We all have secrets, fears, and shame that we would like to avoid facing to our dying day. Though we may not identify with her particular *plot* problems, we will connect in every other way to her *story* problems.

This is important to remember while you are plotting your script. As long as the story emotions are true, the plot can be anything you like.

So now you reach the point of choosing a plot and a story.

How should you choose what to write about?

Well, you've heard this before and you're going to hear it again. Write what you know about. But I am here to tell you that that is a deceptively complicated proposition.

The "what-you-know-about" which you will write about is not what you know about fixing a car or sailing a boat. It is what-you-know-to-be-true-and-valuable-and-meaningful-and-important-and-worth-living-for. *The "what-you-know-about" which you must learn to write about is your own emotional truth.* It is precisely your personal wisdom that supports and validates the story you tell.

No plot, no matter how clever, is worth anything if it doesn't ultimately connect your truth to mine.

The question every writer asks over and over again is if he is wise enough today to write. Not smart enough. Wise enough. How strong is that wisdom. How thoughtful. How deep. How generous. How individual is that wisdom, too. And how much will others learn from that wisdom.

Being wise and being smart are two different things. Maybe you haven't given that a lot of thought, but now is the time you'll have to, because being smart isn't enough. Being smart won't help you be a good writer. You can possess all the knowledge in the world and stink at writing. But if you are wise, I can pretty much guarantee that you will be a fine writer. And if your protagonist trades his knowledge for wisdom he will eventually solve his greatest problems.

The difference between knowledge and wisdom isn't just semantics. The difference is real, and it has everything to do with emotional conditioning. Knowing something is one thing. Knowing how to use that knowing is another. Knowing how to use that knowing selflessly is wisdom. Wisdom is the application of knowledge with love.

We learn to love through our experiences, and we learn to be wise by learning to express what we learn in those experiences lovingly. Not romantically lovingly, but lovingly in the sense of emotional generosity. The richer our experiences, the greater our chances to gain true wisdom become. Some lessons take a long time to sink in and the wisdom isn't very clear early on. If the use of our knowledge does not expand the quality of our lives and those lives around us, then our knowledge has not been expressed as wisdom, and as such is worthless. Its value is only in its application. Much like money. Having a lot of it doesn't mean a thing if you don't know how to spend it.

So your hero will learn some tough life lessons because you will force him to learn if he is to survive. The plot, with its intellectual and physical obstacles, will teach him that he's limited intellectually and physically. The story, with its moral and emotional challenges, will teach him that his moral and emotional capacities are, on the other hand, unlimited. Not only that, but also that his newly discovered moral and emotional strength... his spiritual vigor... can save his physical and intellectual ass. If he is like most heroes, he will not learn this lesson quickly or easily.

And, if he is like most heroes, you are likely to notice how much like you he is. This is because ultimately you will be writing about the things you know best... the things about yourself you know to be true…remember? So your hero should be a lot like you since his emotional truth is your emotional truth. If your hero is not a lot like you, then stop and go back until he is.

In your script your hero may not share a single experience of yours, but he may have reacted the same way to his experience as you had to yours. It is the reaction to life that matters. It is the development of oneself by virtue of those reactions that matters. It is the universality of those reactions that makes us all so similar, though we may seem so dissimilar otherwise. It is in the moment of choosing our reaction that binds us. It is in the moment where loss is faced and felt that our spiritual brotherhood is created. For it is in that moment of loss wherein we are soul-bound. We have all lost dignity. We have all lost faith. We have all lost hope. We have all lost love. We have all known what those losses felt like. We have all wished someone would have felt them with us at the time. Now, as you write, the time has come again. This is your chance to right a wrong. This is your chance to give back what has been taken. To your hero. To your audience. To yourself.

It is the time now to develop a plot in which you force your hero to face the losses of his early life through the discovery of the defenses he has built around them to forget them. For what your hero has suppressed in order to survive a long time ago must sooner or later rise to the surface again. Because what protected him once will not protect him forever.

In your physical plot you will create incidents that will result in expected reactions. In your metaphysical story you will create incidents that will result in surprises.

In your hero's physical world, what goes up must come down. In your hero's metaphysical world, what went down must come up.

When everything comes up, the truth will come with it. And the truth, as they say, will set your hero free. It is in this freedom that the happy ending is found.

When. Where. How.

We have seen classic stories told a hundred different ways. Through the centuries the works of many great authors and playwrights have been interpreted and misinterpreted, placed and misplaced in varying locales, and burdened with differing intentions. Great tragedies have been retold as comedies, and vice versa. Ancient tales have been rendered contemporary. Black characters have been made white, and white have been made black; men have been turned to women, and women to men. But the story remains the same. Still entertaining, still powerful, still meaningful because if the story is good in the first place, chances are it will remain good in any case.

As you decide on your story and your plot you must choose the when, where, and how. These are the period, the location, and the genre in which your film best plays. Through these choices, a good story can get even better.

When

The "when" of your screenplay is something you must decide based on the story material just as much if not more than the plot material. Telling your story in the context of a particular time in history can emphasize your point dramatically. This is because the psychological or emotional subtexts about which you are writing can be much clearer and more powerful in one set of circumstances than another. You want to match the internal story you're telling with the external world in which you set it. If the match isn't a good one, your movie can sink quickly. Most of us start off with a very certain time in which our film story takes place. It could take place in a time long ago (The Dawn of Man; Ancient Rome; the Old West; the sixties, or just last summer). It could take place in the future (science fiction), or it could take place today.

The reasons for choosing the time go beyond historical accuracy or nostalgia. Some film ideas simply work a lot better in a particular era. Other times in history were simpler, for example, and therefore may be a better time frame in which to tell a subtly complicated personal story. Today we live in a very open society where personal problems can be aired publicly among friends and professionals without embarrassment or condemnation. This wasn't always so. If you want to make it more difficult for your protagonist to wrestle with intimate, personal angst, place her in a time when confronting them, indeed even admitting to them, was impossible without suffering serious consequences.

When this dynamic is ignored, a film will usually not work. Filmmakers have tried to place classic Western plots in outer space only to face disappointing results. Even though the plot works, the story does not because what was emotionally true in the Old West is completely outdated and irrelevant centuries later. Too much water has passed under the social bridge. Values have evolved. People have evolved. Without reconciling the story to the plot no plot can be realistic. Without realism (the truth) all believability is lost. Even though the audience may not know exactly why the movie doesn't work for them, they will know it doesn't work, and they will say so. This applies to films that are total fantasies as well. Emotional plausibility is absolutely essential to success. So you can see that considerable thought must be given the timeframe in which you choose to tell your story. The period can enhance your story perfectly or intrude on it fatally. Be careful.

Period pieces can be highly entertaining simply on their ability to transport the audience into another, magical world. But on a practical note you must remember that period pieces are a big headache for the studios producing them. The extraordinary costs involved in reconstructing another time and place—period wardrobe, vehicles, buildings, sets and set dressing—cause many studios to hesitate getting involved. So you must be practical, too. If your film doesn't need warring armies to make a story point, then drop the grandiosity. Simple is better.

Where

Movies take us to faraway and wonderful places, and your film can do the same. But keep this in mind—far and away to you may be very different from far and away to me. The backyard behind the house where you grew up and played doctor with little Suzie can be far and away to me and just as fascinating and romantic as Paris in April, or as dark and haunting as Saigon in winter. So don't feel forced to put your story in a phantasmagorical location. Especially try not to place your story in a locale you personally are unfamiliar with. Studying atlases and travel books will not suffice when it comes to needing the nuances of a place to add to the story's power.

Your locale should be considered more than a colorful place. To have any value at all, the locale you choose should be treated as another character in the film—a very important character. Try to make the "place" of your film so important that the film would suffer were it placed anywhere else. All that being said, Paris in April by itself will not save a bad story, or make silly writing romantic.

To help you with the idea of "place" as an important character in your film, think of examples that worked well for you when you saw them. I think of how perfectly placed the film *Witness* was in the bowels of a big city and the tranquility of the Amish country of eastern Pennsylvania. Each location spoke directly to the emotional life of the characters inhabiting them. Lancaster in particular played as important a role in the film as any character. The farming community framed the love story and strengthened its emotional truths of simplicity as humility and honesty as faith. The power of stories lives in particular places. Find the power in your story and place it exactly where it works best, scene after scene after scene. This doesn't just apply to cities or countries. It also applies to interior spaces. Does your scene play better in the bedroom than a restaurant? On a rooftop with the city glistening in the distance better than at the kitchen table? Walking through a city park than in an elevator? Or does being "stuck" in an elevator serve the tension in your scene exactly as you like? These are the writing decisions—the filmmaking decisions—that are a lot of fun to make.

Give serious thought to "place." I have put a story I'm developing in several different locations—in different countries—to see how it affects the emotional power of the idea. I found one place to be exciting but overwhelming, and another more subtle but eventually more elegant, and more of service to the emotional journey. Not surprisingly, the more satisfying location was also one with which I was intimate and it helped me enormously to taste, smell, and feel the places while I was writing. Things flowed better for me because they felt natural where they were. What I knew of the place—what I remembered—colored each scene. I was actually in a heightened emotional state as I wrote because the memories energized my imagination.

A big part of this, too, is creating a world for your film through which you lead the audience. It will be an emotional journey, so make your locations work for you by adding to those emotions. Dark, scary. Wet, dangerous. Loud, violent.

How

How you want to tell your story is a matter of style.

Fred Astaire had style. Magic Johnson has style. What is your style?

We will all tell a story differently because we are bringing our own experiences to it. But we must not think of style as "being different" in a forced kind of way. If we are honest about who we are, our style will be honestly different. Let's never be different for the sake of being different. That would get in the way of being honest. And your reader and viewer will smell dishonesty a mile away. Like we said, good writing is honest writing. So seek to be different honestly by seeking how you honestly feel about what you're writing. Let your feelings get in there. Let your passion be felt. Those will be the differences that evolve into your style. It is your comfort zone, too, because it is a natural approach to your writing, rather than something forced.

Your style, therefore, is not a way for you to show off. It is probably just the opposite. It is your sincerity. Your depth. You only have to be aware that style and form can detract as easily as enhance your story if you aren't careful. Watch your emotional build. Don't get too passionate too soon, or everything will start to feel equally crucial, and your emotional build will flatten out. When this happens you will find yourself trying to "top" yourself scene after scene in order to reinvigorate the build until you can't "top" yourself anymore or until everything becomes unbelievably huge and silly. When this happens, your story is lost forever. So remember, you don't want your film to be about your style, you want it to be about your ideas. Restraint and intellectual depth are the hallmarks of great style.

If you're worried about your style, give it time to develop. Think of it as an interpretation of how you see the film in your head as you write it. With each story you tackle using your emotional style, you will imbue your film with its greatest personal richness. It is precisely such personal richness your audience will come to identify as... your style.

This creates, finally, the vital link between who you are and what you write. A certain idea will seem especially cinematic to you because you are particularly capable of giving voice to its heretofore, mute emotions, and vision to its barren horizon. Suddenly, then, the once-elusive proposition of "writing what you know about" becomes a natural and creative act in which your uniqueness qualifies you as its writer.

Once you get in the habit of doing this, you will realize how important it is for you to do. If you don't give voice to these ideas, who will? If you don't write with these lofty intentions, why write? The need for you to tell your stories, and the need for people like me to hear them can and will be met. Don't give up.

Character-Driven Plot or Plot-Driven Character

We should avoid getting caught up in semantics or in catchy phrases that confuse more than clarify what we mean. So, in plain English the plot and the story—the event and the character—are inextricably bound. Each drives the other at one point or another. The reason it is important to understand this is because you—the writer—are in charge of deciding who and what does the pushing and pulling.

As you do this you must also maintain a balance in your screenplay. You cannot allow one part to so completely dominate the other that you risk the audience forgetting about either one at any time. At all times be aware of the tug-of-war between the external challenges and the internal turmoil in which your protagonist is engaged. One feeds the other. One, you can say, creates the other. An action creates a reaction. When this synergy isn't working in your screenplay the unfolding events will lose their unique power and any potential for a cumulative emotional effect. The script will feel "episodic" and random as if you were writing it with no aim in mind. First this happens, then that happens, then this happens. You pile up scenes and sequences, but your audience isn't becoming engaged. Instead, what you have to create is a script in which every scene exists only because of what happened in the scene before it. One scene gives birth to the next, even if the scene involves a different set of characters in a different location. This is because the second scene's genesis is found in the emotional content of the first scene, and then builds on that.

Your script must always be building emotions.

The reasons for this are critical. As the first scene's set of emotions gives rise to the second scene's set, the audience rides with them. Your goal in doing this is to have them make a visceral connection between scenes, not an intellectual one. As they follow the plot they will intuitively relate to the deeper meaning in your story. And the meaning of your story, *that is to say the whole reason you are writing this in the first place,* is always found in the emotional architecture of your film, not in the action plot structure.

The plot should be thought of as the motion picture.

The story should be thought of as the emotion picture.

It is a difficult job to create a plot that forces your film's character to consider more than just physical reactions and physical changes. You must create a plot that forces him to face making internal changes. These will be much harder changes for him to make. No one likes to change who he is, or rather who he has become, which is frequently not the person he started out wanting to be. This kind of change comes at a very dear price and most heroes are not willing to pay that price without a fight. So you must make those fights really tough for him. After being beaten down a few times, he will consider facing the internal changes you put in front of him, presented to him usually by his mentor or co-protagonist. He will change begrudgingly at first, not fully convinced it's the right thing to do. This process of changing on the inside is referred to as his story "arc."

Change is inevitable. Growth is optional.

Why change your hero on the inside? You want your hero to be a different person—a better person—by the end of the film. His growth is what makes his effort heroic. And, practically speaking, your audience will be disappointed if they don't see that change in him. Seeing the change in him tells your audience that the trip was worth it. And it lets them know that if he can rise above trouble and come out a better person, maybe they can, too.

Think of heroes who have done this in films you have enjoyed. For me, young Che's enlightenment in the remarkable *Motorcycle Diaries* was breathtaking and meaningful. There was Bogart's reversal in *Casablanca*, Michael Douglas's maturation in *Wonder Boys*, Hugh Grant accepting responsibility in *About a Boy*, and even Tom Cruise's redemption in *Jerry Maguire*.

If reestablishing his career as a sports agent were the only thing

Jerry Maguire had to worry about we would have been watching a very dull and unsatisfactory film. His real challenge came when he was forced to choose between success in business and success in love. He had to risk becoming a better human being in a business that viewed such a thing as a weakness. From that point forward the film took on new meaning. His efforts became more courageous in a different and unexpected way, and the story became more important to the audience than the plot. Suddenly it didn't matter if he got rich; it only mattered if he got the girl.

The victory is in the plot, but the happy ending is in the story.

Viewed in this light, the struggle you create for your protagonist is double-edged. You give him a problem that threatens his way of life if not his life, and you offer him a solution that exposes his secrets if not his soul. Hidden in the problem are the keys to his past. Hidden in the solution are the keys to his future.

As your film progresses, the actions in the plot and the discoveries in the story as a reaction to the plot are interwoven at all times. Don't let them wander on their own. They will get lost if they do, I promise you that. Personally, when I structure a script I think of the plot and the story as not just traveling side-by-side, but rather braided, as one would braid strands of string into a stronger cord. As one plot string curves away and wraps out of sight, another story string comes into view. They tumble and twist, always together. And I want my audience to remain aware that the first element is right behind what's in front of them.

And speaking of strings:

Everything comes with strings attached.

We know that everything in life comes with strings attached. As a screenwriter, make this one of your Golden Rules: each time you introduce a new element or a bit of new information or a new character into your protagonist's life make sure it comes with strings attached to some little thing you can reveal later.

Sometimes it just has to be a thin thread, but it makes life complicated for him by raising the dramatic impact of the introduction of new characters and the information that comes with them, as if there were a clue hidden nearby. And it puts your protagonist in a world where nothing is as simple as it first seems. This keeps him on his toes, and it keeps the audience on their toes, too.

Stylistically, strings also have the effect of connecting everything and every person to something unknown. The unknown can act as your undercurrent. We all live with a lot of unknowns: we all know what it's like waiting for the other shoe to drop.

Connecting people and information in your script is essential. If an event or a character can be yanked from your screenplay without tearing the fabric of plot or story, then it deserves to be yanked. If you see this in your outline or script, do the yanking right away. Don't wait. The sooner you clear your plot and story of clutter, the better. The longer you wait to do it, the harder it will be to do.

Remember we have a finite number of pages in the script and none of them can be wasted. Unlike novels where side trips can be taken, screenplays must stay rigorously on point at all times. Because of that your audience will be constantly bombarded with layers of information. At any one moment you may be asking them to absorb the tone of your dialog, the weight of the silences between the lines, the exposition of a clue, the emotional context of a subtle sideways glance, the color of your film's palette, and the texture of the musical underscore. Your script is dense by design.

Your storytelling should be complex, but it should never be confusing.

Make this distinction in thinking and writing: complex and complicated are not the same things. Complex will keep the audience thinking. Complicated will simply piss them off. If you're going to make anyone's life complicated make sure it's your hero's not your audience's. Clarity, brevity, and elegance are your tools. No unnecessary dialog, no unnecessary scenes, and no b.s. Especially no b.s.

There is never a legitimate reason to lie to your audience. If you state something as a fact, then it is a fact. If you say that your hero, an undercover cop, is a sober alcoholic then you cannot allow him to drink in a scene in order to fit in better while he's infiltrating the mob. Make not drinking another one of his problems if you like, but don't cheat it.

Never let your reason for writing be money.
Write to fill the page and write to fulfill your dreams.

Write to fill the page	*Never write just for this*

1. This will make you happy.	1. This will not.
2. This will bring admiration.	2. This will not.
3. This will get you your next job.	3. This will not.
4. This can change things.	4. This cannot.
5. This will last forever.	5. This will not.

An infamous case of lying to the audience occurred on the CBS television drama *Dallas*. Born out of greed, the network and its partner, Lorimar Productions, decided to bring back the character of Bobby Ewing from death hoping to lift their Nielsen ratings. This is always a problem on television. There is no easy way to raise someone from the grave, but Lorimar's choice was especially amateurish and disdainful. Having led their faithful audience through an entire thirty-episode season built around the aftermath of Bobby's death, the producers added one final scene to the last episode of the season. They chose to have Bobby's widow awake in the morning, go to the shower where she finds Bobby showering (what?) and tell him that she had the damnedest nightmare. She dreamt Bobby was dead!

CBS and Lorimar tossed out the entire season's story, a story they asked their audience to believe each week, as something that never really happened. They knew the audience would be upset, but they also believed the audience was dumb enough to come back and watch next season, anyway. And they were right. The audience came back. The ratings justified their decision as far as they were concerned. But the rest of the world saw it for what it was. CBS and Lorimar made a shamelessly lazy and condescending decision based on quarterly reports rather than quality programming. Their notoriously undignified decision caused the show not to be remembered as one of the most successful primetime soap operas ever to air, but instead as a laughing stock. Money will do that to people. And people will do that to your script now and then. Sometimes there's nothing you can do about it. Sometimes there is something you can do about it. And when that happens—when you can do something about it—you better damn well do it. Because writers are better than that, and you are better than that.

Your world of characters and the strings attached to them.

When you introduce your characters you will want to attach strings to them, too, strings that hint at who they really are underneath it all. You do not want to stop the action in order to tell us something about your protagonist's past; rather, you want to weave it into the action organically. Stopping the action to explain what's going on is not only weak writing, it's very frustrating to your audience. This especially holds true at the end of the script. It is a sure sign of an unsuccessful film when a set of characters has a final scene in which they explain to the viewer everything he just saw.

Witness—written by William Kelley, Pamela Wallace, and Earl W. Wallace, and starring Harrison Ford and Kelly McGillis—is a great example of the use of strings attached to characters and situations from beginning to end.

In the film, Book (Harrison Ford) learns the identity of the murderer from the Amish boy Samuel, the witness in *Witness*, but with a BIG string attached. The murderer is a fellow cop in Book's department. This string alters the normal way Book handles the case. He goes with the change because he has no choice, but he believes he'll get the job done and things will soon return to normal. He is wrong, of course, because this is the first step of many that will continually take him off course. Little by little his life will change dramatically.

Soon, during the course of being off course, Book is shot and is given a safe place to recover from his wound by the Amish widow Rachel (Kelly McGillis). This too comes with strings attached. In order to appease her he must give up his gun. This may not be a big deal to you or me, but to a cop who survives in a world of violence with it, it is a very big deal indeed. The gun represents his way of life. Remember what we said earlier that the protagonist's problem has to include a threat on his life or way of life. In Book's case, it's both.

When Book regains enough strength to get out of bed, he must do so with another string attached. He has to dress as a member of the Amish community. The clothes are a poor fit and he feels silly in them, especially when Rachel comes into the room and sees him. But two important emotional shifts take place behind the gentle humor in this scene.

First, Book is humanized. He is forced to conform to something with which he is completely uncomfortable, and this humbles him in a constructive way. I want to make clear that he is humbled, not humiliated, and that the value in this humbling is the exposure of a personality capable of sweet self-deprecation heretofore dormant beneath the tough cop exterior. It surprises him and it surprises her.

The second important emotional shift belongs to Rachel. Certainly a painfully shy woman in the presence of a strange man, she finds comfort and some safety in the humor of the moment. She has let her guard down, as he has. It is a subtle moment for them to share, and it is significant precisely because it is shared. More important for her is the fact that the last time she stood in a bedroom with a man was with her recently deceased husband, whose clothes these undoubtedly were. So you can imagine, as you watch her watch him, what's going on in her mind and in her heart. It is an eerie and evolutionary moment for each character, gracefully laced with allure and potential.

In the film, Book's problem becomes Rachel's, then her problem becomes his when her family and community react to her involvement. This forces them to have to work together to help solve each other's problem. And all the working together gradually and tenderly creates a third problem: their mutual attraction. His problem and her problem now become *their* problem, and at this point in the movie—the midpoint in all good movies—the story changes direction. It is no longer a murder mystery, it is now a love story. Which is a much more interesting mystery anyway.

You will want to pack your script with these kinds of very creative and thoughtful observations, especially regarding the human condition. It is in the human condition where the universal themes of the story can be recognized and actually felt. Such writing connects the audience to the film on a deeper and more satisfying level. As you put your script ideas together, aim to create this kind of emotional linking.

No one in your script can live in a vacuum.

Most screenwriters, in my estimation, are either not aware of or misunderstand emotional structure, and they miss their opportunity to create a work of simplicity and subtlety and power. Promise yourself now that you will not be like the rest, and that in every scene you write you will stay conscious of the emotional structure that binds your plot and story. And that when you can you will write with strings attached, and that you will pull them now and then to confound your protagonist and reveal more exposition by way of his reaction. You will do this because you know that if everyone is connected, moving one person will shuffle all the rest, and often create an emotional tug-of-war.

Another way of looking at this kind of connecting is to compare an incident you create in the script to tossing a pebble into a pond. Whenever something happens to one character in your script, see how far you can push its ripple effect into the other characters' lives. No fish in your pond should remain completely unaffected.

The Population in Your Pond

Just as it is important to know everything about your protagonist, so it is for your other primary characters. While you want to invent a cast that is fascinating and provocative, you have to keep them real within the context of your story. Even if your film is fantasy, science fiction, or magic realism you are still creating your reality. And within that reality everyone must stay true. For example in the Superman movies there exists a well-defined reality. Gotham City, for the purposes of the stories, is very real, and the population of the city never doubts for a moment that their lives aren't authentic, or that there isn't a guy with a cape flying around saving their butts. Reality is what you say it is, but once you say what it is, you can't screw around with it just because it's easy or convenient to do so in order to solve a script problem. If you do that then you will violate the legitimacy of your characters and invalidate any truth you want them to express.

Your protagonist

The person around whom the plot revolves, and whose experience is the focus of the story is your protagonist. He is your hero, and it is through his evolution we will learn and grow.

Chances are you know your hero very well. If you do not, stop right now until you know him inside and out. You may not know everything that's going to happen to him yet, but for now that's okay.

Your hero should be your hero. Don't write a film about someone because he's interesting or because he's important unless you are passionate about him. In this context knowing him means more than knowing *about* him. It means having a deep understanding of what makes him tick. Understanding his heart and soul, as cheesy as that may sound, because it is his heart and soul that the movie is about.

When you look deeply into your hero you will see a lot of yourself in him. His flaws and his strengths. The more you identify with your hero the more passionately you will write about him. Be careful, however, that you don't become so in love with him that you allow him to become a saint by emphasizing his strengths and minimizing his weaknesses. It is a common mistake, so keep your eye out for it. Stay objective.

This will hold true when you portray your antagonists. Often we tend to paint them pitch black, allowing them few if any redeeming values. Be aware of this rookie mistake, too.

The most important thing you must know about your protagonist is what his journey means to you, because he is the personification of your film's theme.

Your antagonist

Villains can be great fun because they can embody an amalgam of so many of your own personal enemies. But you cannot allow your antagonist to be a fool. He must be complex and real and smart. The antagonist represents your protagonist's greatest fears, capable of bringing out the worst in your hero. And your hero knows this. And what is it that makes this fear so great for your hero? It is this: Your hero sees so much of himself in your antagonist that it scares him and weakens him. It is your job, and a critical one, to show how much alike the protagonist and antagonist really are. The dramatic conflict rests in their similarities, and what those similarities mean, more than in their differences. In fact, it is an over-simplification to think of your antagonist only as a villain. It is possible to have an antagonist who is a saint. What makes the antagonist an antagonist is that he is antagonistic, not evil necessarily. Being a pain in the ass and being evil are two different things.

The antagonist can also be, in theory, something far bigger than just one other human being. It can be the government, or "the system," or corporate America, or the Catholic Church, or apartheid, but it will have to be personified in order to create dramatic conflict on a personal level. So you will create a character or group of characters that will represent the element of corruption or threat that directly involves your protagonist.

The man who stabbed Tom Cruise in the back in *Jerry Maguire* wasn't the enemy, per se. He did, however, represent what was wrong, what was corrupt, about the life Jerry Maguire found himself leading. His sense of values had gradually eroded in his career environment, and that erosion crept into every other aspect of his life. Somewhere along the line money became more important than morals. Jerry wasn't a bad guy, really; he was a good guy leading a not-so-honorable existence. The competitor who aced him out of his promotion, and then fired him, personified the ultimate end position Jerry was headed for. This is important to delineate because it focuses the solution on the problem, not on the particular personality that represents it. In other words, even if Jerry could somehow get rid of the other guy, the real problem, which is his own moral bankruptcy not his monetary one, wouldn't be resolved. This is the kind of set-up you will aim to devise for your hero, too. And your hero, just like Jerry Maguire, won't be able to do it alone. He will need help. Enter your other fish in the pond.

Your co-protagonist

Most protagonists have lost their way and haven't yet noticed. The daily-ness of life, the same-thing-day-after-day-ness he accepts as normal gives rise to the gradual adoption of habits and an unconscious accumulation of attitudes. Like you and me, your protagonist becomes formed unwittingly without a master plan or check system. Now, in the face of failure or threat, whichever you devise, he learns from a sympathetic co-protagonist that he is ill equipped to defend what is really at stake.

The co-protagonist usually starts off in the piece as someone who is not fond of the protagonist. The co-protagonist almost immediately challenges the protagonist on every level. The protagonist can't wait to solve his problem quickly and put this person out of his life forever. But, boy, that is so not going to happen.

Creating confrontation and wariness between them allows each to learn about the other in a heightened emotional state. The idea of sailing rough seas together, with no other option than to work together in order to survive, forces them into moments of personal exposure. Revealing themselves, exposing vulnerability or weakness just makes things worse. But while they fight on one level, something else is happening on an internal level. And it scares them.

In the film *African Queen*, with a screenplay by James Agee and John Huston based on the novel by C. S. Forester, Rose, played by Katharine Hepburn, starts out as an antagonistic pain in the ass to Charlie the boat captain, played by Humphrey Bogart. It is also fair to say that he is an enormous pain in the ass, as well. As their dangerous journey down river proceeds they become partners fighting against the same monstrous Nazis even while they fight between themselves. The question becomes who is the bigger enemy? Tough exteriors crumble under extreme pressure, and their fears are exposed. They are forced to deal with them in order to survive. They have to stop fighting each other, and help each other instead. This is the beginning of their "real" journey, an internal journey toward truth. It is a wonderful and uplifting journey, as all journeys for truth are, and in the end they overcome those fears, and of course, fall in love.

Had their relationship started off on great terms, we would not have had a very interesting movie. In fact, we wouldn't have had a movie at all, because their trip down the river might have captured some viewers' imagination, but it couldn't capture our hearts. Watching Charlie and Rose fall in love under the worst of circumstances made for a vivid and powerful human story. Nothing in this film would have worked were it not for its solid emotional structure.

We said very early on that your plot could take place almost anywhere in the world as long as your story was solid. I've never floated down a dangerous jungle river in Africa, I've never chatted with professional athletes in their locker rooms, and I don't know how long I would last trying to live the simple, beautiful life of an Amish man on a farm. But I know what personal struggle is. I know what falling in love feels like. And I am no different than the rest of your audience. Give me a good story and I will buy a ticket.

Character and Conscience

Historically, social competence, either universally or locally, goes through cycles from great strength to complete collapse and back to strength again. When we consider our screenplay's subject material we must consider it in the context of the place in that cycle in which our particular society finds itself in order to keep our story relevant. When society is functioning at its peak, everyone is king. When society begins to falter, everyone looks for the thing that is missing that will bring peace and prosperity back. Depending upon your point of view, we're either in need of a good war, or God.

Events such as September 11, the wars in Afghanistan and Iraq, and the bludgeoning natural disasters of hurricanes and tsunamis awaken the world. It may be such an event, one with world-changing impact, or it may be an event significant only in your protagonist's life that awakens him. But awaken he must. Your protagonist must be driven from his comfort and complacency. Suddenly his need for something more than a quick fix rears its ugly head. He is compelled to seek something more lasting; something more meaningful; serenity or sanity, or both.

The incident at the beginning of your script should trigger his awareness that this trip is going to be different, and that it is going to test him in ways he hasn't been tested before. He knows he can't just look for an easy way out. He must look for the "right" way out. And this "right" way will cost him.

But here's the caveat:

He doesn't know the right way.
Though he may not always know what is
right, he does always know what is wrong.
You must make him realize that just be-
cause he doesn't have the answer doesn't

mean he mustn't go forward. He must go forward, reluctant as he may be, substituting his conscience for his confidence. He has to do the right thing.

As the screenwriter you have to remain vigilant about this. You have to create a set of values that your protagonist exhibits without making him sound like a saint. Making statements about character, about morals, is the hardest part of writing a script, because it so often appears condescending and aloof. Dialog dies when we judge. It turns to lecture. True, people lecture in real life, but you may not lecture in your script. Instead, you observe and make observations. Many times you will make the observations without dialog, using images only. Which is rarely confused with lecture.

The importance of the writer's observation can't be overestimated. It is the key to objectivity, and objectivity creates relevance.

When we judge, objectivity is compromised. You could say that when we judge we aren't being relevant. We are merely being opinionated. Observations and opinions are mortal enemies. Opinions aren't drama. So get over yours if you want to write drama.

Observing objectively takes practice. It takes patience, understanding, and compassion. The human condition makes room for folly and forgiveness. And so must you. We write about our protagonists and antagonist, not to judge them, but to show what it is like to be human.

No one is perfect in our screenplays. The goal of the hero is not to be perfect. The goal of the hero is to realize his human potential, a potential that has been sabotaged by life's mischief. Your story is about that moment in his life when the issue of fulfilling life's potential slaps him in the face and demands to be dealt with. It is a moment or incident that commands his immediate and undivided attention or else even worse things will happen to him. And it requires action that is always counter-intuitive.

He is facing an unpracticed journey. And he will be in desperate need of guidance.

Enter your mentor

You must make sure your protagonist doesn't turn tail and run at any time during this life-challenge. One way of insuring this is to create a series of incidents that force him farther down the road of danger and away from the safety of home. Another way is to create a character referred to as the mentor whose cinematic purpose is to prevent the hero from ever retreating. The mentor forces him to go forward through the worst times, through the toughest challenges, until he reaches his goal or dies trying.

Our first instinct, and a common mistake, is to present the character of the mentor as a know-it-all. Some wise old fart with a long beard and cane. Please don't do that. If you do, the moment your mentor shows up on the screen everyone in the audience will know who he is and what he's going to say. That, in and of itself, is the kiss of death.

We want to surprise the audience as we introduce characters and situations. We want to keep them on their toes and keep them guessing. We don't want them to be aware that the mentor is mentoring. There might even be times when the mentor isn't aware that he is mentoring. This happens when young Samuel befriends John Book in *Witness*. At first it may seem that Book is mentoring Samuel, but really the opposite is happening. Samuel is the personification of the trust and innocence Book has lost and now seeks. Later, Eli mentors Book in the ways of the nonviolent world. So when you consider your Mentor, create situations that are subtle and allow them to build slowly. Maintain the element of the unexpected, and maintain the forward movement of your plot and story.

The mentor represents the protagonist's highest aspirations.

He personifies the kind of moral person the protagonist wishes he could be, and he mirrors the protagonist's spiritual center.

This is tricky stuff, Mr. and Mrs. Writer. Because, while the mentor is allowed to give the protagonist all the encouragement in the world, he isn't allowed to give him any answers. And the reason is simple. The mentor's answers are the mentor's answers. The protagonist must find his own.

Learning how to find the answers is the lesson being taught.

The dynamic of mentoring in screenplays is different than that of mentoring someone in business, or in the arts or sports. The dramatic mentor is a guide to the protagonist's conscience. When your protagonist struggles through your story and makes it to the point where he openly wrestles with his own conscience, usually late in the second act, he will do so because the mentor successfully conveyed to him the importance of reclaiming his own worthiness above all else.

The protagonist will be prompted by you, the power behind the mentor, with clever plot incidents that point to the higher aspirations of his younger life. Childhood dreams of a quest for soul-goodness, and of the people he admired and wanted to emulate, will come back to him in a flood of disconnected memory fragments. If your protagonist's childhood was anything like yours or mine, it was the goodness in others that enriched it.

I remember some great people, and I'm sure you do, too. People I wanted to be like when I grew up. I wasn't excited about their law practices or dry cleaning businesses, but I was moved by their warmth and generosity. Those gifts of patience and attention were my hope, and I had no reason to believe I wouldn't echo them when I grew up. Then life happened. I put those dreams aside as I grew older and was taught to focus on how much I could earn, rather than how much I could contribute. I studied profit margins instead of purpose. By the time I became learned, I had forgotten my hope.

That kind of "learning" probably happened to your protagonist, too, and set him on the path of indirection. A long, dusty, dangerous, and disagreeable path, on which he was battered and disheartened in the battle to earn capital instead of esteem. Character and conscience were not matters that occupied much of his time during that phase of his life. He might have formed habits that he substituted for character, which were built on need rather than honor. And when you create a situation in your script where the going gets tough and his world starts to collapse around him, the only thing that can save his butt is exactly what he doesn't have... the courage to change. That takes real guts. And it takes real faith.

The journey your hero must take is that one from fear to faith. From self-dependence to trust. From doubt to belief. It is a long and hard trip.

But your hero must not take this trip alone. You must take it with him.

In order to set up the story of a person seeking those things that were quieted in youth, or damaged by some trauma and put off limits emotionally years earlier, you have to imagine him having them first. You have to put yourself in his shoes and feel how painful the traumas that robbed him of emotional surety must have been. It's a smart idea to take a long walk all alone and attempt to live the heartaches and brutalities he must have suffered. Feel them if you can. Bond with your protagonist. Get upset when you write about the abuses and heartbreaks in his childhood. Ask yourself where the hell the people in his life who should have defended him were, and get angry at them. Understand why he became the person he became as a result of all of this.

This process is important, and the inquiries and powerful responses you will feel are legitimate. You are his caretaker, and you must remain his caretaker from fade in to fade out. You will know what it must have been like for him. You will know how the anger and resentments born of those events now rest uneasily just beneath his skin. It will not take much from you to write events and conflicts that will boil them to the surface.

The effects of those events from his past manifest in his everyday behavior. The behaviors you invent will be the clues to his past. At first they may seem simply like habits, good and bad. But gradually your audience will pick up on the emotional story you are telling beneath the plot.

When you bring him to a particular crisis in the script you will be able to sight the difficulty he has facing it through his personal history. Being subtle with this exposition is critical. You have to drop bits and pieces of his habits that reveal his history a little at a time *before* the crisis occurs that brings them full bore to the surface.

The bits and pieces may be in his behavior in the privacy of his home, for example. They may be in his choice of art, or music, or wardrobe in an attempt to distance himself from the tastes of a parent of whom he is now ashamed or from whom he is now estranged. They may be in his diet, unhealthy to the point of physical illness or overly healthy to the point of absurdity. They may be in the people he chooses as friends late at night behind closed doors. They may manifest themselves as sexual addiction, or drugs and alcohol abuse. He may hate all sports or he may be obsessed with them to the point of berating his son to become the best on his team. His history is told through these visible and telltale elements of his acquired personality. When we examine them, most especially when you "test" them under stress, they will reveal his psychological profile. And those revelations will ultimately lead to the inevitable surprise in the climax.

By including this kind of information as part of the fabric of his scenes, or the "wallpaper" as it's called, you will be accomplishing two important goals. First, you are creating a complex and interesting character: one with depth and credibility. And, second, you are telling his story visually with intrigue and nuance without anyone having to verbalize it. Remember this is a visual medium, and the more you can show rather then tell, the more satisfying your film will be.

In *The Fabulous Baker Boys* we could see the distinct differences in the brothers in almost every facet of their physical and emotional traits. We also see that these differences are a constant source of conflict for them. They can't solve their differences without breaking up their act, but they don't dare break up their act because they are both afraid of what the future might bring without the other. So they must live within that particular denial system of brotherhood, trapped in their co-dependence.

The device of exposing each brother's personality, especially how they view each other, tells us not only what each is like individually, but defines their complicated relationship as well. They seem to communicate at their best through their music. This has been true since they were kids in high school playing bar mitzvahs. And as the years passed, this communication style became a crutch for them. It became, ironically, a way of not communicating.

By dropping in these "personality clues," the writer, Steve Kloves, lays the groundwork for the inevitable fireworks ahead. He constructs each character through the subtleties of their habits. From Beau spraying his bald spot with scalp polish, and keeping track of every cent in their bank account, to Jeff's love affair with cigarettes, whiskey, and jazz. Beau's sense of responsibility is in complete opposition to Jeff's more tragic surrender. These details, doled out in bits and pieces along the way, foretell a disaster waiting to happen. How long can this fragile dynamic last? The answer is, as long as they are afraid to change. If either changed, the dynamic that was their career could come crashing down. And that would expose them. And that exposure would be too painful to imagine. So the bits and pieces set up the story, through tremendous conflict, of the resistance to change.

When Michelle Pfeiffer joins their act, the balance is thrown into chaos. Her presence brings their worst fears to the surface. The bits and pieces that define each character become more pronounced under the stress. Acting out of fear, Beau cuts his brother verbally, telling him to keep his hands off of Pfeiffer and stick to his cocktail waitresses. It is a terrible put-down, but fear brings out the worst in them. However, because of the groundwork laid down earlier, Beau's behavior is completely understandable and believable. Jeff's reaction is retaliation. Not wanting to believe seducing cocktail waitresses is the pinnacle of his sexual prowess, he seduces, and allows himself to be seduced by, Ms. Pfeiffer. And, as in his brother's case, Jeff's behavior is believable and in character. It would have been a lie if he hadn't bedded the blonde.

Creating the character's emotional structure supports the dramatic action.

Here is a writing exercise I'd like you to try now.

Write a two-page scene between two people. Invent any two characters you want. They don't have to be characters you've written about before. It is a scene in which the two characters lead up to and then make love together for the first time. During the scene Character One learns that Character Two's parents were murdered. But you are not allowed to let Character Two ever say so, and you are not allowed to let Character One show or tell Character Two what he or she has just discovered. You have to hide the information in the scene and you have to allow it to be discovered subtly and organically. The epiphany *must* effect an action that otherwise would not have yet occurred. Under no circumstances are you allowed to have the discovery derail the love scene.

The scene accomplishes two goals. First, it moves the love story (plot) forward in a very meaningful way. They are deepening their commitment to a relationship that may be loaded with complications or risks. Again, that's up to you—it could be an illicit affair, for example. The second accomplishment is the revelation of a critical emotional footprint (story) that will come into play in both the plot and the story later on. Maybe she has to have the lights out, or maybe he has to keep his socks on, but whatever it is, it has to send a deeper emotional or psychological signal.

The thinking behind this exercise is to show how more than one thing must be going on in a scene at one time, and that those things can be very, very different. We spoke earlier about making your script dense. This is an example of creative density.

Writing this kind of dense scene is not as daunting as it first sounds. If you keep your faith in yourself (what's good for your characters is good for you) you will discover the opportunities popping up all around you in scenes and sequences to lay the groundwork or drop in clues. You will be subconsciously aware of the need to expose your hero's information here and there, and this awareness will carry you through. You will develop a story sense, which is knowing when and where to say what and to whom for the greatest dramatic impact. In a later chapter we will discuss methods of organizing notes on these clues so that you don't forget to use them.

The antagonist and the co-protagonist

Your protagonist will need a lot of prodding to do all his soul-searching. And he will also need understanding and support. Two other central characters in screenplay structure are the antagonist and the co-protagonist. The antagonist forces the protagonist to take action and the co-protagonist encourages and supports that action.

The antagonist is the plot initiator in most cases. He is the one who drives the situation of change onto the protagonist. He is The Joker to Batman. He is the corrupt cop—all the corrupt cops—in the police force chasing John Book in *Witness*. He is also the corrupt cop in *Leon: The Professional* who is after Leon and Matilda.

Sometimes the antagonist isn't a person. Sometimes "society" is the villain when it has taken its toll on the protagonist to the extent the protagonist is not living the life he imagined he could. Examples of this are in *Wonder Boys* and *Lost in Translation*. In each case the antagonistic force that the protagonist faces is composed of fear and disappointment. In their stories life is beating them up with its ordinariness, not with any one particular event such as the murder in *Witness* or *The Professional*.

Genre will have its influence on this. You may be developing a murder mystery, for example, so your antagonist is personified in a clear way. Or you may be developing an idea along the lines where your protagonist is forced to go home to a parent's funeral and face a lot of old ghosts. In that case the incident puts the protagonist on the path but the incident itself isn't antagonistic, rather the entire mini-culture that was the source of great pain and rejection is.

In either case, the antagonist is responsible for keeping the pressure on your protagonist to leave his comfort zone and deal with a matter he would rather not. And remember, as we noted earlier, the antagonist need not be someone who is a total butthead. He can actually be a lot like your protagonist. The difference in their lives may only be that at a particular fork in the road, each took a different turn.

If the protagonist is being pushed or chased into a situation by the antagonist, then the one who encourages and supports him through the process is the co-protagonist. Sometimes there is a tendency to give the co-protagonist a mentor-like authority, and this is wrong. The mentor is someone who has his or her own answers. A co-protagonist, one who often starts out as a co-antagonist, does not have her own answers and will be seeking them just as the protagonist does.

The co-protagonist shifts from a co-antagonist stance when he or she comes to the realization brought on by the protagonist's search that he or she needs to do some searching, too. So, while the co-protagonist is helping the protagonist seek his goals, the protagonist is, in a way, forcing her to do some soul-searching as well. This becomes the mutual search to which we alluded earlier that, when heightened by the threat of the antagonist, leads to a mutual emotional experience that gives birth to an equally emotional attraction.

The missing gene of happiness

The role of co-protagonist is a great film role usually. The character is often as conflicted as the hero, but with far more humility and grounding. I like to call it a quality of warmth that the audience gets and likes. I also like to refer to the co-protagonist as the character who carries the hero's missing gene of happiness. That is to say she has an abundance of those rewarding human qualities the hero lacks. And he dislikes her for it.

It is this difference in personalities that gets them off on the wrong foot at the start. On the surface there are such conflicts of interest and points-of-view that it would seem impossible for them to agree on anything. Beneath the surface, however, there is an undeniable attraction. Both the conflict and the attraction should be evident from their very first encounter.

It's up to you if you want the conflict or the attraction to win out.

Deciding on character strengths and flaws can be progressive.

When you create your characters it is okay to start off with generalities. For example you may say your co-protagonist is shy or introverted, though you're not sure why or to what extent yet. But you know she's quiet and you like that about her. You may use other characters to comment on that quietness as a sign of her humility and maturity.

Gradually you can sneak in exposition revealing where the shyness came from as you get to know her. You will surprise us with her personality's dramatic and emotional roots as you develop them in your own mind and in your own time. You don't have to have your characters figured out completely from page one. Actually, it's better if you let them grow on you and tell you a little about themselves as you write.

You will see that this kind of development faith is a big part of all writing. You have to trust your writing. You have to trust that the answers will come if you just keep at it. I want you to also remember that there is no absolutely right answer when it comes to developing your characters. You can go in a hundred different directions with them and still have a stirring and gripping movie. Don't waste your time looking for the perfect solution. There is none.

In the case of the humble girl, you may decide that her humility is more complicated than most people think, and a result of a tragic event rather than a great personal achievement on her part. It could be the consequence of an abusive and humiliating childhood, for example. Or abandonment. Her shyness might be her defense against being hurt in a relationship again or being abandoned again. So her shyness is really a form of withdrawal. This of course is very unhealthy and leads to deeper emotional problems eventually. As you can see, what was thought to be an asset is really a liability. And it is something she is unwilling to take a hard look at until you make it a necessity in your story. When she does face it, she will go through as much pain as your protagonist. And their suffering will be the stuff of their bonding.

Keep your characters "down to earth."

With all the characters you are going to create, and all the problems you are going to give them, it is easy to portray one or two as bigger than life. This is okay only if the story is about a personality that is bigger than life. Otherwise, keep your characters right-sized. Make them people I can believe I'd run into in the course of my life. They can be exceptional in some ways—one may be an extraordinary concert pianist, or another may be a Medal of Honor winner—but the bottom line is that all people, great and small, are just people. If I can't relate to them as one person to another then you are putting up a barrier hard for me to overcome. I want to meet solid, real people. People I can love and people I can hate, but most of all people I can believe are real, with real problems I can understand.

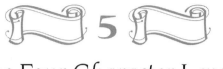

The Four Character Levels

What Makes Us Different Makes Us the Same

When I get up in the morning I am bursting with confusion. A chorus of screaming monkeys swings in the hollow of my skull, each voice demanding my attention. They are as unreliable and ill-informed as they are strident, doing nothing more than creating confusion and predicting defeat and misery in the day to come. I should never listen to them. But I am normal. And I listen. Maybe they are the legitimate voices of my ghosts clamoring to be heard, or maybe they are just the clowns in my Big Top brain. They are the reason, when I awaken, my thinking is usually at its worst.

I have discovered that if I sit quietly in my pajamas for a bit before I engage with family or friends I am far less likely to confound them or embarrass myself. When the monkeys quiet down and I regain enough mental equilibrium, I shower, dress, and speak. On my good days I make sense.

I am not alone.

I am not always what my thinking tells me I am.

I am not always what my words might suggest.

I am not always my manners or lack of them.

I am never the same person I was yesterday.

But I am always me. And I consider myself normal because I know that you are probably a lot like I am. And your protagonist is a lot like you. He might be a mess, but he is normal, even though normal doesn't always mean healthy or completely evolved.

Your story starts by finding your hero in an unsettled state.

When you create your protagonist make sure you create a part of his character that has always confused and scared him. It's something that scares him enough to avoid engaging it. It is the part of him he least understands, not for lack of brains but for lack of a consciousness or willingness to unearth it. There are parts of him he is ashamed of and he'll be damned if he could tell you why or what they are. You must create demons lingering in his subconscious that frighten him. He cannot define them, but he knows their threat like he knows the back of his hand.

Imagine your hero waking in the morning with the same disheveled thoughts as you or I. If you start a movie or a sequence in the movie with him on the bus to work, remember that he had an hour or more at home before this and ask yourself what it was like. Maybe there's nothing there for you to play with. Maybe there is. Maybe there was something in the tone of his wife's voice that causes him to suspect she's having an affair. Maybe the local ball team lost to the team in the cellar and the sure bet has him dodging the bookie's call. Maybe his kid was sick in bed, and he's worried he's getting sick too often. Could it be drugs? Maybe he felt a new pain in his chest while showering. He starts to count the years until his retirement and wonders if he'll make it or if he can afford it. He walks out the door past the table with yesterday's mail still there: the orthodontist bills, the private school bills, the back taxes. He has a choice. By the time he walks to the corner he can choose to take a deep breath and climb aboard the damn bus with the rest of the faithful, or he can throw himself in front of it.

Our Character Levels

The illustration of our hero on the next page gives us a look at how he might relate to the outside world on different emotional levels. He doesn't always, in fact he rarely opens up completely. And when he does open up he opens up to different people in different ways. This isn't to say that he is being deceptive. Most of the time he is being forthright. But most of the time he is being judicious, too. He doesn't want just anybody knowing all about him. There are levels of privacy and there are boundaries he keeps that are emotionally healthy most of the time.

Then there are those times when he plays around with the boundaries. He uses them and abuses them especially if he can gain power or control. He shows enough of himself to be liked, or to be elected, or to take you out for dinner and dancing and whatever may follow that.

There are honest boundaries, though, that he constructs and tries to

The Four Character Levels and the Nature of Their Emotional Connections

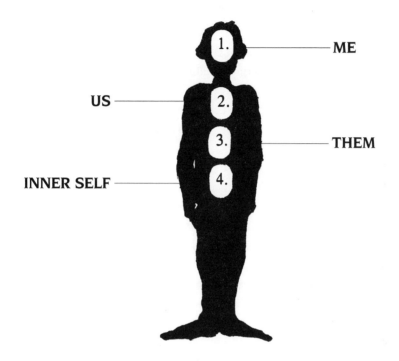

1. Individual.   Outer layer uniqueness. Character traits. Surface personality.

2. Familial.   Morality. Secrets. Sickness. Habituated belief system. The seat of guilt.

3. Social.   Cultural. Otherated. Environmental. Deep-rooted yet changeable. Obligation pressures.

4. Emotional.   The real deal. How your character honestly feels whether he/she is aware of the feelings or not. Hidden behind neuroses. Dedicated to individuation and compartmentalizing.

honor and those are the ones I'd like to focus on now. The four emotional levels are generalizations of course, but I use them to demonstrate the layers of emotions your characters are constantly dealing with.

Level one: the individual character level

The most visible character or emotional level is what I call the *Individual* level. This is the public presentation of your protagonist and what defines him or her as an individual in his community. It is his outer personality the rest of the world sees according to the way he manages it. It is a portrait of his physical makeup, his character traits, and his uniqueness. It is the way he walks and talks, the way he laughs and cries. This is the cover by which the book will be judged. You will introduce us to your protagonist on this level in most cases.

Some protagonists are just naturally wonderful on this level. We've all seen the kind of man or woman protagonist at the start of a film who is thoroughly likable, carries himself or herself with elegant ease, looks a person in the eye when he speaks, and remembers his friend's birthday.

If the protagonist is a woman, she has the long, shiny, healthy hair and the exquisite, athletic body. Clothes, even old rags, drape on her with eye-popping allure. When she walks away from us, we watch her every step until she is over the horizon.

If it's a guy, he is so casually handsome that it's unfair. His voice is an aphrodisiac, and his eyes see a woman's secrets. And she likes that.

But if your protagonist is not Mr. Perfect, and he is normal like you and I, he will sometimes struggle at this level. No matter how well he holds it together on the outside, he is continually influenced by one or more of the other character levels on the inside that could knock him off balance in a heartbeat.

In *Witness* for example, we meet Rachel who is comfortable and confident as she presents herself—her *Individual* level—in her Amish community, even in the aftermath of tragedy. Her presentation is based on her core beliefs. When she is forced into the situation of sustaining her outer self in the hostile and highly uncomfortable environment of Philadelphia's mean streets, she becomes self-conscious, and calls on her core beliefs to protect her. She demands to go home. Home, where her outer and inner selves exist without conflict. The comfort of her identity can only be found in the environment in which it was created.

Likewise, when John Book, the tough cop, is forced to stay on the farm, in Act Two, his external persona is not effective anymore. The *Individual* level he formed is suddenly transparent to those people, the Amish, who now populate his world. Being a tough cop means nothing to them. They see the person beneath the cop exterior.

The common dread for any protagonist is that in a new and strange environment he will be seen for what he really is. His fear is based on some inexplicable lack of faith in himself, or an unnamed shame.

This is the main reason any protagonist does not want to make his journey.

In your protagonist, indeed in all of us, there is a healthy need for this public mask. It serves to identify and protect us. But, as time passes, it can become more than a mask. It can assume the identity of the person it represents. We have all run into The Phony. The Phony is the guy who is so consumed by his outer portrayal that he believes his own lie. Unless something dramatic happens to him, something that will uncover the lie, he will be lost forever.

The protagonist's *Individual* level is a protective shield, first and foremost, born out of the fear of being seen in a less than perfect light. When you create your co-protagonist, you will be bringing to the protagonist a person who will see through his *Individual* level and challenge what's beneath it. This will be the beginning of the exposure of the protagonist's more intimate character levels. It is the function of Rachel's character in *Witness* as co-protagonist to expose Book.

Level two: the familial character level

The second emotional character level is the *Familial* level: the source of our core beliefs. It is the wellspring of the best of us and the worst of us. We are as healthy at this emotional level as our family history permits. We may have been lucky and been brought up in a loving family. Or we may have been average and raised in a loving dysfunctional family.

Think of the influence family has on a person from birth to death. Almost every opinion formed early in life is over dinner or on the way to church or in the hushed cynicism of deserved punishment. It gives me the chills. The best we can do sometimes is to acknowledge that those who raised us did the best they could.

A childhood is filled with damaged blessings.

You, of course, must consider your protagonist's childhood. He has become the person he is today because of it. In *Witness* we see very clearly the family traditions that have shaped Rachel, and we see how they are shaping the next generation in the person of Samuel. I would venture to say that their family is a microcosm of the entire Amish community. In Rachel's family, which is a loving family, the simplicity of their lifestyle helps a great deal in keeping things in perspective. The focus is on what is important and meaningful in their humble spirituality. Humility is balanced with a pride in their work and their faith. Rachel is known and judged not by her outer appearances—the *Individual* level—but rather by her interior qualities. This is the intent of their uniformity, and it works well on that level. We know what to expect from Rachel in terms of her behavior in most situations because it is consistent with her beliefs.

John Book, on the other hand, is not as simple to "read." His childhood experiences are hidden deep within. In Book, the writers have created a character who is living on the outside. His *Individual* level has become who he is. He doesn't want to discuss what's going on inside of him because he doesn't want to think about it or acknowledge it. To some women perhaps, this presents an attractive, strong, silent type guy. But to Rachel it represents a man in denial. We get only a glimpse of his past through his relationship with his sister, and the revelations she in turn discusses with Rachel about him. He is an enigma. As the protagonist, this is a good thing. It means that the writers can now devote the entire story in Act Two to unraveling his mystery.

So, when you create a character that is a stoic son-of-a-bitch, who refuses to cry during a three-hankie movie, maybe he has some issues your co-protagonist should deal with before she says "I do." A person who isn't emotionally accessible is a ticking time bomb.

If you were to ask your protagonist how he feels about his family and his upbringing you might not get the whole truth from him. This is because he doesn't really know the whole truth himself. He prefers not to know. And he believes he's doing just fine in life without knowing. It's your job to create a scenario in which he isn't doing fine anymore, and that forces him to take a look whether he likes it or not. But you can't ask him to take a look if you, the writer, are not willing as well to take a look at your personal *Familial* level.

So here's the next writing assignment.

On one side of a sheet of paper write down how you are different from your mother. On the other side of the same paper write down how you are like your mother.

Don't rush this. Take a good look at yourself. Be honest. You may even find yourself changing your mind about how you've thought of the similarities and differences you've assumed for so long. After you've taken a look at yourself, take a long, gentle look at your mother. Sometimes pain obscures the truth or misplaces blame.

The family truth

The *Familial* level refers to the nuclear family living under one roof. This is where the family truth is. Every family has a family truth. It may all be a pack of lies, but it is the family truth nonetheless. It is usually more opinion than fact, greater intolerance than tolerance, and more selfish than selfless. It seems innocuous while it develops, but it is actually very dangerous.

Sniping, that all-American expression of jealousy and ignorance wrapped in ridicule, is the epitome of a graceless mind. It is falsely authoritarian and a prime example of substituting emotional honesty with sarcasm. Sniping gives life to fear.

The fear-based family truth creates mass amounts of guilt. Comparisons work silently on children especially, establishing their first experience with anxiety. Comparing one person to another is an awful practice. In a family where love is the ideal condition, comparisons—which are judgments in sheep's clothing—should be banned. When a parent asks her child why she can't be more like little Suzie down the street, the damage is done.

Comparison very often tiptoes in on gossip. If disingenuous gossip is tolerated at the dinner table by his parents, the child believes two things. One: gossip is okay. And two: if we talk about our neighbors, then they probably talk about us. Gossip is hearsay, and hearsay is not okay. Hearsay is borderline defamation that establishes a subconscious mindset of "them versus us." This gives birth to the life-long worry of "what do others think of me?" And we know that seeking the answer to that question is man's biggest waste of time. And it is also the primary reason we form our *Individual* level in the first place. This is how the first and second layers, the *Individual* and *Familial* levels are connected.

The connections don't stop there.

Level three: the social level

The third emotional character level is the *Social* level. We are social animals. The influences from society are great. Cultures differ so much yet they all provide the same things in the end: human connection, validation, appreciation, love, comfort, and pleasure. But society can also bring pressure to bear. We have obligations in society, and standards to meet. We can be bullied by society if we are not careful. Boundaries, just like those in our family relationships, can be tested constantly. Society can also challenge our morality. As tribesmen and women we have roles to play that come with responsibilities, and when met, set roots deep into the community that subsequently create a sense of security and satisfaction.

The danger the *Social* level represents to the individual, and to your protagonist especially, is its ability to corrupt one's morals. The profound attraction of social acceptance often turns obsessive in nature. Gradually, almost unknowingly, we lend more importance to being accepted by our peers than by meeting our own personal standards. The quest for acceptance and success causes us to compromise our own boundaries. As we do this we devalue our core selves. This capitulation is the source of many problems. The deterioration of personal boundaries sets us up for much greater problems in the future. Many times the price of admission is a loss of self-esteem or worse.

When we examine this level in *Witness* we see that all the pressure brought to bear on Book comes from his police chief and fellow cops— his *Social* level. He can alleviate all his problems by simply going along with them. But he would have to completely abandon his morals to do it. What makes this surrender so difficult for Book is that it will cost him the only family he has.

We see Book able to thrive in this police family in Act One. But by the end of Act One everything changes. He sees the corruption and he must make the decision of a lifetime. The writers force him into this situation, and then they offer him an alternative level three in the society of the Amish. But in order to thrive in the new *Social* level he has to change. A deep change. Deeper than he's changed before. Because it's not a change on the *Individual*, *Familial*, OR *Social* level. It's a change on the most basic level. The Fourth Level.

Level four: the emotional level

When all is said and done, everything we see, everything we hear, everything we feel, everything we taste, everything we do affects us emotionally. Thomas Merton said "Every moment and every event of every man's life on earth plants something in his soul. For just as the wind carries thousands of winged seeds, so each moment brings with it germs of spiritual vitality that come to rest imperceptibly in the minds and wills of men." Powerful stuff.

The fourth level is one over which we have the least control. It is not ruled by will or logic. It is not ours to boss around. It alone is responsible for releasing what I call the conscience response. Our emotional responses are tied to our sense of fairness and our belief in goodness. Our *Emotional* level is the level most in need of constant refinement because the imprints of experiences are constant. As each moment in our lives brings its germs of spiritual vitality to rest in our minds or will, we are responsible for developing an awareness to receive them, and a spiritual mechanism to transform their value. We cannot go through life oblivious to what is going on around us. We cannot go through life without being held accountable to the greater good, even if we're not aware of that obligation yet. We cannot, either, go through life denying how we feel, or especially denying that we don't know how we feel. Sooner or later, driven by dotage or pain, we begin to ask those almighty questions: Who am I and what does my life mean?

The entire Act Two of *Witness* is dedicated to this question. Both Book and Rachel must examine who they are, who they want to be in the future. The entire Act Two of *The Professional* does the same. Leon and Mathilde search for their realities and worthiness. In both movies their individual quests create a bond as a couple. It is an everlasting bond, whether they remain together or not, because it is a bond created on the most important level. It is not an Individual bond, or a Familial bond, or a Social bond. It is a profound uncorrupted Emotional bond, pure in its need and innocent in its demands.

When you create your plot your job will be to force a situation on your hero and his co-protagonist wherein these almighty questions will be asked. Your characters have to reach the point where they trust each other. Based on their mutual trust they can move on and face the unknown.

Remember the guy we talked about earlier who leaves his house in the morning with more questions than answers? When he climbs onto the bus of faith in the morning he has reached a breaking point unless he can tie all his problems together in a way that explains their value rather than their threat. Beyond the worries of whether or not his wife is having an affair, beyond the question of whether his son is on drugs, and beyond the pressure of the unpaid bills, he must believe that what he doesn't know is as viable as that which he does know. And that he doesn't always know what he thinks he needs to know. Artemis Ward said, "It ain't the things we don't know that gets us into trouble. It's the things we know for sure that just ain't so." Always having the answer does not guarantee happiness or jackpots. Trusting the process is far more important than needing to know the results.

If your protagonist, just like the guy on the bus, doesn't take the time to nurture himself, he will surely pop. The answer to Who am I lies not in the intellect, but rather in the soul. It is a spiritual question that requires a spiritual answer. It cannot be found on the shelf at the market. The secret of life is not found resting on our outer layer, our surface personality. The secret of life does not exist in the mystery and sickness of our family. The secret of life has nothing to do with our culture or environment. The secret of life has everything to do with how we honestly feel about our worthiness and our worth.

It is important for you to monitor the constant and subtle changes that take place on the four character levels of your characters as they move from scene to scene, and from act to act. This is not as difficult as it sounds. If you make sure that your characters learn something in each scene, and that that knowledge changes them in one way or another, then you're doing well. A critical element in Emotional Structure is the awareness that each scene adds to the protagonist's knowledge, even if the knowledge isn't the answer he thought he was looking for. At least he knows more at the end of a scene than he did in the beginning. There are few exceptions to this rule.

When he learns more, he changes. As he changes, his relationships with other characters change. He cannot have the same conversation with his wife on page thirty that he had on page ten because he is a different person by page thirty and would be asking different questions. If he's clever he won't have to ask any questions at all. If you create the right behavior for both of them based on their character levels the answer to his question could be in her actions rather than her words. They could be talking about the weather but their body language could be saying something else. Actors and directors like this kind of writing in your script because it gives them a chance to tell the story with pictures. Then, by the end of that scene he and she will be different again. And so on. Every scene will have character growth because every scene has to have an epiphany.

As these changes pile up, the protagonist will become less comfortable with the idea of ignoring how he feels. He will become less willing to hide his true self behind a facade. This is because once he is exposed to the truth, it can never be denied again. When he takes the next step and adopts his newfound truth, he will transform knowledge into consciousness. Which is the same as turning change into growth. This is huge.

And here is why.

Harmony

Once the fears are faced and dealt with, the Four Character Levels realign. As they do, they come into an Emotional Harmony. In other words, the insides and outsides match. What you see is what you get, and what you feel is real. Your protagonist becomes whole.

When we first meet the Amish of Lancaster in the opening of *Witness* we get the immediate feeling of a community, a society, that is at peace. At One. This is precisely because their philosophy is to create a true harmony between their interior and exterior lives. It is living in the ultimate truth. We all feel that "something special" when we watch the film. We all wish our lives could be that simple. That is the attraction of a harmonious emotional life. And that is what turns the hero around in the end.

This is what happens to Book at the end of *Witness*. He finally accepts that there is a better and more peaceful way to live life. This growth in him brings a new strength and determination with which to do battle. A battle he can win today that he could not have won yesterday. And, ironically, he wins the battle without his gun. Unarmed, he simply states the truth: you can't kill everyone.

Your bonus

All of this change and growth is not just about the characters you create. It is also about you. Every time you create a character or write a scene you grow, too. Every sequence and act you write will make you more capable of writing the next sequence and act. Just as you ask your hero to trust his process, you must trust yours. The first act will be good, the second act will be better, and the third act will be the bomb.

Trust your growth.

Part 2

Structure: Not Necessarily a Necessary Evil

A Three Act Structure Overview

As you begin to develop your script it will be necessary to envision it in three parts: the beginning, the middle, and the end. This is the simplified broad stroke version of your plot and story. There are different structures for the various genre of film, but no matter which genre you choose, without some kind of plan your screenplay is likely to be a complete mess.

Many screenwriters, fledgling and seasoned, resist the idea of structuring their work fearing it will turn their artistic endeavor into something mechanical and inflexible. But this is giving structure a bad rap. Organizing your artistic effort only makes it better.

Think of it as a wide-angle view of your concept from start to finish before you write it. You want to imagine the film in your head, not in great detail, but in sweeping strokes that tell you what your beginning, middle, and end is going to be like. In fact, a good analogy to a screenplay outline is the painter's sketch. If you have had any experience in painting you know that you develop your composition with a series of sketches first. You want to see your options, and you want to get it down to just what you like before you commit it to the oils on a large canvas.

Writers do the same thing. The purpose of sketching your idea out is to see all the options available to you and to develop a sense of what your film "feels" like. When we sit down and work on our painting we don't start in one corner and complete the painting in that corner then move to another corner and complete what has to be painted in that corner until we've filled in the entire canvas. We sketch out the whole vision in pencil on the canvas first. Then we work with paints on the entire canvas at one time, not just one corner at a time. By doing this we maintain our vision and can see how everything is connected with the use of colors and shapes and themes. The work is cohesive.

Ditto with script structure. We have to make sure our writing is cohesive and we can't do that by painting in one corner at a time. That would be like writing a script without an outline. It is foolish to think that we can write scene one, scene two, scene three, and so on up to scene one hundred and eighty-two and think it's going to be cohesive. More likely it will be incomprehensible.

So if you hate the idea of writing an outline before writing your script, get past it now. Put the book down, stand up, raise your arms and whine at the top of your lungs. Now sit back down, take a deep breath, and get to work. There is an easy way to do this and we will break it all down into simple, logical steps in the following chapters. For now I want to stay with the overview because I want to introduce you to all the wonderful things that go on in a screenplay of which most people aren't aware.

Overall length

Until recently the typical screenplay was around 120 pages in length. Though that is still acceptable, the trend has been toward slightly shorter scripts. And I am personally glad to see the trend. I like to keep my screenplays well below 120 pages. Somewhere between 100 and 110 pages feels nice and tight and fast moving. I'd like to suggest that you try to keep your screenplay at that length, too. Anything more than 120 pages and you will meet resistance at studios and agencies.

As I mentioned earlier, the executives at production companies and studios have a lot of reading to do. When they lift a script by a new writer and it feels like the Manhattan Yellow Pages the first thing they do is flip to the last page to see its length. If it's 130 pages or more, chances are they will suspect it is over-written, and won't take it seriously. They may read the first twenty or thirty pages but unless those pages are fantastic they will toss it on the rejection pile. If it's more than 130 pages I can almost guarantee you it will land on the rejection pile without being read at all.

That may sound unfair and callous, but the truth is those executives only have so many hours in a day to read an enormous amount of material and come to decisions involving millions of dollars. They cannot afford to waste a couple of hours reading anything less than a very professional script. If you expect their careful consideration and professional opinion, then the least you can do is be careful and professional, too.

Put first things first.

To ensure that your script is tight and professional you need to write an outline first. The outline will help you see how the plot and story lay out. It will help you edit your work up front so that you can drop scenes that aren't needed before you write them. The three-act structure is above all else a magnificent editing device. As you lay out the scenes in acts one, two, and three you will be able to see where you're being redundant and where you're missing some important information. You can see, too, if your story is slowing down to a crawl in places and if it will help to bring in a bit of action to keep things moving. Or the opposite: sometimes we get so excited about writing an action piece that we forget to slow down and let the audience catch its breath.

The classic dramatic structure is three acts. In a 110-page script the first act is about twenty-five pages long. The second act is roughly fifty-five to sixty pages long, and the third and final act is the shortest, often only twenty to twenty-five pages. Each act has its own function and responsibility.

Act One

Act One's function is to introduce all of your main characters, your theme, point-of-view, your genre, your time and place, and your style. By the end of Act One you must state the protagonist's problem. This will tell us who and what the film is about. The first act must be gripping and completely engaging. You will grab or lose your audience in the first fifteen minutes of your film, so your opening has to be smashing.

That's a lot to accomplish in twenty-five pages. There will be no room for side-trips and no allowance for squandering valuable pages on things that do not address those specific goals. As you can imagine, trying to write twenty-five great opening pages that will do all the things mentioned above without the benefit of an outline would be making a difficult task almost impossible. Sketching out first what has to be in the twenty-five pages will help enormously, and save a lot of time and effort.

We will break down Act One further in the following chapter because each group of pages—the first ten, the second fifteen—has specific functions. For now, let's stay in the wide-angle mode and simply say that the first twenty-five pages set up the whole movie.

By the end of Act One when the protagonist comes up against his big problem it will be clear to the audience what kind of movie they are going to see. They will have met their hero, the hero's co-protagonist, the antagonist, and the mentor. They will have seen the protagonist and the co-protagonist in their home settings and have learned about their private lives and personal problems to some small extent. They will have seen them meet over a particular problem, and disagree on how to solve that problem. Having been forced together, they will see the protagonist and co-protagonist attempt to solve the problem and make it worse by their attempt. They will see them encounter a major crisis and moral dilemma that their attempt has caused and that thrusts them reluctantly on a journey together they don't want to take.

So the first act ends in a major crisis that tells the audience what the movie is going to be about. It forces the protagonist to step outside of his comfortable world to solve the problem. He thinks he'll be able to solve it and get back to his comfort zone without too much difficulty. But he doesn't know what you have in store for him in the second act.

Act Two

Act Two, the center and centerpiece of the script, is where the story overtakes the plot. This is the section of the film that is really the guts of the film. It embodies the theme of your story through the personal journey of your hero as he changes and grows in order to defeat the antagonist in the climax. Act Two is the E-motion picture, and the film within the film.

In *Witness* it is the story of Book and Rachel trying to figure out each other while the world spins around them. In *The Professional* it is the story of Leon and Mathilda trying to cope with first love while the violent and corrupt world spins around them. In *Wonder Boys* it is the touching unrequited love between Michael Douglas and Frances McDormand amid the chaos and comedy it causes. In *The African Queen* it is Bogart and Hepburn being Bogart and Hepburn and falling in love under fire.

These middle sixty pages are the meat and potatoes of the film. This is the part of the movie everyone will remember because this is the part of the movie to which everyone can relate. Everyone has tried to figure out his life or fallen in love. Maybe not under fire, but it's still falling in love. The second act is the most important part of the film. The first and third acts can still succeed even if they are flawed, but the second act cannot. You film will fail if the second act fails.

The second act is longer than the other two acts combined because it has many more jobs to do. It is an enormous undertaking. That is why a well thought-out outline for this act is essential.

In the plot in Act Two the risks and dangers you threaten your hero with continue to escalate. Page after page the odds become greater, and the defeats more profound. Simultaneously in Act Two's story you explore each character's emotional reactions to the events and the deepening complexity in their relationship the exposed emotions create. The protagonist starts Act Two fully resistant to any change. You have given him a big problem at the end of Act One and all he wants to do now is to solve it and go home. But you have a few things in mind for him first. He winds up going through defeat and fear, he reexamines his life, loses faith, finds faith, becomes willing to change, commits to things he's never committed to before, almost dies, almost gives up, but stays the course and fights the good fight. At the end of Act Two the fight to fulfill his quest turns bitter and grim. He is standing at the precipice facing a life and death situation.

So you see what I mean by suggesting this is the most difficult act to write. Not because it is longer, but also because it is so damn complex. It is very easy to get lost in the second act. A lot of films do. Without a solid emotional structure going into this act, it will fall on its face. That's when the middle becomes the muddle. We will spend a lot of time working on this act in later chapters. Now, back to the overview.

Act Three

Act Three begins as the protagonist faces his final and greatest challenge. It is at this point he engages in the fight of his life and for his life. It could be with swords on a pirate ship or with words of love so difficult to speak, spoken for the first time. Every great battle is different, and every great battle produces greatness. We will want to make your hero's battle profound and beautiful. Your hero's victory signals the finale to the physical plot victory. His display of courage is something he never could have done before this journey. The battle has been won and the antagonist you introduce in Act One has been defeated.

Now that the plot is ended, you must end your story. It is here, in the final few pages of the script, we create the film's resolution. Your protagonist must face the other battle and resolve it: the battle going on inside his heart and soul. The resolution is reflective, a taking in of the experiences with some perspective and imagining the new life he or she is about to lead from this point on.

Will they stay together, as Michael Douglas and Frances McDormand do in *Wonder Boys*? Will they find it impossible to stay together, as Harrison Ford and Kelly McGillis determine in *Witness*? Will they forever be better off but heartbroken as Bill Murray and Scarlett Johansson are at the end of *Lost in Translation*?

Act Three opens up our protagonist and co-protagonist's lives to all the possibilities ahead of them that had been denied earlier. Sometimes those lives are led together, and sometimes not. Sometimes one or both of them die. It's up to you to resolve their stories in ways you feel are the most honest and moving.

Act Three tells us what this story has meant not just to your characters, but to all of us. It tells us what we have to consider in our lives, just as the characters in the film considered them in their lives. It tells us we are all part of the human family. It tells us that we are okay, that we are human and fallible and lovable and forgivable. It wraps up your thoughts on the film. It reiterates your point and your faith in your characters and your audience. It is a simple, delicate, thoughtful, and profound ending.

THE BEGINNING

PAGES 1 THRU 25

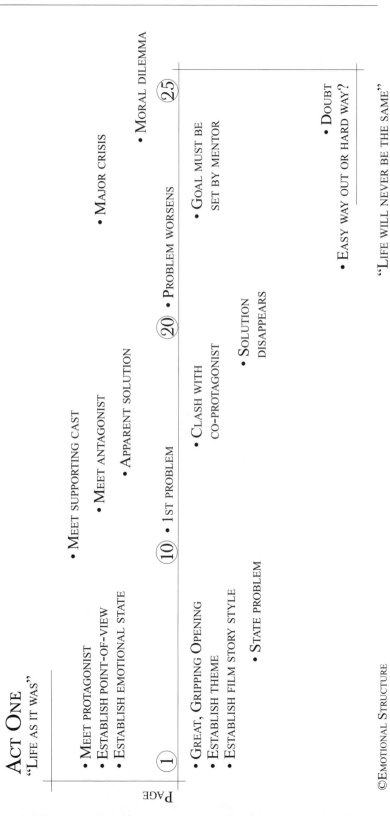

ACT ONE
"LIFE AS IT WAS"

- MEET PROTAGONIST
- ESTABLISH POINT-OF-VIEW
- ESTABLISH EMOTIONAL STATE

- MEET SUPPORTING CAST
- MEET ANTAGONIST
- APPARENT SOLUTION

- MORAL DILEMMA

(1)

- GREAT, GRIPPING OPENING
- ESTABLISH THEME
- ESTABLISH FILM STORY STYLE
- STATE PROBLEM

(10) • 1ST PROBLEM

- CLASH WITH CO-PROTAGONIST
- SOLUTION DISAPPEARS

(20) • PROBLEM WORSENS

- MAJOR CRISIS

(25)

- GOAL MUST BE SET BY MENTOR

- DOUBT
- EASY WAY OUT OR HARD WAY?

"LIFE WILL NEVER BE THE SAME"
END OF ACT ONE

PAGE

©EMOTIONAL STRUCTURE
PETER DUNNE

THE MIDDLE

PAGES 25 THRU 85

ACT TWO
"LIFE TORN APART"

- PHYSICAL ACTION TO HELP CREATES RISK & DANGER

- SUFFER LOSS
- ROUTE ALTERED

- NEW DANGER DEFEATS OLD WEAPONS
- COMMIT TO WIN

- CO-PROTAGONIST OFFERS ANSWERS AND ELICITS ACCEPTANCE
- NEW REASON TO STAY & FIGHT

- DEEPEST FEARS ARE TESTED

- FACING DEATH

- CLIMAX

- HIGHER PURPOSE

- TENT POLE SCENE

㉕

㊺ (55)

⑧⑤ (85)

- EMOTIONAL RESISTANCE
- FEARS ARE REVEALED

- CO-PROTAGONIST FEUD
- DOUBT-DISTANCE

- EMOTIONAL TURMOIL
- FIGHT/FLIGHT MODE

- CO-PROTAG BONDING
- FEARS CHALLENGED
- APARTNESS THREATENED

- EMOTIONAL DEFEAT
- LOSS OF FAITH
- MOST VULNERABLE

- CO-PROTAG COMMITMENT
- EMOTIONAL UNION
- CHANGES BEGIN
- GROWTH IS PAINFUL

- REBUILD OR DIE
- ALONE AGAIN BUT ALONENESS IS SAD — NO LONGER A COMFORT

- EMOTIONAL SET BACK
- BREAK UP & GIVE UP
- WILLING TO LOSE

- COMMIT TO LOVE
- FAITH DEFEATS FEAR

"NEW SET OF EMOTIONS"
END OF ACT TWO

PAGE

©EMOTIONAL STRUCTURE
PETER DUNNE

THE END

PAGES 85 THRU 110

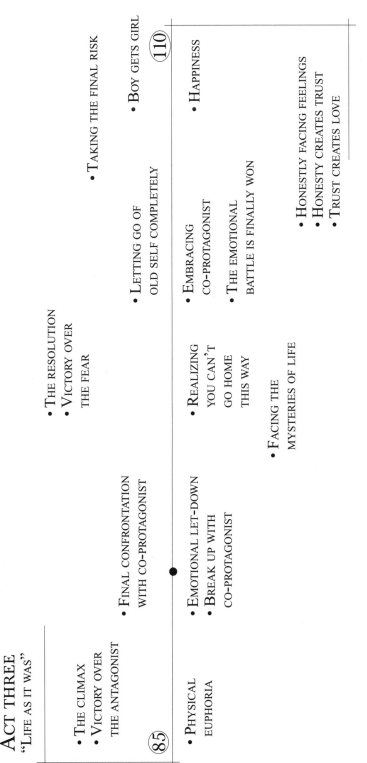

ACT THREE
"LIFE AS IT WAS"

- THE CLIMAX
- VICTORY OVER THE ANTAGONIST

- FINAL CONFRONTATION WITH CO-PROTAGONIST

- THE RESOLUTION
- VICTORY OVER THE FEAR

- LETTING GO OF OLD SELF COMPLETELY

- TAKING THE FINAL RISK

- BOY GETS GIRL

(110)

- HAPPINESS

- PHYSICAL EUPHORIA

- EMOTIONAL LET-DOWN
- BREAK UP WITH CO-PROTAGONIST

- REALIZING YOU CAN'T GO HOME THIS WAY

- FACING THE MYSTERIES OF LIFE

- EMBRACING CO-PROTAGONIST

- THE EMOTIONAL BATTLE IS FINALLY WON

- HONESTLY FACING FEELINGS
- HONESTY CREATES TRUST
- TRUST CREATES LOVE

THE END

(85)

PAGE

©EMOTIONAL STRUCTURE
PETER DUNNE

The Case for Brevity

When I first undertook writing years ago friends would ask what I was writing about. Try as I might, I could never get the answer down to anything slicker than a sort of stultifying State of the Union address. If you are like most writers you are familiar with the sickening feeling that overtakes you while you stumble on with your explanation even as your friend's eyes glaze over. It seems the more you try to clarify things, the murkier it all gets. Suddenly you begin to doubt your idea, or if you even know what the hell you're talking about. The same thing will happen to you when you're writing your script unless you take the time now to crystallize your story and theme. If you start to question your idea while you are writing the script you will often abandon it.

Thus the case for brevity.

Albert Einstein said that no idea was so complicated it couldn't be explained in a couple of sentences. The way I look at it, if the man whose ideas were certainly more elegant and complicated than any of those seeping out of my little brain believed in such pithiness then who am I to argue?

As you think about the film you want to write, think of it in terms of a short, summarized review in the Arts & Leisure section. Reduce the concept down to as clear and concise a pitch as you possibly can. This is hard to do at first, but you'll get the hang of it. The more I practiced putting my ideas down in three tight sentences, the clearer my own understanding of my ideas became. Not only that, but as I went on to write the scripts I remained more aware of the development of that idea and became less likely to wander away from the primary, two or three sentence concept.

One sentence at a time

It is a necessity in the business to be able to pitch your idea to a producer or studio executive in a quick and entertaining way. Not only will they get excited about your film, but they will get excited about you, too. If you know your idea as if it were second nature they will trust you to stay on point with it and deliver what they're buying. Studios will invest a lot of money in you and your idea, and having confidence in your concise thinking is critical to their comfort in making that investment.

In reducing your idea to three sentences you need not worry about stating the climax or resolution in any detail at all. The fact is you may not know exactly how your film is going to end until you get there. What you must know at this point is the kind of story you want to tell. The act of writing it will answer a lot of questions for themselves. For the three-sentence pitch you need only introduce the protagonist, his great challenge, and what the challenge reveals to him. In other words his emotional arc and the "point" of his story, and what enlightenment the story offers to the filmgoer.

Here are a couple of examples I've worked up. Within each of them there is enormous latitude for the author to invent scenes and situations till the cows come home. But knowing the direction and goal of the film will keep those choices on the right path. After you've given these some thought, put this book down and try working on yours for a few minutes.

Broken Flowers

Broken Flowers, written by Jim Jarmusch, stars Bill Murray as a committed bachelor who is told in a letter from an anonymous past lover that he has a grown son searching for him. Murray's pursuit of the woman who wrote the letter turns into the pilgrimage from hell in a series of face-to-face encounters with all the women who once loved him, but whose love he abused and abandoned. Though he never learns who mothered the son he has yet to meet, he does learn the painful truth about the damage his inability to love and be loved has caused, and what he must do to change that in the future.

Wonder Boys

We have all been "stuck" before in dissatisfying jobs, in stifling relationships, in frustrated artistic endeavors, but few of us have been as "stuck" as Grady Tripp in Steve Kloves' adaptation of Michael Chabon's novel *Wonder Boys*. Michael Douglas portrays the university professor whose pitiable existence finally collapses in one hilarious and chaotic campus weekend celebrating the achievements of his students, whose work has surpassed his own. Realizing his own failures are the price he has paid for succumbing to his fears rather than believing in his dreams, he must take the leap of faith that has haunted him all his life.

I began a screenplay of my own with this three-line description:

Indirection

Scott Peck is doing just fine in the Big Apple taking City College courses during the day and driving an ambulance at night, until his mother calls from Muncie, Indiana, to tell him his kid sister ran away from home. Desperate to find her, he reluctantly teams up with a sarcastic and beautiful street-savvy stranger in a hunt against the clock, against the odds, and sometimes against the law. Their urgent pursuit across a patchwork of cities and towns, pavement and pasture, high rises and silos becomes a search for their own runaway hearts in an American social landscape devoid of the love youth needs.

You can see I left myself a lot of room for invention and incident. You may also notice a pattern here, that the three sentences often reflect the beginning, middle, and end, or acts one, two, and three of the film.

My desire to write a story about America's youth came from my own childhood experiences, and from witnessing the experiences of my children. I have felt for some time now that "society" isn't holding up its end of the deal to love and protect her vulnerable youth. Instead, "society" seems bent on treating them merely as a desirable consumer group. And that scares me and angers me. I couldn't afford to use my script as a political soapbox condemning demographics, though, so I had to create an adventure story and a love story (yes, Scott and the pain-in-the-ass girl who helps him do absolutely fall in love) within which my political points-of-view could be exposed.

The first sentence

Start thinking about how your idea could overlay one of these examples. Do you see the beginning of your movie? Do you see your hero living his or her life and then *something* happens that pulls him out of that life? In its broadest strokes the first line in your three-sentence pitch tells me who the story is about and what happens that yanks him out of his life as he knows it and sends him on a trip he's never wanted to make.

In my story about young Scott things are going along just fine until his fifteen year old sister runs away and he knows he has to go after her, and we know his life is never going to be the same again.

So now work on your first sentence. Set up who he is and what event happens that's about to alter his life forever.

The second sentence

The second sentence reflects the body of your script and the essence of your story more than the plot. Again, you don't need a lot of detail since most detail will have to be worked out as you write the script. But you have a general idea of the things you want your hero to encounter, and the challenges you are thinking of putting in his way. So this sentence refers to those experiences and the effects they are going to have on him, both the human costs and the spiritual gains.

Think about your second sentence and work on it for a while. It's not an easy one to write because a lot has to be said without detail. Take your time working on this and try different approaches. Don't forget that this part of your pitch refers to the very essence of your idea. This is the heart and soul and guts of your film, so do it justice.

The third sentence

Finally, your last sentence speaks to the resolution of your film, which is the point of your story and the universality of your concept. There is a tendency here to wax philosophic, as if to say your film is too, too special. Be aware of that tendency and express your belief in the importance of the story without sounding self-important.

So take the time now to work on your third sentence, and then go over the whole three-sentence pitch a few times. Try different approaches until you are happy that your approach reflects your feelings about your story and your commitment to its resolution.

Three Acts in Three Pages

Now that you have reduced your idea to three sentences you are ready for your next step...which is to *expand* the three sentences into three pages. There really is logic behind this approach. Writing three pages without the three-sentence guideline can become a world-class, time-wasting struggle. One, I believe, that rarely leads to the clarity you can achieve with the three-sentence base you just developed.

The three pages serve as a brief analysis of your three acts. They will begin to demonstrate the connection between the action in each act emotionally. The three pages are mostly focused on the story rather than the plot. This three-page treatment will be used to hook an agent or producer if your three-sentence pitch did its job. For the record, the greatest percentage of the page count will be dedicated to the second act.

Page one, Act One

In my story *Indirection* I will establish Scott's life at work and play, and I will show what it means to him when he hears his sister has run away. He takes it very hard and is committed to giving up his life temporarily in order to find her at all costs. Simultaneously I plan on introducing the co-protagonist, the pain-in-the-ass streetwise girl who will eventually help Scott, in her own plot and story. The two will cross paths in an antagonistic encounter, and then very guardedly agree to go on the search for his sister together, he for obvious reasons, she for reasons she hasn't yet disclosed. The girl will be more of a co-antagonist at that point, much as Rachel was to John Book at that point in *Witness*.

Another example, just for fun, might be watching the guy we were talking about earlier who gets on the bus in the morning wondering if his wife is having an affair, if his son is a drug addict, or if he'll ever get out from under all the debt. The guy's having a terrible day and it hasn't even begun yet.

He's riding the bus when it comes to a stop and a beautiful woman bounds on board and runs down the aisle. A grizzly man jumps on after her. As she races past our guy she flips a package in his lap, then jumps out the back door and runs away. The grizzly man stumbles out the door after her. The bus starts up again and people go back to reading the paper as if nothing happened. But something certainly did happen. Our guy opens the package surreptitiously.

And so on. You get the idea. The first page, representing the first act, is the set-up for the film. It should be a grabber. It should make the studio executives want to see the picture.

Keep it unique.

As you expand on your first sentence you will invariably go into greater detail than necessary. That's okay. Don't edit yourself right away. Overlay what you're thinking about onto the model we're talking about and see if you get across the most important elements. First, who is the story about? Second, what is the story about? Third, what incident incites your hero to leave the security of his world and jump off into the unknown?

For the sake of clarity try not to use the movie ad or *TV Guide* hyperbole. Focus on the inherent excitement in the drama without overselling it with exaggerated Madison Avenue lingo. Your story idea is unique, you must believe that, and you must sell it based on that.

Act One may or may not take up all of one page, but Act Two will more than likely make up for that.

Page two, Act Two

This is the body of the work. Now you will expand on that second act sentence and elaborate in broad strokes once again the kind of incidents, or twists and turns, and danger and thrills you have in mind that will teach your hero his life lesson. Again, a lot of this will be worked out as you develop this act, so for now we want to hit the highlights. Remember that the reason behind all of these challenges is to get him to realize he has to change if he is to grow, and he has to grow if he is to be victorious in the climax. The incidents you want to focus on in this three-page pitch are only those that scare him, thrill him, or force him to change. You also have to animate the co-antagonist's dilemma by showing us how having the protagonist in her life has her changing as well. What is it about him that brings out that need in her? Just like Book and Rachel, Bogart and Hepburn, Leon and Mathilda, Michael Douglas and Frances

McDormand, your protagonist and co-protagonist effect change in each other, because ultimately they are honest with each other. Nothing works like honesty. You can't go into great detail, obviously, but when you do think of something or some incident that you don't want to forget, put it down on paper and put it aside to use later.

I was thinking about the guy on the bus.

He's sitting there looking into the package of several hundred uncut diamonds. Is this the answer to his prayers? Pay the bills. Send the kid to rehab. Let the wife have everything and leave the country? Rio? Monte Carlo? But up ahead as the bus comes to its next stop he sees the same Grizzly Man. As the Grizzly Man gets on the bus our guy jumps out the back door, runs into a high rise office building, and into an elevator. The doors close behind him and he heaves a sigh of relief. As the elevator rises, something pokes him in the back. He turns slowly and is eyeball-to-eyeball with the beautiful girl who tossed him the diamonds. The elevator bell pings and she whispers, "This is our floor."

This sort of stuff is a lot of fun and should be jotted down and saved for the outline. When in your Page Two, Act Two page you refer to your character running into a progressively complicated series of events, this is one you'll want to use when you get there. Always write these little bits down when you think of them. Don't think you'll remember it later on. You won't.

Page three, Act Three

Finally, on the last of your three pages you will expand on what you've decided are the climax to the plot and the resolution of your story. The climax is about defeating the bad guy. The resolution is about the lasting emotional consequences the victory has on your protagonist and co-protagonist. One is external and the other is internal. One is the physical ending and the other is a metaphysical ending. One is the human gain and the other is the spiritual meaning.

The sketch on the canvas

Once you have written your three-page treatment you will see your film with greater clarity. This in no way means you won't change it several times during the process of writing the script. This is the sketch on the canvas. This is your way of seeing all the corners of the painting at the same time. You will do much pushing and shoving things around, shuffling events and consequences from one corner to the other. This is to be expected because this is what the process is. You will see the emotional picture much sooner than you will see all the parts to the plot. That's when you know you are doing good work. The story is what's important. The plot is only there to service it.

These are brave and bold strokes on your canvas. They are the truth.

Indirection

I've written a three-page treatment for my idea *Indirection*. I know that a lot will change once I go to the next step of development with this, but I also know that I'd never get to the next step if I didn't have this to guide me and to keep me on track. Take a look at it, and then continue to work on yours until you are satisfied.

Sample Three-Page Treatment

Indirection
by Peter Dunne

INDIRECTION is the story of a young guy who teams up with an unlikely and beautiful stranger in a desperate search for his fifteen-year-old runaway sister. It is a search against the clock, against the odds, and against the rules. But more important, it is a search for what causes all of us to run away from the things we hide inside.

SCOTT PECK rooms below street level in a hovel on the Lower East Side. With a day job behind the wheel of an ambulance, and most nights in classes at City College, he lives like a king. It wasn't that long ago he was riding in the *back* of an ambulance, his drug-riddled life hanging by a thread. A hundred-and-twenty in County, followed by another ninety in drug and alcohol rehab, and a lucky break getting into school and getting a job got him to this high point in his life.

Then his mother called from Indiana with the news that his kid sister, RED, had run away from home. Scott knew he would have to run after her, and that his search would take him back to the streets that would surely kill his sister if he didn't find her in time. And it's on the streets where he meets a hardheaded delinquent named MIDGE who was the last person to see his sister, and who might be the only one who can help him. So he makes a deal for that help, and teams up with the beautiful stranger on a road trip as mysterious as it is dangerous. A trip for which there are no maps.

Red Peck, fifteen and fed-up with her divorced mother's raucous sexual second-wind, feels there's no place for her at home anymore, with so many of her mother's boyfriends coming and going. She leaves Muncie to strike out on her own, to find independence, to find joy. Red's journey, though, goes from bad to worse, from dream to nightmare, and Scott's intuition that a girl as young and naïve as Red wouldn't stand a chance alone on the road is right.

As Red's journey spirals downward into danger, Scott and Midge follow the traces of her trip and any clues she leaves behind, but every time they get close to finding her, she seems to disappear again. As the frustrations and tensions mount, Scott and Midge, both stubborn and both running from their own ghosts, find themselves on a journey neither of them bargained for. It is a journey of having to face those ghosts, and coming to grips with past mistakes.

And as the trip unfolds we discover that Midge's reasons for helping Scott were not so altruistic. She had her own self-seeking reasons to make the deal to help, and uses Scott's dilemma to settle a score with a drug dealer who killed her brother. As she does this, she risks losing the trail of Red for good. By the time Scott realizes he's been betrayed, they have not only lost a lot of ground on Red, they nearly get killed in the process.

But Scott is not completely innocent either. The more tense and angry he becomes, the more obvious it is that he's hiding his own guilt that he betrayed his little sister, and could very well be the reason she ran away in the first place.

Meanwhile the streets continue to victimize Red relentlessly. Robbed, assaulted, hospitalized, and so traumatized she suffers from amnesia, Red wanders alone and frightened, desperate to remember who she is and where she belongs.

Scott and Midge's clashes raise the emotional stakes for each of them. The more honest they are forced to be with each other, the more they begin to trust one another, something they haven't allowed themselves to do in a long, long time. And the more they trust each other, the more they are attracted to each other. And out of that, to their surprise, comes an intimacy that excites and scares them. With a newfound commitment to the bond between them, they kick their race after Red into high gear and eventually track her down and save her from near death.

Red, still amnesic, listens to Scott tell her about her life, where she lives, where she goes to school, and shows her a picture he carries with him of them together when they were younger. She stares at the picture, then thanks him for making such a great effort to find her, but she's not ready to go with him or anyone else just yet. The answers she's looking for aren't in the past because she's not trying to find the person she was. She's searching for the person she wants to become. A local family offers her a safe place to stay, and she accepts it, knowing that someday, when she's ready, she'll come home again.

Scott is shocked. Midge, on the other hand, understands Red's decision. After all, Midge and Scott are now faced with the same problem. Neither one of them can go back to the way things were, either. Why would they want to? Too much has happened to them. Too much has changed in them.

So where *do* they go? If they can't go back, she says, they've got to go forward, too. Maybe they should go together, he says.

There are no maps for that kind of trip, she says. He shrugs; sometimes that's a good thing.

Beginning at the End

This may sound ludicrous but trust me:

Even the most general idea of how you want to end your story is a great beginning.

I know I would have been lost when I was developing the idea for *Indirection* if all I thought about was the great trip the brother and the street girl were going to take without first deciding where the film story would end. Experience has taught me time and again that knowing the story's end directly impacts every development along the way.

The brother and the street girl would have wandered aimlessly for many pages. I had a lot of ideas for scenes but none of them would have amounted to much unless and until they became a part of a greater story, a story with a purpose. Learn this about your project: If everything is going to add up to the ending, then obviously you must know what the ending is going to be. There is no way around it. None. Period. Don't be stubborn. You'll only waste a lot of time and effort.

You may feel that you could end your film in a number of ways. I wasn't sure, for instance, if I wanted the brother to find his sister. Or if he did find her, if she was alive or dead, or somewhere in between. I wasn't sure if I wanted a happy ending, a tragic ending, or something in between. I wasn't sure if the brother should survive the trip, or die trying to reach her.

Think of all the ways you could end your film. It goes without saying that the way you end your film is the way you want the audience to remember your central ideas. So now you can see how important it is to know that answer before you can begin to build toward it.

I'm sure William Kelley, Pamela Wallace and Earl Wallace struggled with the same issues deciding on an ending for *Witness*. Seeing Book and Rachel get married and raise Samuel in the peaceful hollow of Lancaster would have been a nice Hollywood ending, but it would have been a poor choice. It would not have been true to the theme of the film. It would have cheapened it, and it certainly would not have won the Academy Award.

So I worked on the ending of *Indirection*. I knew the point of the story I had in mind was to put the brother on a journey of self-discovery. I did that by disguising it in a plot of his sister taking off on a journey of discovery, and by chasing after her he is forced to take his. Ironically, he winds up taking the trip his sister set out to take. I wanted him to take the journey because I wanted him to face a part of his past he had buried and was determined to deny. I planned on plot incidents to force him to face his devil. Since the guilt he buried had to do with his sister I knew I had to have a scene at the end between them. Therefore, I now had a few choices made for me. First, he had to find her. Second, she had to be alive. Third, he had to deal with his guilt. I still wasn't sure how it would go from there, but it was enough of an ending in my head to get started writing toward.

I went to the beginning and started him on his journey knowing he had a secret he was guilty about. I knew that somewhere along the way the streetwise girl, Midge, would pick up on his guilt and get him to open up about it. I had the feeling that she would be the one to make him face the truth with his sister. I also figured I had to create a secret or an emotional ghost for her as well. I knew that if during the trip he helped her overcome her innermost fear, that at this point she would have the strength to shepherd him through his fear. Keep in mind that when I say know the end, I mean know the end of your story, not your plot.

It's okay to start your script and not know how the plot will end, but you cannot start your script and not know how your story will end.

I've always had this hunch that when I'm disappointed with the ending of a movie it's because the writer thought he'd figure the story out once he got there. And then once he got there, it was too late to figure it out. Faced with having to rewrite the entire movie or stretch credulity, he stretched. Which is a stupid thing to do.

Never compromise the end of your movie.

When you know the ending of your story, you can start outlining each act with a new confidence because everything will be headed in the right direction. And that right direction can be as curvy and creative as you can possibly make it and still be on target. Knowing the end creates opportunities for you to invent tricks and traps without losing sight of the goal line. This applies not only to the development of film scripts, but to dramatic television scripts as well. In fact, this is especially critical in television because you have a precise number of minutes of "air time" to end up exactly where you must. Knowing the ending to your drama, and having an outline to get there on time, are absolute necessities in dramatic television writing.

In the case of *Indirection*, knowing my protagonist had a secret he was ashamed of kept me thinking and looking for it. Once I decided on what his secret was I could drop clues along the way and create particular behavior that would betray him. I also wanted to make his secret, his fear, something the co-protagonist could relate to in order for her to help him with some degree of familiarity.

In my script I wanted to end Act One with Scott and Midge striking an agreement to hit the road, but not before a heated argument about why his sister was stupid enough to run away. This argument serves two important purposes: first, it sets up their relationship as antagonistic, which is vital. They have to start out not thinking much of one another so that we can turn that around into a love story later on. Secondly, the argument foreshadows each character's secret. Hidden beneath the surface of the argument lie their resentment and anger toward the injustice that makes kids think they have to run away in the first place. Each knows that running away is not a solution to the kid's problem, yet each knows it is sometimes the only option available. Why and how they know this is the basis for each of their secrets.

Scott's secret, which he is loathe to confess to Midge, is that he ran away from home when he was his sister's age and now feels he abandoned her and caused her to follow in his footsteps. As much as he wants to find her to save her from harm, he also wants to find her to relieve himself of the guilt he feels. At this moment in time—and it is the reason he argues so vehemently with Midge—he doesn't know if he's angrier with himself or his sister.

It will be my intention to have Midge see through his altruistic bullshit and challenge him to admit the truth. This is an example of the co-antagonist shifting to the co-protagonist. She's becoming fond of him because she can trust him. She wants him to do the right thing. She won't let him shy away from it now matter how hard it is for him. And this is an example of how the co-protagonist keeps the protagonist on his journey, not allowing him to turn tail and run. He may run after his sister, but if he's running away from the truth his journey is for naught.

That is why I say:

Knowing your ending keeps your characters emotionally honest.

The ending of your film is what the audience takes home with them. They will either love or not love your work based on your conclusion. They say the first impression is a lasting impression. Well, in my book so is the last impression. Some films end so elegantly I will watch them over and over again. As I do, I take notice of the emotional structure all the way through the film that leads inevitably to the final scenes.

I love the gently compelling ending Sophia Coppola created in *Lost in Translation*, a warm and intelligently comic tale of two lost souls wandering the turf of their individual broken-hearted worlds finding solace in their similar quandaries. They attract each other, as like-wounded people do, and charm the pants off each other, figuratively speaking, and risk a friendship that is as open as it is intimate.

As isolated buddies, they listen to each other, unlike their respective spouses who do not listen, and they understand each other. This reflects the logic behind the title. *Lost in Translation* refers not to the linguistic and cultural misunderstandings they encounter in Tokyo, rather to the lack of understanding and appreciation they endure in their respective marriages. All any person wants is to be heard and understood. And this is what Ms. Coppola's audience found hitting so close to home.

How many of us feel we are not listened to by those we love, or when we are heard are misunderstood? Though Bill Murray is wonderfully funny and Scarlett Johansson is completely captivating, I believe the emotional chord the film struck with its audience is the reason for its enduring popularity.

Bill and Scarlett's emotional honesty

We see that Ms. Coppola decided from the very beginning that the couple wouldn't solve anything by having an affair. It would make matters worse, and more important it would cheapen the characters. She was wise enough to know she could let them fall in love as a result of their openness and honesty, but she also knew it would be dishonest love if they slept together.

This is good, adult, independent film drama. I can pretty much assure you that the ending would have been tampered with were it made for a major studio.

Sophia Coppola was able to take these two charming characters on a wonderful trip and slowly build to the ending she was sure would work.

There were no false beats in the entire script as a result. The ending was an inevitable and delicious surprise. I will never know how she made such an expressive and haunting comedy-of-the-heart with so little money. It is a testament to her artistic strength and I admire her greatly.

Leon and Mathilda's emotional honesty

In a very different film, but with an equal regard for the truly dramatic adult romance, Luc Besson knew he could let his protagonist and co-protagonist *fall* in love without ever *making* love in *The Professional*. Because he knew his ending before he began Besson was able to taunt and tease the love and lust out of his characters without violating the boundaries of truthful behavior.

His was the story of romantic awakening while Coppola's was a story of romantic maturing. Each is a brilliant film in its use of emotional structure.

Leon and Mathilda expose their fears to each other through a series of forced incidents. They are wary to reveal their feelings at first because when they have done so in the past they have been hurt. Trust is their main issue. And like I've said before, you can't have love if you don't have trust. And you can't have trust if you don't have honesty. Once they cop to the truth and build a trust the floodgates are open for the emotional reckoning that calls itself love.

When we are introduced to Mathilda we meet a seemingly tough and independent, street-smart young girl. When we meet Leon, we see an emotionless, cold-blooded killer. Then the script forces the two together and we watch each character being exposed in ways they have never allowed themselves to be exposed before. We learn that what the fearless hitman actually fears, and what the self-sufficient girl actually craves, are the same thing: intimacy.

Mathilda's impenetrable exterior is cracked wide open when her family is murdered and she rushes to her mysterious neighbor, Leon, for safe harbor in complete fear and desperation. Leon sees a helpless little girl for the first time, and in that tormented moment makes a decision to save her. It is a decision that alters the course of his emotional story, and ultimately, his life, because he reveals to her and to us that there exists beneath his ice-cold exterior a person capable of compassion.

Leon allows her in, giving her temporary protection, with the proviso that she leave as soon as she can. But she really has no other place to go to, and she is still traumatized by the nearness to the site of her family's slaughter just down the hall. It is at this point that they are each "taken out of" their safe worlds and dropped into a new and uncertain world. Here, in this emotionally complicated, new environment, their old ways of doing things can't work. Her toughness doesn't impress him, and his threats don't scare her.

Mathilda needs to stay longer, but acting tough isn't loosening Leon up. She needs new tools. She realizes being a child and a tomboy have to be exchanged for something more mature and seductive. As she explores this, she finds her vulnerability and femininity will work as the new tools. Her way of reaching him is to explore her untapped seductive nature. It begins to work, but the tragedy accompanying it is the forfeiture of her childhood for womanhood.

Leon, on the other hand, is frustrated by his inability to throw her out or even kill her. His violence doesn't threaten her because she has been living in an unstable and violent family environment all her life. Leon has to find another way of dealing with her. He opens up his child-like heart and mind to adapt to hers. New tools, hidden beneath the weapons of killing, are untapped emotional arms for living. Mathilda pulls these emotions out of him by engaging him in kids' games. He is initially incapable of accessing his own innocence, an innocence long lost, but he gets caught up in her enthusiasm, and his own silliness surfaces. It is a breakthrough for him and their relationship. It is intimacy. And, as they relate on a more intimate level, their attraction builds. When the need for each other evolves into a wanting for each other, they have reached the mid-point of the script. A story of violence becomes a story of love.

Book and Rachel's emotional honesty

As we pointed out in *Witness*, the writers knew the protagonist and co-protagonist could never happily marry in the end. Knowing that, they could not allow Book to take advantage of Rachel sexually when she exposed herself to him while she bathed. The writers knew that if they allowed him to make love to her he would have to stay with her, and that would never have worked out. They devised that scene, and other scenes of physical and emotional attraction to advance the notion that no matter how much we want things, it isn't always best to get them.

Seeing his carpentry skills at the barn raising, the raw physicality he displays quenching his thirst and spilling the drink down his chest, his affection for her son, Samuel, and his disarming goofiness dancing by the light of the headlights in the barn all tease her and us. The cumulative effect of these observations work to make the ending that much more painfully but emotionally honest.

Unrequited love bruises our hearts but we forgive it for doing so because we recognize that it is honorable and eternal.

Back to the elevator

Remember the fellow with the diamonds? We left our poor schlub in the elevator with a gun sticking in his ribs. He's been at the mercy of circumstances, and it's been a lot of fun torturing him, but we have to stop before we go any further and decide what the end of his story will be.

Great openings are a dime a dozen. Great finishes count for more.

Who is this guy? And who is the antagonist? Is it the chick with the gun in the elevator? Or is she the co-antagonist at this point? If she isn't the antagonist, who is? Is it the grubby guy who's after her? Time for us to decide on three important items. First, who is this guy? Second, what personal "journey" is he about to take? Third, what's he going to learn from the journey (what's the ending)?

First, let's say the guy is normal. He's doing what every guy thinks he's supposed to be doing. He's holding down a job, he's faithful to his wife, and he loves her and the kid. But he's lonely and worried. That's what I mean by "normal."

What he wants most is to know he's enough. Enough for his wife, for his kid, and maybe even enough for his boss. Who among us likes feeling "less than" everyone else? How many times have we been put down, purposely or not, when we were younger, to the point where we begin to believe we are not enough?

We have been compared to others all our lives. We have been told that failures are wrong. We have been led to believe that failure is a sign of weakness or lack of character. And that those who succeed are simply stronger than we are. By the time we are adults and settled into a career and home life, everything we wear or drive or eat signals the world how weak or strong we are.

And that's just crazy.

If what our guy wants most is to be enough, then the end of the story must deal with that. At the end of the movie we will have made him enough. That could mean that he is enough already and just didn't believe in himself, or that he has to figure out how to be enough if he isn't already.

The plot with the chick with the gun in his back can take him all over the world. The plot journey can be exciting and dangerous. He'll see things and feel things and taste things he's never before known. The chick with the gun might even fall in love with him. And in the end—in the plot—he will have a choice. He can go on living the high life with the fortune that's come his way and the chick with the gun on his arm, or he can go home to his "normal" life.

The choice he makes will be the point of your movie.

This is where a lot of screenwriters go down the plot path to find an ending for their film instead of going down the story path to find the resolution. The answer isn't in Paris or Rome. The answer may not even be back at home. The answer isn't in the plot, therefore it can't be in the location. The answer is in the story, and the only location that matters in the story is deep inside your protagonist.

He has to choose the answer that will validate his newfound "enoughness."

When enough is enough

When I say that a person is enough I do not mean to say that he or she is merely adequate, I mean to say that he or she is complete. It is this completeness that satisfies the resolution. And it is a lesson for all of us to learn. We are all born complete. We are all enough, and what's good for the hero's resolution is also good for audience satisfaction. Being enough is the emotional connection the audience understands.

When enough is the theme

So if we were to build the script about our guy from the back forward by saying that in the end he accepts and celebrates his "enoughness," the emotional structure in the script will be based on every possible facet of what being enough means.

We have to disguise it of course, and be subtle and calculating to build our case piece by piece. We have to shift the chick with the gun from co-antagonist to co-protagonist, and as such pressure him to dig deep to find out what happened to the completeness he was given at birth. What event or series of events occurred in his life that caused so much distress he forfeited his emotional base? Does he even know he's forfeited it? Why is he incapable of or unwilling to do something about it now?

These are the interior, metaphysical questions that form a sweeping and gentle emotional story. We don't want to rough him up. We don't want the co-protagonist to bitch, bitch, bitch. We want her to *understand* him, because, when the co-protagonist understands the protagonist anything is possible in their relationship.

Beginning at the end creates freedom not restriction.

Once we know where we want to wind up we not only have the theme of the film, but we also have the answers to the questions being posed throughout the script. The whole idea of beginning at the end is to create a target at which you aim all your action and emotion. Knowing the end does not limit your options; it increases them. And it makes writing your script easier and more creative.

It would be wise for us to go back to our three pages and review them in the context of Beginning at the End.

Choosing an Emotional Opening

We have a choice when we open our film to be big and noisy and action packed, or to be intimate and quiet and passive. To open with a splash or with a tear. To open with a laugh or with a cry. To open with a tragedy or a celebration. But there is one thing we don't have a choice about in our opening. It must stir us. It must grab us by our ankles and run its long fingers up our pant legs. It must nibble at the back of our neck. It must turn us on or turn us inside out. It must give us the chills or warm the cockles of our hearts. It must reach our emotions. That is its obligation.

Every great film opening must be emotional.

I'd like you to think of some of your favorite film openings and how they grabbed you emotionally. We said we could open noisily or quietly as long as we created an emotional undercurrent. Let's look at examples of emotional openings, some noisy and some quiet.

Noisy

First the noisy openings. Horror flicks are famous for emotionally noisy beginnings. *Scream*, written by Kevin Williamson, is a wonderful example. A beautiful young woman trapped in a house all alone, a frighteningly evil phone call, a desperate chase, and finally a murder calculated for its brutality. This gets our juices flowing and our hearts pumping, no doubt about it. I noticed how everyone in the theater reacted to this opening. No one just sat there unmoved. Most of the women screamed, and most of the men laughed. Nervously.

Another gripping opening came in *Basic Instinct*, written by Joe Eszterhas. How can we ever forget that beautiful blonde astride her bound-to-the-bedpost lover bringing him to the orgasm of his life? And then, as if knowing he'll never be as satisfied again, eliminates any possibility of future disappointments by heartily plunging a dagger into his chest a few times. First the opening turns you on with its brisk sexuality, and then it freaks you out. Eszterhas gets you emotionally, and you're happily ready for the rest of the film because the opening tells you a lot about what kind of crazy things are in store. A good opening will engage your audience right away.

Not so noisy

Sometimes you will want to open your film with a more delicate approach to emotion. We can use a slow, visual story-telling sequence to emotionally interpret the mood and temperament of the particular place or time. The opening of the film *Witness* is a prime example of this.

Here, the writers and director worked as one to create a particular storytelling style, a style that is strong visually and spare verbally. They started their story with stunning imagery of Rachel's world. It is a visual symphony of a time and place into which the audience is invited. The bucolic grace and peace, even on the worst of days—the day of a funeral—is more than comforting, it is benevolent. This is a world that does not need words to describe it, because it is experienced viscerally. This is a lovely, quiet opening.

Rachel and her son Samuel's world is then set against John Book's world of noise and violence and a total lack of grace. Their sensibilities directly contrast the harsh malevolence of life in the modern city. Then the violation of Samuel's innocence at the witnessing of a brutal killing merges universes and brings to a head the opening of the movie by encapsulating its theme. Violence cannot bring peace; only peace can bring peace.

The writers' and director's confidence is indeed powerful. The two worlds, so different, are each introduced in a sequence involving death, which places the two societies, perspectives on *living* as its central thesis. You can readily see why the choice of a quiet opening was essential, therefore, because time is needed for all of this to be taken in by the audience.

Or, as Sophia Coppola chose in *Lost in Translation*, we can set up an appetite, a hunger if you will, for something. In her case she created an appetite for a connection emotionally charged with its alluring close-up of Ms. Johansson's youthful charms intercut with Mr. Murray's weary mug. Both portraits speak to the similarity of the emotional distance between their own presence and the isolating and emotionally barren environment in which they've been dumped. Only a few minutes into the film they ride down the same elevator in the same luxury hotel and steal a glance at one another. And we are hooked. We are suddenly rooting for them to get together. That is the emotional bond Coppola created with her opening sequence. Nothing noisy or splashy, just solid, visual storytelling.

I also love the quiet opening of the film *The Station Agent*, a flawless and elegant character study written and directed by Tom McCarthy. With little or no dialog we meet the protagonist and learn his problem in a sweetly sympathetic and mood-setting sequence. He brings us into the world of a man who disconnects from everyone around him and is all but ready to stop living until he meets a woman who is doing the same thing. By daring to engage with her, and by showing her all the reasons *she* should not give up, he exposes his own strengths, and his own reasons for not giving up. By saving her, he saves himself.

McCarthy's protagonist is Finbar McBride, a dwarf played with distinction by Peter Dinklage. Finbar's life has been defined by the size of his body rather than the size of his heart. His burden, though painfully visible, is very much like our own. We all have been hurt by others' perceptions of us, and we have subconsciously built walls around ourselves to prevent, or at least minimize, further insult and injury.

Finbar awakens to the similarities others share with him, rather than their distinct differences, when he encounters the soulful but impenetrable Olivia Harris, played wonderfully by Patricia Clarkson. Olivia suffers quietly and deeply over the death of her son and the ruin of her marriage. She cannot get past her grief, and she cannot allow anyone to get too close to her.

She and Finbar are two of a kind who sense a strong mutual attraction almost immediately, but because of the walls each has thrown up, they can't reach each other. The irony is not lost on Fin. And he must face his own demons before he can help Olivia face hers. Two people, so completely opposite in so many physical and social ways, find rich and rewarding similarities where it counts. Each takes a leap of faith. Each risks further pain and humiliation by opening up. But the emotional structure of the script doesn't allow the characters any other choice. Not to risk means not to live. It is a sheer and delicate premise, and using a quiet, almost contemplative opening suits the film perfectly.

The point in choosing your opening scenes and sequences is to determine what will maximize the emotional exposure to your characters and their lives as we find them.

All the entertaining plot action in the world is worthless if it isn't grounded in the interior story. Action alone is shallow and won't last for more than the minute it's on the screen. We have seen this in the popular films of the 1970s and 1980s that starred action figures Sylvester Stallone and Arnold Schwarznegger. Once the opening is over you can take a nap until the climax in another ninety minutes or so.

You want more from your opening than muscle and mumbling.

You want more from your hero than posing. You want intelligence within the entertainment. You are not interested in the actor's vanity. You are interested in the character's value. You want to make a powerful, gutsy emotional statement that has nothing to do with libidos or pectorals. You want to write a film, not simply a movie.

Setting the Emotional Table

There are many ways we can set the emotional tone of the film in the opening. It's important to be consistent from the very beginning. It's lazy writing to have a huge, hysterical, action-packed opening only to then settle down into a movie that never sees any action again. The emotional tone in the opening should reflect where your heart is on the subject. This is a visual invitation to a story that is important to you and you want it to mean something to your audience. It is a promise, not an opportunity to trick them. You want to make sure they know what they're getting, and you want to make sure you can deliver it. Everything you put into it will count. You will undoubtedly go back into the opening time and time again during the course of writing the script and add or change things as your story develops. If you have an honest opening, going back into it will be easy.

Opening choices

You will have choices in your opening involving the placement of scenes, the time of day or night, the dialog or complete lack of it, a point-of-view, style, character introductions, and genre. You will find that each of these choices will enhance the story you want to tell. I think it's important for you to have as much fun creating your opening as possible. This is the freest you may be for a while, so I recommend stretching your imagination. Surprise yourself with your thinking. Take an approach you haven't entertained before and see where it takes you. You have your ending in mind, so you know where you have to go. There are countless points from which you can begin your story. Try jotting down different ideas and see which ones start to feel exciting and different to you. Trust your instincts and trust your talent. See if opening your movie in a crappy hotel room works better for you than in a private jet over the Black Sea.

I'm back to our guy in the elevator with the chick with the gun.

Let's say we don't start the movie in the morning with him getting ready for work and walking to the bus station. Let's see if we get something more out of the situation by opening the movie at night—the night before the morning's action. What's he doing at night that can be more internal and personally revealing? Is he putting his kid to bed and wondering where his wife is? After the kid's in bed do we see him clean up the dishes in the kitchen and throw away food probably meant for her? Does he sit down at his desk in the den and go online? Are the overdue bills on the desk here? What does he check out online? Does he go to his bank account and see what's left in it? Does he see credit card expenses that he didn't know about? Does he go to a legal advice site regarding do-it-yourself divorces? Does he check out private eyes who follow wayward wives? And while he's doing this does a pop-up appear with a sweetie in a bikini selling cheap flights to Rio de Janeiro? Do we see him pause? For a long time? And then do we see him smile and type away? And then do we dissolve to the morning where he's going through his routine and leaving for the bus?

It's just a different way to go. I'm not sure it's the best way, but I do think that this is the time in development to explore these kinds of options and see what you find. See what tickles you, or scares you, or makes you cry. If it does that for you then chances are it will do that for the audience.

In your opening, every story beat has a contribution to make and a statement to enhance.

Many filmmakers like to use the opening credit sequence as a mood setter. I think this is a solid and practical idea. This involves all of the elements in a film coming together to set the pace and tone. It can be as fast or as slow as you want. It can be anything you want, as long as it is honest, and as long as every beat is necessary and expressive.

By the time your opening sequence (with or without titles) comes to an end your audience should be totally engrossed.

I find that history also has a place in the opening. I like to hide bits of the protagonist's personal history in the sequence. It may seem unimportant at the time and as if it was mere window dressing, but to me it's money in the bank. A photo here, an old hat there. Maybe a pet parrot, or a faithful dog at the protagonist's side. I can't tell you how many times I've been surprised by how important that little clue is later on. Maybe it's just because it's in my head all the time, subconsciously, and drifts to consciousness when prompted by merging events later on. Whatever prompts it, it is always a happy occasion when that happens, and I give myself every chance of it happening by dropping these bread crumbs whenever I can.

The Emotional Power of Personal History

These visual nuances, even if they are never called on again, do still add color and information about the character in an unobtrusive way. Looking for these details in your opening can be a lot of fun, and the details can start to tell you something about your protagonist that you hadn't thought of before.

I have found subtext in these details and I urge you to spend the necessary time to find subtext in your details, too. The way a woman prepares for a dinner date can tell me a great deal about her if the subtextual details are well placed. Her preparations can forecast her expectations. They can also underline her self-esteem by the amount of care she applies. Does her appearance matter to her as much as she thinks it might matter to someone else? Is she distracted? Bored? You can tell me so much about her and her date before she even leaves her bedroom!

Does she take great care in every detail? Does she apply perfume to the most intimate places? Does she stop for a second in front of the full length mirror and decide to slip out of her panties? Does she check her purse for condoms? And then, finally, does she check the pistol in her purse to make sure it's loaded? Does she take one final look and then head downstairs where her date is waiting, and do we find out that her date is her husband who is reading a bedtime story to their four-year-old? Does this feel odd? Could she be planning the murder of her husband? Is her lovey-dovey kiss goodnight on her daughter's nose a deceit? What the hell is going on? I don't know, but I want to know.

Your opening exercise

You've been thinking about your script idea for a long time. You probably are more comfortable with how the film opens than with any other part. And that can be a problem. If we get stuck on our opening, that is to say if we have fallen in love with our opening because it's so cool, and we don't want to change it or think it needs to be changed, we are making trouble for ourselves.

I have read hundreds of scripts with great openings, cool openings, that could not carry the script beyond the next ten pages. I would be willing to say the great majority of the scripts I've thrown in the reject pile had wonderful openings. The problem is no matter how great the opening may be, it is worthless if the writer can't build a movie on it. I am confident that over half of the writers' pitches I've listened to had a great opening followed by the writer telling me he hadn't worked out the rest yet. When I was very new and stupid in the job, I bought into the writer's fantasy that the rest would come. I paid for the development of the scripts where the rest, if it was coming, was still a light year away. Yes, the opening was great. And then the whole thing turns into a cow pie.

Loving the opening of your script so much that you are willing to follow it down the road to wherever it takes you is idiotic. It is not a writer's thing to do. It is an undisciplined wannabe-writer's thing to do.

You are not that person. You will write an opening that is more creative and more entertaining and more intelligent because you know that it works for you, you don't work for it. It has a job to do, and that job, most of all, is to lead you down the road you choose to the ending you know and love.

I have seen logic go out the window in order to maintain the direction of the opening simply because the opening was cute. I have seen characters ruined because they had to conform to the same bad idea.

Everything in the opening must obey your ending.

True, you are a long way from the end of your script. But you know how you want to end the film and from the first frame you should be focused on that. Because you will do that and you will find the focus enlightening and extremely helpful, you will be pleasantly surprised at the ending's reciprocation for the opening's good faith. It's got a power of its own, the ending does, and it will reflect back on the opening of your script with a tip of the hat and a thanks.

The opening sets up the ending, and the ending brings it all back to the opening. This is the cyclical nature of film storytelling. It gives everything a sense of completeness and it helps make very clear the questions that have been answered by your protagonist's adventure.

If your protagonist goes back home at the end of your film, he or she will find a completely different experience there than that one of the opening. It may not be that anything at home has changed. But we know your protagonist has changed forever. Whether your protagonist can survive in the old world we found him in on page one is anyone's guess. I often wonder what happened to John Book when he went back to the precinct. I wondered how long it would take him to quit and seek a more meaningful or peaceful existence. I also wondered how happy Rachel and Samuel were going to be with her new husband.

I wonder how long it will be before Scarlett Johansson dumps her hubby. I wonder what ever became of Mathilda once she graduated from her high school. Is she a hit lady out there somewhere? I wonder these things because your hero can't go back. And I like that. I like that the story you tell me is true to your thinking and that someone has changed and grown and is headed for a better unknown.

I think that's good writing.

10

Connecting the Beginning to the End

Let's take the obvious first. We have seen many movies that start and end in the same place, or the same circumstance. That's nice. It's a little on the nose for me, but it works, and actually sometimes it is the very best decision. It makes it crystal clear to the audience the changes that have occurred and the gains that have been made by the journey the hero made. We have to be careful with this, though, because we don't want it to appear as if we are treating the audience as a bunch of dummies who can't figure it out for themselves.

In *Emotional Structure* we are referring to a different kind of connecting. We want the beginning and the end to have the same kind of feeling, sure, but there is an even more important connection. In fact, it's more of a reconnection. It is the broken being repaired. It is the spirit being renewed. It is empowerment returned two-fold. It is a mended heart, a soothed soul, and a reassured conscience. It is a healing. It is the opposite inside out.

It is a fear overcome by a new faith. It is courage. It is willingness. It is promise.

These are the important connections that a strong Emotional Structure brings to every script. A broken person is whole again. And the reason I say whole again goes back to our understanding that we were once a great deal better off than we are now. We were perfect once. Then life happened. And although we can't ever be perfect again in this lifetime, we can at least head in that direction. I don't mean anal perfect, and I don't mean we want to make our heroes saints. I mean we want to bring our heroes through the dark times with valor.

Foreshadowing

Foreshadowing the difficulties that are about to come is a smart idea. It can be done without being heavy-handed and if it is done artistically it will add a great deal to your opening. Foreshadowing doesn't have to be literal. It can be shades of trouble. It can be hints of the dangers that lie ahead in other shapes and forms. But we should also make an effort to foreshadow the resolution in some way. This would be a much more subtle assignment. But there is an extremely important reason for foreshadowing the resolution.

As William Goldman puts it, your resolution should be an "inevitable surprise." Well, the inevitability comes from the subtle foreshadowing very early in the film, and always in the first act. Hopefully it won't be such a strong statement that the audience will have it in mind for long. But when the resolution in the final act harkens back to it, they will smack their foreheads and say, "Of course. It had to be that way."

You've already given great thought to how your story ends. You know in a general way, but a solid way, what the emotional resolution will be. You have decided what fears your protagonist must and will overcome in the end. So now it's your job to make those problems and his fears squirm beneath the surface of his behavior early on. It may take all of act one to put the pieces in place but you will have from page one to page twenty-five to fill in his emotional profile.

Places we've been

As you work your way through the twists and turns of the plot in Act One you will find places to drop in the notes of personality and history. More than anything the audience will want to know what's going on inside your protagonist. What he's made of and what makes him tick. They are going to try to figure him out from the moment you introduce him. You have to satisfy them with peeks at his internal layers. The more they get to know him, the more they will care about him. But you can't give everything away too easily. Keep them guessing.

It is the process of guessing that keeps the audience involved and engaged. As they put their thoughts together, the elements of your drama will have a deeper impression. This is important because the deeper impressions will be lasting impressions, and they will be those impressions that tie things up at the end.

Look at *Lost in Translation* again. It is the story of loneliness in the middle of millions. Scarlett Johansson lies alone in bed in the opening frame. She is just as alone at a table in a bar with her husband and several of his cronies. She is alone walking the crowded streets of downtown Tokyo. She is a prisoner in her hotel room with nothing to take her mind off of her problems no matter what she does to amuse herself. She takes a train to a mountaintop temple: ancient and awesome and far from the madding crowd. There is a staggering elegance in the way things grow in the foggy-green forest. There is a gentle quality in the landscape architecture that soothes her soul. There is wisdom. And there is sacrifice. All of these are matters of her heart. They are longings. They are so out of reach to her in the world in which she lives that it pains her to have them. What she doesn't realize is that she is the embodiment of all of these treasures. She is elegant and beautiful and gentle and soothing and soulful and wise. And so it follows that it is okay for her to feel alone.

This is the great lesson for her in the film. Aloneness need not be lonely. It can actually be gratifying and enriching. She needed to learn that she was not unlovable, which is what she attributed her loneliness to, but rather she was lonely because she was unloved by those who abandoned her emotionally. Being unloved is a lot different than being unlovable. Learning the difference is the point of the film. For us as an audience that point saves our lives. We are all familiar with being unloved. And we all know that we are lovable. From the first moment of the film loneliness was the theme. Not unrequited love. Not extramarital affairs. Not an indictment against marriage. When some ask, "Why didn't they just hop in the sack?" I know they missed the point completely.

Coming full circle

The beginning and the end of *Lost in Translation* are very similar. He's riding out of the city, just as he arrived, in a limo as the frantic neon city dances outside the windows. She is left alone again. But she is happier now than she has ever been because his affection for her validated her. She is a little less afraid of her feelings and of the reality she can no longer ignore: her marriage is a bust. She has the will and the strength to change that now. It is a beginning. It is a second chance. It is enough.

And all of this, every beat of the ending that makes any sense at all, was set up in the beginning. From the very start the film has a point of view and it stays committed to that point of view, and elucidates it throughout the charming and complex story.

Rainy days and Sundays

I would like to suggest a great way to spend a rainy day. Find a copy of Sophia Coppola's script in the bookstore or online, buy it, and read it. Then, on the next rainy day go out and buy the DVD and watch it without interruption. Get comfortable and let it take you away. Then, on the third rainy day watch the film again, this time with your script in hand and study the two together. Stop and go and look for the smart style that holds all the clues to this human mystery. Check out her act ends. Compare the scenes in the script to their final interpretation on film. And you will find, as I did, that it just gets better. This exercise is not only educational, it is encouraging and inspiring. Take the time to do it. You won't regret it, I promise.

Anytime you see a film you like, study it. Buy or rent the DVD and stop and go with it. If you can find the script online or in a bookstore, get it. You will find this to be extremely helpful. When you work on your script you can overlay your idea onto one of the film's structures you like and see how it works. It's a great way to jump start your writing. Once you get going, you will customize the structure to fit the particulars of your idea. Your structure may wind up being an amalgam of several of your favorite movies, and that's just fine. I would never recommend that you copy another film. First of all it's stealing, and secondly it's a stupid idea.

Each film must develop its own telling.

As you put your ideas together for your script you will notice a natural way of telling the story take hold. This is a gift from the gods. Don't fight it. Don't be guilty of feeling so strongly about an approach or genre or style that you won't change it no matter what. Writing a screenplay is still writing no matter how you slice it. It cannot be forced.

Writing isn't mechanical; it is deliberate art.

The deliberate focus is always on the importance of the subject you're treating. The topic means something to you or you wouldn't be taking the time to write about it. You can be seduced into putting greater importance on its presentation, its slickness and hipness, instead of credibility and profundity. You can fall in love with cool ideas that aren't necessarily good for you. You must stay focused.

The Connecting Second Act

The second act, you will see, has a life of its own. And for good reason. It has a job all its own. It should be obvious to everyone, but it isn't. Its function is to explore the emotional territory that is exposed at the end of Act One and that is resolved at the end of Act Three. Many writers presume that Act Two is simply a continuation of the plot begun in Act One, but that presumption has ruined 95 percent of the film scripts crisscrossing the country in FedEx bags.

The second act has far less to do with the plot and everything to do with the story. The plot, which rules the first act, is completely at the service of the story in Act Two. Take all of the films we've been talking about along with your own idea and you see the pattern of Act One setting up the plot, Act Two exploring the story, and Act Three resolving the plot and story together.

Witness is a police/murder mystery film in Act One. In Act Two it is a love story with the police story plot pushed into the background. The only time the police story plot shows up at all is when the love story needs it to accelerate its action and to raise its stakes. In Act Two the love story explores the human strengths and weaknesses that are exposed by the plot. The conclusion of Act Two shows that humanity not firepower is the only way to solve the plot.

Body Heat, written by Lawrence Kasdan and starring William Hurt and Kathleen Turner, is the opposite structure of *Witness*. Love becomes a crime. It starts out as a passionate affair and turns to a story of murder. In Act One the couple succumbs to an illicit affair. In Act Two the affair grows in fury and desire to the point of no return. They want each other so much they conspire to murder her husband and live on her inheritance. In Act Three the illicit affair becomes the real crime, a crime of the heart.

The Thomas Crown Affair starts out as a crime story (Act One) evolves into a love story (Act Two), and both are tied together in the end when love conquers all (Act Three).

An act of intimacy

Make a note of this and tape it onto your computer screen: The second act is an intimate act. No matter what's going on in the action plot, whether it's taking place in a war zone or in outer space, the story in Act Two is a story of personal angst and discovery. It is a very intimate fifty or sixty pages because so much is revealed about the protagonist and co-protagonist. It is a magnifying glass on the heart and soul of your lead characters, and it deals with the visceral responses to the plot each exhibits. We learn in this act just what each person is made of. Strengths drift to the fringes and weaknesses take center stage. That is because the weaknesses are the emotional footprints of fear.

It is during Act Two that we learn what our hero's real fears are. Act Two, remember, starts with your protagonist leaving his comfort zone. He may think it's only temporary, but we know better. As he moves out of his comfort zone you will expose to your audience the first signs of his fears…those things that have caused him to stay where he is, accepting being stuck rather than risking something else.

This is a mystery story in itself. Act Two is filled with revelations and is a powerful emotional act. It will be up to you to craft a second act that uses the threads of the action plot to push the emotional issues forward. This goes back to our earlier discussion of weaving the plot and the story together, inseparable and dependent. As the elements of the plot, for example the bad cops after John Book, drift into the background we focus on the foreground story accelerated by the police threat. The response to the threat is the gist of the story. Does Book's response reveal courage or fear? Does Rachel's response to his courage cause an emotional response in her?

These are the intimate issues they will deal with, as your characters will deal with the ones you devise. But it takes guts on their part.

Intimacy is bravery.

I say this because there is great risk in intimacy. We open ourselves up to all kinds of criticism and judgment when we let our guard down. One reason we always find that a protagonist hasn't revealed what he reveals in this story before is because he was burned the last time he revealed something deeply personal. Admitting our own fears and asking for help is a hard thing for a lot of people to do. It's easier to tough it out. Or to take another avenue. But each time we do that we make it harder on ourselves to ever be able to do that in the future. As a result we get stuck in our own defenses and we suffer for it. And we know it deep down inside even though we are completely unwilling to admit it to anyone. Unwilling until you force the situation on him by creating a plot situation that makes being open and honest his only way out.

Your protagonist must take his great leap of faith in Act Two. He must reveal himself to his co-protagonist and risk everything in the hopes that she will understand, and that she will not betray his intimacy. This is the great act of bravery in your script. He may stand up and wield a sword against the dragon later on, but it will be an act of bravery that pales in comparison to his earlier act of confession.

Moral courage is the basis for all courage.

You cannot have your protagonist face The Big Bad Guy and defeat him until he has defeated the fears that put The Big Bad Guy in his path. This is why the second act is such a different kind of storytelling than the first and third acts. The feat you must accomplish when you outline and then write Act Two is to keep it within the tapestry of all the plot events and to mingle their purposes so that they are seamless. The second act is a weave of the physical action and metaphysical journey into one smooth tale.

WE ARE ALL AFRAID TO COME
OUT OF OUR SHELL.

The second act is the most difficult act to figure out because it needs such a comprehensive and delicate structure. In order to keep your second act vibrant and vital you must develop a story strategy that creates density without creating confusion. When we get to the chapter dedicated solely to Act Two we will study techniques available to choreograph those central fifty pages into a divine dance.

Act Two is the place where most scripts die. Where most writers give up. The whole point of understanding the real purpose of Act Two is to avoid either of those fates with your screenplay.

Act Two is the movie within the movie. It has to be considered as a separate animal. We are going to learn how to do that and you will never have to face the muddle again.

Part 3

Emotional Structure: The Internal Landscape

11

The Journey through the Middle

Getting through the middle sixty pages of your script can be the hardest thing you do in your life. Ask any screenwriter. The pain and frustration are caused by the belief that the middle of the script is a free-for-all. That it amounts to fifty or sixty pages of incidents. Fifty or sixty pages of one action sequence after another and one joke after another. Cinematic padding. The idea that anything can be put in these pages just as long as it leads up to a big climax is ludicrous, of course. Nothing could be further from the truth. The middle of the film is not filler.

The middle of the script *is* the movie.

If anything, the beginning and the end of your script only exist to service the middle of your script. Not vice versa.

The *only* way to look at the second act is in terms of its emotional content. This is not the way it is looked at by most writers, and it is the primary reason that for most writers the middle of the script becomes the muddle. This is the most important guidance I can give you:

> **If you aren't dealing with the emotional undercurrent of the characters' relationships in Act Two, then you aren't writing the movie. You're doing something else. Usually something bad.**

The second act is the story beneath the plot. It is the emotional story that gives the plot meaning. We spend twice as many pages and twice as much screen time in Act Two as in the other two acts combined. We do this because it is the most important act in the movie. And since its basis is emotional, and most writers don't look at it that way, it needs its own special structure. It does not conform to the action/plot structure. Its nature is different. Its nature is epigenetic not episodic.

Emotional structure

The simplest way to approach the center sixty pages of the script is to consider its sum a small movie within the larger movie, connected to the larger movie by the dangers and manipulations of the plot. Those dangers and threats continue to push the protagonist farther from his comfort zone in the plot and closer to confronting those things in his past he denies exist or matter to him.

The whole point of the movie will be to reconcile an injustice.

By reconcile I mean reconcile. I do not mean revenge. Revenge is worthless because revenge doesn't change what has to be changed.

Each of us, every man, woman, and child on earth carries some suffering in the heart. While it is brave and Christian to manage the suffering and move on, it is also unhealthy. We were not meant to be hurt. We were not meant to exist in a damaged and unfulfilled emotional state. We were meant to be whole. We are meant to be honored. And if the world doesn't completely honor us in the way Heaven had hope, then the very least and the very best we can do is to honor ourselves. This is not psycho-babble. This is the basis of human recovery. And the whole damn point of your script is someone's human recovery. That is what reconciliation is. If the point of your script is not some human's recovery, then go write poems. Poems don't deal with recovery. Poems deal with the unrecoverable.

Healing the hero

Suppose you have a protagonist, who, when he was just a little kid, lost his mother in a terrible accident. At the wake, his father tells him to be a brave little guy and not to cry…to be strong. The kid has just lost the most important person in his life and his father is telling him to be a strong little man. Today, your protagonist would probably still be dealing with that issue subconsciously, along with all the other problems it has since created. He is most likely incapable of expressing sorrow, really, or acknowledging loss. He is probably unable to commit to love unconditionally since the only love he ever had was taken from him and denied. On the surface it may sound like I'm describing a cold and reclusive person, but you'd be surprised how many lovable, successful, and popular men and women fit this mold. Because this kind of memory is hidden so deeply it can't be detected on any practical social level. You can go back to the illustration of the Four Levels of Emotions to visualize what I mean.

This may not seem like the makings of a movie, but it is. If, in the middle of your plot and story, his habits, which are his defense mechanisms, are challenged and he is forced to change them, then he is getting dangerously close to exposing what he has been denying for a very long time. You can put Jerry Maguire in this category. He is handsome, lovable, successful, popular, sought-after, and incapable of filling the need to love. This is the need he denies. He can tough it out. He can do it on his own. But, the truth is none of us can do it on our own, nor were we meant to have to do it on our own.

It is not enough to be loved in this world. You have to be able to love too. You cannot be complete or fulfilled otherwise.

Look at John Book. He's never had a successful relationship. The only things he trusts are his own skills and his gun. What happened to him? Where did the distrust in other people come from? He doesn't know it yet, but he is going to learn from a very simple and trusting woman that trust is the basis of love. If John Book can't trust anyone, how can he possibly love anyone? If he can't love anyone, how can he ever be a complete and happy human being? The fact that he falls in love with Rachel by the end of the film tells me that he is now capable of trusting people again. This may ruin his ability to be a cop, but it opens the doors to many other and better things in life in the future.

Now do you see the stuff that makes a film a film? These are universal themes. Not a soul in your audience will be untouched by these familiar truths.

Your hero's journey, which is all of Act Two, is to go back to the place that needs healing and to heal himself.

Archbishop Desmond Tutu said it best:

**"Without memory there is no healing.
Without forgiveness there is no future."**

And as I have said, though less eloquently:

The past holds the problem. The solution holds the future.

Take your pick.

The job of the sixty pages is to first acknowledge that there is a memory to be found. We expose the protagonist's discomforts and fears when he's forced outside his own world. Though he will downplay them or deny them outright, they will be there for all to see.

As the incidents in the plot (he's being chased by the bad cops) pull him deeper and deeper into the problem, he will also be drawn deeper into a new place where his tools or talents can no longer solve the problem. The defenses that were developed as safeguards to emotional sanity in one world do not apply to the world where what is being hidden must be used. The defenses no longer provide safety. They are no longer an asset. They are a liability. And no matter how hard it will be for him to deconstruct his defense system, he had better do it or die. Cool, huh? This is what emotional structure is all about.

The whole point of the plot is to draw these fears from deep within to the surface. Once they are exposed, the story takes over and makes him deal with them. Though the plot pressures may be physically imposing and even life threatening they are not there to actually kill your hero. They are there to reveal your hero. The poison arrow is just motivation.

The plan from the opening pages of your script is to engage your protagonist in two life and death battles—the physical battle and the metaphysical battle. At first he will only fight the physical battle because he is good at it and has won before. But this time you've made it different for him. You've changed the rules. You've put him in a position where he has to fight with a serious disadvantage. He accepts the challenge because he's confident. He soon learns, however, that the talents and techniques he depends on in battle will not work for him this time. The enemy is very different from those in the past. The enemy is within.

Now his second life and death battle is with his own denial system. Your job in the second act is to tear apart his defense system and make him fight with his hands, so to speak. He has been avoiding this confrontation very carefully, so you have to develop your own scheme carefully as well.

Your ally in this plan is your co-protagonist. You and your co-protagonist must have a very special relationship. Between the two of you,

you are going to tear your protagonist apart and paste him back together again. As a reward to your co-protagonist you will let her have a little fling with the protagonist, maybe even a big fling with him. Maybe even let her fall in love with him. As long as she gets him to admit his fears, face his fears, and overcome his fears.

Fear. The enemy within.

No matter how brave your hero is. No matter how many battle ribbons he won in the war. No matter how many home runs he hit. No matter how many risks he has faced, bravery cannot defeat fear. Bravery can defeat the enemy but it cannot defeat the fear of the enemy. The only thing that can defeat fear is that thing which is the opposite of fear, and bravery is not the opposite of fear. The opposite of fear is faith. No matter how brave your hero is, if he doesn't have faith he will never win the interior battle.

Faith in this regard does not mean singing hymns in the chapel. Faith in regard to Emotional Structure means the recovery of self-belief. It means forcing your protagonist to take a leap of faith and trust someone else until he can trust himself again.

There are many examples of heroes in films who are brave and daring in many ways. They are quite pleased with themselves and their lives. They see no reason to change. And your protagonist should be no different until he meets your co-protagonist. Your co-protagonist is responsible for getting the protagonist to see the error of his ways. This may seem unfair. After all, the guy is happy with his life, and doesn't need anyone coming along to tell him he has to stop what he's doing and get some faith. But it is more than fair in the long run. He just doesn't see it yet.

It may cost your co-protagonist a great deal to teach this lesson. It could even cost her her own life. But she has no choice. It is her duty to teach. That is every good co-protagonist's duty.

Your theme

The *The Thomas Crown Affair* remake, written by Leslie Dixon and Kurt Wimmer and starring Pierce Brosnan and Rene Russo is a great study in second act Emotional Structure. Once Rene shows up and challenges Brosnan to play the game with a different set of rules, everything changes. The film is a lot of fun to watch because the cat-

and-mouse game they play is so delightful and clever and sexy. But beneath all the superficial catch-me-if-you-can stuff another story is playing out. It is a love story, and aside from its provocative nature and steamy love scenes, it is a love story based on hope. Something important is missing in each of their lives. Something they are too tough and self-sufficient to admit they need to examine. Each one dare not even say what they are thinking, because for some reason it seems that would be a weakness. And what they are thinking is this: Can I love and be loved? Can I open up and trust this guy, this girl? Can I dare to hope that a wonderful and real relationship is possible for me? If the film is about stealing art, it is also a film about the art of loving that was somehow stolen from each of them. They must curate this art now, but it will mean looking for answers they may not like.

That is the real dare. That is the theft with which the film must deal.

And so that becomes the theme of the film. As the writer you must remain aware of this theme in everything you do or say. It needn't be on-the-nose at all. It can be very subtle and off-center and it can be packaged in a humorous moment of self-deprecation, or in a moment of passion between the sheets. That's your call. Mix it up.

Do not be afraid.

At first the sheer number of pages in the second act can give you pause, and now that you see what has to go into all of those pages, the pause may be closing in on angina. But don't be discouraged, and don't give up.

I have an easy way to deal with Act Two: I break it up into three parts, a beginning, middle, and end, and I literally treat it as a film-within-a-film structurally. I can break those parts down even farther if I like until I clearly see very manageable sections and sequences. I reduce it to parts I can see and write without panic. Like everything else in my life, I have to take writing a page at a time. If I look at the whole deal at once, not just the 120 pages, but all the angles that have to be considered within them, I would be so scared I'd never begin.

This film-within-a-film is simple, and it is not about the plot. It is about the story beneath the plot and only uses the inventions in the plot to service the emotional story. It begins to lead me to where I have to go. It isn't about inventing crazy twists and turns, it's about digging deep inside a person, and that is very doable if I just chill.

The Emotional Journey

I have designed a chart for you to keep in front of you while you are writing. (See next page.) It is a very basic but necessary road map for the emotional journey your protagonist takes. It is designed for you to take your film's theme and your film's plot and story and, using your imagination, overlay your concepts onto them.

Let's take my film idea *Indirection* as an example, and then I want you to spend some serious time plotting your film the same way.

The chart shows us that we must establish the protagonist and co-protagonist's lives as they know them now. We show each one in his or her environment and establish a little bit of history. Each character is *emotionally settled* in life. If you were to ask them, they would tell you they are okay. They know who they are and they are okay with that. They are proficient at what they do. They are confident.

In my script I will introduce the protagonist and co-protagonist, each in his own world and each confident (maybe over-confident) in his ability to survive in that particular world. When I bring them together through a plot device they will immediately clash. I won't want them to like each other at the beginning. I want them to develop that through the course of the film.

I will refer to my other chart of the Four Character Levels and think of these characters in the terms of those levels. What kind of a world do they live in? How happy are they in it? Where is their family? Where have they been and where do they think they are going? These are important questions to ask because by the end of Act One, somewhere between pages twenty-five and thirty, I am going to yank them out of their respective worlds. In the plot I am going to send them on a road trip to find his little sister, but in the story what I am really doing is sending them out in an unfamiliar world to see if they can find *themselves*.

The middle of the script, Act Two, will be spent watching them try to cope outside of the worlds they were comfortable and confident in. As I create their journey I will look for ways that force them to expose more about themselves than they want to. The plan, we have said all along, is gradually to peel the onion. And remember to create these disclosures or revelations through their behavior, not speeches. For example, in my script the co-protagonist Midge has never been outside of her native New York City. I want to show that by her actions. I want to see

THE EMOTIONAL JOURNEY

• WHO I AM • WHAT I KNOW	• WHAT I KNOW DOESN'T WORK	• WHAT MUST I KNOW	• WHAT I DON'T KNOW NEARLY KILLS ME	• CAN I CHANGE?	• WILL I CHANGE?	• CHANGE
PAGE	30	45	60	75	90	105
• I AM UNIQUE • I AM ALONE	• REJECTION	• I AM NOT UNIQUE	• REGROUP	• RECOVERY • ACCEPTANCE	• REASSESSMENT • RE-COMMIT	• GROWTH • I AM NOT ALONE

her drink in the changing landscape as they get farther away from the Big Apple, and additionally I'm going to create a beat where she *tries* to read a road map in the car to help sell that idea of being in unfamiliar territory.

Putting your protagonist and co-protagonist together as much as you can is definitely the objective here. When it is difficult to do, make that difficulty part of the suspense and tension just as the writers did with Book and Rachel in *Witness*. What could have been a problem for the writers became an asset because they used the notion that Book and Rachel shouldn't be together as a tool to elevate the emotional intensity when they were together.

The first step in changing someone is to strip him of his confidence.

I want you to be able to strip your protagonist and co-protagonist of their confidence, too, because that confidence is a false confidence. It is one that was cultivated out of fear. It was designed to shut in rather than let out feelings. Now you will cleverly design scenes that will reveal the chinks in the armor. You can design scenes a hundred different ways to accomplish the same goal. So your hands are not tied by structure, they are free to do as they will. I can't emphasize this enough:

> **Now that you know where you want to take your characters emotionally, you will also know how to construct a plot to serve that purpose.**

This second act, the one that scares the heck out of everybody, has a very clear and simple path if we stay focused on the Emotional Structure instead of random action sequences. If we know what the story needs—the character de-construction undercurrent—then we can create any film we want to satisfy that need.

I think of the midpoint of the script, which is also the midpoint of the second act, as the moment when my film changes complexion forever. In the case of *Indirection* I am going to use the midpoint to turn my story that is focused on finding the little sister into a story that is focused on Scott and Midge "finding" each other and falling in love.

This excites me no end. By the time I'm in the middle of my script I love my characters and I want them to love each other, too. And I love seeing people learning how to open up without shame, and as a result allowing love to come in to displace it.

The instant the film turns from the first half to the second half it also turns from a specific adventure to a universal quest. It changes from a unique set of circumstances none of us may have ever encountered to a set of circumstances we all have encountered. The film becomes a personal story for the audience.

This is also the half of the film where you will be speaking more from your heart than your head. You will be "writing about the things you know." And as you do that, dear writer, you will find that the second act is not your enemy anymore. In fact, it will be your favorite part of screenwriting. The second half of the script is the most intense and the most dense, and the most fun to write. You will look forward to it.

In the second half of Act Two the protagonist's quest changes because the antagonist changes.

Another very important thing to remember in the second half of the script is that the antagonist changes, too. True, there might still be the cops chasing Book, or in my case the clock ticking in their race to find his sister is certainly still there. But the real antagonist for Scott and Midge resides in their emerging feelings. As we said, the enemy is within. What they are fighting now is the thing that shut them down and never allowed this kind of love before. They will have to fight this enemy with new skills because the old ones won't work. They will look to each other for the answers, and in the act of looking the acquisition comes automatically. This is because in the act of asking is the act of constructive humbling, and when we are humble we are teachable. Each person will have to acquire those skills in a hurry, and they will have to take the great leap of faith to use them. This is the great battle, not the one with the bad cops.

At first they will use them incorrectly and they will get in deeper trouble. The reason they will use them incorrectly is because they will try to use them the way they used their old tools. And that won't work. There is no shortcut to complete surrender. They have to let go completely. When, finally they trust each other, they will trust themselves. And when they trust themselves, no one or no thing can scare them again.

What a truly great victory. For you and for your characters.

12

Creating the Story's Emotional Environment

We portray emotions not with words so much as with language. The language of film is unique and powerfully effective. When they say a picture is worth a thousand words that goes double for motion pictures.

We portray heat not so much with fire as with perspiration. We portray desire not so much by consuming as by tempting. We portray a time by how it felt. We portray a place by its sounds and smells and colors. We portray true love by sacrifice. We portray pain by hope. As writers we do not write *about* feelings, we write feelings. In order to do that of course, we must feel.

A *house is not a home.*

When I choose a home for one of my characters I choose one that says the most about her emotions. It is a space for her heart and soul more than her body. Although it might be interesting to describe her condo's palette and the furnishings and expensive artwork, it doesn't characterize her. It tells me how she relates to the world on the outside, the first level on our Four Levels of Character chart. Nothing is revealed about her really, except how she wants to present herself to the rest of the world. This is her public persona, and we all have one. It's calculated to please others as much as oneself. We have to go to the details to find the real her. Those are the details I like to create. I have to put things in her life and in her environment that reflect her spontaneous choices. The *spontaneous* choices are the subconscious truth. We may find something that reveals part of her past, for example, or an aspect of her personality she doesn't show to the public.

Lorenzo Semple, Jr. found this in his script for *Three Days of the Condor* based on the James Grady novel. In a scene in that movie Robert Redford notices that the black and white photographs on Faye Dunaway's apartment wall have no people in them. They are stark cityscapes without humans. They express a soul-sadness and a loneliness she doesn't admit to the world. What does this say about her, he wonders? She is lonely, that's for sure. And people are not her favorite subjects. Does she even like other people? Redford challenges her on this and manages to peel away a layer of her secretive character. It is a well-crafted scene and an intelligent revelation, and is an example of the kind of emotional exposition that makes a film more complex and interesting.

If your heroine is comfortable in her home, nesting in it, that tells me a lot about her. I will get the impression that she is comfortable in her life and in her choices, and that she doesn't have to force a public persona.

Shane Black creates a temporary home for Bruce Willis in the opening of his film *The Last Boy Scout* that is nothing but Willis' crappy, old car. But it is a powerful statement and it tells us all we need to know about Willis and the state of his affairs. It's a wonderful idea.

Clothes make the woman.

Clothes are an extension of the home, socially speaking. How you dress your protagonist can tell us a lot about her. If you describe your beautiful heroine brushing her hair off her forehead as she chops firewood on her ranch early one autumn morning wearing old jeans and her favorite flannel shirt, I get a very clear picture that she is self-confident and self-sufficient, and probably not a phony. What man doesn't fall in love with a beautiful woman who chops her own firewood? If that's what you want me to do, to fall in love with your heroine from the first frame, then you've succeeded.

If she joins some of her ranch hands for a cup of coffee in a tin cup (not a ceramic Starbucks latte cup) when she's finished, then she can do no wrong as far as I'm concerned. You don't have to put another word in the description to tell me who she is. You are telling me all I need to know by her actions and attitude, and how a person dresses is an attitude.

Emotional companions

Let's follow her up to the ranch house, shall we? As she walks across the field a couple of her working dogs join her. Their relationship is great and she begins to jog with them. Dogs, especially dogs whose master is a mistress are very emotional props. If you've had such a companion you know what I mean.

Horses are emotional companions. Cats are not emotional companions. Sheep are emotional companions, but I'd keep an eye on the shepherd. Goats are definitely emotional companions. Gerbils are definitely not emotional companions.

You get the picture. Okay, so our cowgirl gets up to the house, kicks off her boots on the front porch—she's a lady after all—and goes inside.

Emotional elements

Water is about as emotional an element as you can get. In this case it's really emotional because your heroine is stepping into the shower. I say shower because I think she saves the bath for the end of the day. Either way, water is a great emotional element.

The swimming pool. The sprinklers' spray. The afternoon cloudburst. The golden pond. The sweat on the pitcher of iced tea. The sweat on a dancer's body. The waterfall and mountain stream. Poipu Beach. Hosing down the car. Hosing down the dog (counts as two). Hosing down the cowgirl (counts as three).

Fire is another emotional element. Candlelight, the glow and warmth of the fireplace, a bonfire on the beach, a gentleman lighting a lady's cigarette, all add a kind of emotion to a scene. Sometimes fireworks.

Wind has a sexiness all its own. It can ring the wind chime. It can lift the hem of a filmy skirt. It can comb her long locks in a convertible. It can wave the flag. It can carry rain and drive snow. It can push the curtains aside in a boudoir window. It can dance with autumn leaves. And it can whistle through the high country pines with a song so magical I get goose bumps.

And that's what we want from any one of these elements—goose bumps.

There are special places and old sweaters and trusted pets and lily ponds and rose gardens and floating candles in bubble baths and silver clouds blowing across the moon above the canoe on the lake.

There is no reason not to use these emotional environments and emotional elements whenever you can. You can choose to place the same scene in a closet or on a rooftop. People can talk anywhere. People can fight anywhere or make love anywhere. Don't restrict yourself. Don't be boring. Be inventive.

Unless there's a hand in the stew, get out of the kitchen.

There are few things worse than a scene played in a kitchen when it doesn't have to be played there. I have nothing against kitchens really, it's just that a couple of cowgirls sitting around the kitchen table talking isn't my idea of cinema. Unless they're stirring the pot of stew and stumble onto someone's hand floating in it, put the scene somewhere that adds to the emotional undercurrent. Using the environment is what cinematic storytelling is all about.

Having said that, please be reasonable. I have watched scenes inexplicably played on the rooftops of houses in the middle of the night. Maybe the writer or director thought it was a pretty shot, I don't know, but it was so disconcerting and distracting that it ruined the scenes. In fact I don't even know what the scenes were about.

The flip side of that would be forcing the wrong kind of emotion into a scene. I have witnessed a scene originally written between a husband and wife discussing their wills in their attorney's office rewritten so that it could be played in the couple's Malibu beach hot tub while they make love. The attorney was relegated to the other end of the speakerphone conversation. I kid you not. Ludicrous? Of course. But the executive producer felt it had been too long since we had seen any flesh and he was afraid the audience would get bored with the scene in the attorney's office. Instead, the audience was simply dumbfounded.

Time and space

The elements of time and space play an important role in the cumulative feelings you can create for your film. If you want to establish another era when the pace was slower, then you have to create scenes in which the slowness of time plays a part. Before the automobile ruined our country, folks used to walk to town or into the big city. Sometimes that took an hour or two, and sometimes it took all day. Make sure you use that in your film in such an era. If it took all day to milk the cow and churn butter, or to cook a meal in the kettle over the fireplace, then let it take all day. It is a visual undercurrent. You don't have to say anything about it, or make any big dramatic point of it, because no one made a point of it at the time anyway. They weren't in the rush we are in today.

What it implies, however, is that for a farmer or a rancher to take the day to go into the city he has to plan on making a special trip. There are dangers on the road, and there is always the loneliness and worry of those left behind. Again, it doesn't have to be hit hard, but the loneliness or worry has a place in the emotional undercurrent in your scenes. Don't waste it.

Space is a precious commodity. It has always been precious. In the olden days way out West space was a given. The Big Sky Country connected a man to the earth in a powerful, almost indescribable way. It was clear that nature deserved a man's awe and respect and love. Today there is a serious lack of even the awareness of such things. When you see the spaces we all live in in our crowded cities around the world it is a wonder we don't all go mad and eat each other.

But the wide-open spaces and the cramped city crypts are powerful visual and emotional elements for us to use. Don't waste these either.

Listen to the heartbeat.

As I write this by the light of a few candles and my computer screen I can hear all the frogs in the stream bed a stone's throw away. It always thrills me to hear the change of day. It's one thing to see it…to see the sun set and the stars come out, but it is a totally different emotional experience to actually hear the day change to night. I forget until that happens that there is a whole set of creatures I am rarely aware of who can't wait for me to turn off my damn Miles Davis so they can serenade one another.

Other than a very brief mention of this kind of thing in your scene descriptions there are limits to how you can write about the heartbeat of your heroine's environment. But it's worth keeping an eye out for and using whenever you can. It isn't a horrible idea to have her mention something like that in her dialog in a scene. She may be tucking the kids in and recalling a story about a cricket—the insect not that horrid ball game—that was triggered by the sounds of the crickets outside the kids' window.

Another element to watch for is the time of year. It can add so much to your story to be in a specific season. Each season has its own powerful emotions attached to it and we should take advantage of those emotions to bolster the emotions in your story. Swimming in the old swimming hole in the summer. Raking and burning the leaves in autumn. Walking through the woods in the snow in winter. Cleaning the house in the spring. These are all natural occurrences that belong in your picture. Sometimes they may only be in the background, but put them there anyway. Emotional detailing is worth its weight in gold.

Nothing is in a vacuum.

Film is extraordinarily expressive. It takes everything around it into account. You must be aware of that at all times. Never write a scene without regard to where it is being staged, at what time of the day or night it takes place, during which season or around which holiday it might be, the presence or absence of other people, the weather, or pressures inherent in the moment.

Every scene you write is unique in all these ways. Every sense and sensation can be used to heighten the mood or elevate the tension. When you have the choice of where to place a scene, enjoy making that choice.

And last, even if it is 100 percent valid, never place a scene in any environment so overwhelming or bizarre that it distracts from the drama. You want the elements of environment to enhance your work, not obliterate it.

13

Barriers, Roadblocks, Broken Legs, and Old Lovers

Nothing can ruin a person's day quicker than an unexpected visit from an old enemy, or a detour in a storm, or a stupid misstep that gets you a free trip to St. John's Hospital and a cast that you know is going to smell like crap in a week. Life happens. And when we write our scripts we often forget that.

We get a plot and story in our heads and then we put our characters through their paces page after page without regard to the fact that they are living in the real world and the real world is going to get in their way now and then. In fact, sometimes it gets in their way at exactly the moment it is least tolerable.

Put poop in your script.

Poop happens. We are tied to too many things for one of them not to blow up in our face now and then. We need to develop a keen awareness of this and use life's little interruptions to our benefit. Keep notes on some of the life interruptions that have amazed you or tickled you. Then use them in your script when you need a diversion or roadblock.

We can look back at our guy who started out his day riding the bus, and before he knew it he was holding a fortune in an elevator with a cute babe poking her pistol between rib number four and rib number five. Where had he gone wrong, he wondered. Well, truth be told, most of us aren't doing anything wrong when poop happens.

Poop can be a minor or major inconvenience. It can make us late to the theater. It can cause us to miss our flight. It can cut our finger and require a few stitches. Or poop can be catastrophic and tragic. We can be on our way from Boston to L.A. and wind up getting no further than the World Trade Center. We can think we're going to see our sons and daughters tonight, and never see them again.

We can visit our mother in the hospital and feel safe. And days later never feel safe again. We can get past some things. We cannot get past others. We are human. Your protagonist is human. He may possess buckets of charm. She may possess a breathtaking butt. But the only thing that makes either one interesting and worth a frame of film is the fact that each is human. And each can and will screw up.

Each is frail. Each is strong. Each is different. Each is alike. Each is part of it all. And each is apart from it all. Each is to his own. And each is owned. Each has needs. Each has dreams. Each will succeed. Each will fail. That's humanity.

In the course of your plot and story you must make sure that your characters are participating in the larger world—in the larger scheme of things. They cannot be isolated from the reality surrounding them, yet in many films (bad ones) you will notice that they are.

Your protagonist and co-protagonist cannot pass through a city like New York without their story absorbing some of its culture. Within that unique ambiance you can construct vital plot points or clues. You can use the city to impart something to your protagonist that he needed to hear and that he could not have heard in any other city.

Using the specificity of a time and a place contributes to your film's reality because it borrows from the actual reality. Remember what Merton told us, that every experience you put your characters through creates a lasting impression on their hearts and souls. It may be a small impression but sooner or later it will hook up with another impression and together they will have meaning. On the other hand, some lasting impressions suck.

What do you want? I thought you died.

Not every relationship ends tidily. Seeing someone you once loved and now hate sweep through your life and create a mess can make homicide seem like a real option. This is usually the case in a romantic comedy, where an old flame blows in on an ill wind and gets nasty all over again. In a comedy the writer has the liberty to talk about things like murder and mean it. In drama the writer cannot be so glib.

In drama when an old flame blows in it's usually not on an ill wind. It's usually on a wing and a prayer, suffering and private. Then, for crying out loud, of all the gin joints in all the world, she craps out in your place and ping go the strings of your heart. She looks at you and the look says it all and your heart aches and your head spins.

I hate when that happens. But it does happen, and as the inventor of events, keep these in mind. You can never tell when an ex-lover is just the ticket to liven up a quiet scene.

Another asset the visit from an old buddy or ex-wife can bring to the table is some historical information the co-protagonist would never have been able to draw out of your protagonist in a million years. The danger is not to make it too obvious. In other words you don't want the uninvited guest to pop in, tell tales, and then take a hike. You will have to be smoother than that. When an "ex" shows up with damaging information the best way to expose it is not by her own volition. Don't make her vindictive and don't make it the point of her visit to disrupt things. Let the information slip out another way or let it be discovered by someone else. This takes the heat off of the "ex" being the heavy and even gives her the chance to straighten things out later on as the good witch instead of the evil witch. Did I say witch?

Turn up the heat.

It isn't easy to construct all the things we're talking about and keep it riveting all the time. Just keeping all the balls in the air at the same time is a miracle. Naturally there are going to be some parts of the script that are less thrilling than other parts. You can't write a story that travels a hundred miles an hour all the time. Things must and do slow down now and then. The audience needs the rest, and the characters do, too. But every once in awhile things slow down to a crawl and it isn't a crawl you intended or expected. You're in the death pages. Everything seems to be dying.

Your script needs an energy boost. When this happens, shoot at him.

If you think things are slowing way down then throw something at your protagonist that forces him to run like hell. Create an incident or conflict. Say he's walking down the street. A lot happens on the streets. A purse snatching or a mugging could do it. If you need something on a grander scale you can always drop a body off the roof to the pavement in front of him. The blood and bits of bone on his pants will get his attention. But not all incidents created to turn up the heat need be nasty.

Your heroine might be dashing across the street late for meeting at a client's when an incredibly handsome Italian lad in a Maserati stopped at the red light calls out to her for directions to a Park Avenue co-op he bought sight unseen. Or she could find a lost puppy and return it to its owner and wind up having a one-night stand with him that to this day brings tears to her eyes every time she looks at her ASPCA lifetime membership card.

The biggest life interruption in your script will be the eruption between your protagonist and co-antagonist/co-protagonist when they first meet. This should be considered in this conversation about roadblocks and course changes because you will want their first clash to ring true. It has to be organic and seamless to what is happening in the plot. For example when Book shows up to investigate the murder and meets Rachel for the first time it is completely organic and real.

In romantic comedies the first incident in which the protagonist and the co-protagonist run into each other is called a "cute meet." "Fate" brings them together, it is presumed. He looks at her and she looks at him and they each know they've been looked at. Good golly goosebumps. For some reason the innocence of a "cute meet" is presumed to imply that their ultimately happily-ever-after-wedding-in-the-park-with-a-little-pooper-in-the-oven finale was "meant to be." Maybe it's just me, I don't know.

Beat up but better for it

On a more serious note, the real reason to set up the roadblocks and barriers on your protagonist's journey is to make him face and overcome fears that will teach him the lessons he needs to learn. We cannot just obstruct his progress for the sake of obstructing his progress. We have to have an important lesson in mind. Not only that, but the lesson learned has to enable him to go to the next level on his quest.

The primary reason to set up the roadblock is to challenge him morally and spiritually. The secondary reason is to challenge him physically. The primary reason for him to overcome the roadblock is to gain emotional and spiritual strength. This is the story's reason. The secondary reason for him to succeed is to advance the plot.

We have all noticed that the protagonist is on a journey that usually beats the crap out of him. During the times of physical recovery between battles he contemplates his fate so far. This is a transition period for him emotionally and spiritually. He usually shares these observations and feelings with his co-protagonist. This is an intimate exchange wherein they expose their fears and vulnerability. This intimacy draws them closer. It is not the victory in the battle that wins the co-protagonist over, for she is wiser than that. It is the admission in times of recovery and transition that he is only human and has doubts and weaknesses that her heart is taken.

The transition periods are the most important development points in your script. These are the times of change for the protagonist. After every

DENIAL

transition and the change it brings, he has the new strength with which he can face the next leg of his odyssey. The discussion of transitions will come up again in greater detail in a later chapter.

Because the barriers you set up are so important to your protagonist's progress we have to make sure they don't become silly. Sometimes we come up with really witty incidents to frustrate the journey but if they make our hero look like a fool we have to change them. We cannot afford to hurt our protagonist's character for the sake of a joke. I've seen this happen and the consequences are irrecoverable.

Plausibility is a key as well. You cannot construct a roadblock so difficult to overcome that it requires your protagonist to don his Mighty Morphin Power Rangers tights. The audience has to believe your protagonist can actually do the thing you have him doing. You don't want your audience clucking when they should be cheering.

When is a roadblock not a roadblock?

Not all roadblocks are big physical or intellectual challenges. And not all roadblocks are constructed by the bad guys. The biggest roadblocks are the ones we build ourselves deep within our psyches. The challenges we face in life are not so grand most of the time. They just seem so. You may argue that if they seem so, then they are so. But that is wrong. What a thing seems to be cannot make it a thing it is not. What a thing seems to be is what it seems. Not what it is.

How else can we explain that when the same thing happens to two different people, one person manages it and the other does not. The thing isn't the challenge. The challenge is the thing. When the challenge calls for inner strength rather than outer or physical strength then the inner strength can come from one of two places. It can come from the place of confidence, and the confidence can manifest what it takes to meet the challenge. Or it can come from the place of denial, in which case the denial facility turns a blind eye, and walks away.

The challenge moment is one of fight or flight. Confidence built on the practice of faith can fight. Denial cannot fight, so it must flight. Sometimes the flights are actually flights. In some circles this is called "taking a geographic." Sometimes the flights are flights of fancy—delusions that are subconscious defense mechanisms.

What it takes for someone to stand his ground when he is scared to death is an act of faith. Faith is an act of surrender, not to the challenge, but to the spirit in whom we put our trust to face the challenge with us and to take care of us no matter the outcome. This spirit in whom we put our faith can be anyone we choose. It can be Allah, or Buddha, or Jesus Christ, or Larry over at Sit'n'Sleep. It doesn't matter.

It doesn't matter because faith isn't religion.

I never understood it when a person would say he was of the Catholic faith, or of the Jewish faith. Faith doesn't have a church. Faith doesn't have a pope or a rabbi. Faith isn't an organization. Faith is a personal spiritual condition.

We will discuss the idea that sooner or later your protagonist has to find the faith to move forward or die in later chapters. For now suffice it to say that I have faith in you and I hope you have faith in what I'm saying.

Connecting the Internal and External Themes

Earlier I discussed the notion that the plot and the story feed off of each other and travel the road together not so much side-by-side as entwined. I described my vision of it as two strands wrapped around each other creating a stronger cord. As the plot strand wraps around the story strand and comes into our vision it occupies the action of the film and our attention. When it curves out of sight the story unfolds behind it and occupies the emotional consequences of the action.

In the plot the protagonist takes action. In the story the protagonist contemplates and subsumes the emotional consequences of that action. Two distinct functions, but each of which would fail without the other. They are the yin and yang of film writing. As such you must always be aware that they are traveling together to support each other. They are not speeding along on parallel courses. They are on the same course at the same time, entwined in a rhythm and flow. They are the rhythm and flow of story and plot.

The work of the plot is to offer situations in which the story can be told. And the work of the story is to give value and meaning to the plot. They are inseparable. They are happening at the same time though one will be in the foreground while the other recedes to the background temporarily. Their growth is parallel. The plot cannot be addressed in any depth separately from the story, and vice versa.

The plot and the story take turns moving the film forward until they merge near the climax.

In Act One the plot drives the story.

In Act Two the story drives the plot.

In Act Three the plot ends and the story begins again.

This is a lot to take in. I wish I were sitting beside you at your keyboard now so that we could discuss your screenplay idea in specifics. We have to try to imagine your idea overlaying the pattern above, and I would guess that trying to picture the whole of your screenplay all at once has you completely frustrated or confused. Do not despair. In the next chapter we will get to the methods that reduce these seemingly formidable tasks into very doable work.

Connecting emotions

The most overlooked aspect of developing and writing a screenplay is that of the emotional balance the plot and the story must achieve. In the lesser action films where plot is master and story is irrelevant, the pace of the film is spasmodic. It is only a matter of budgetary concerns that slows the febrile nonsense. When, for example, *The Terminator* has a scene between the action sequences it is not of any meaningful nature. It's not as if he's going to go soft on us and worry about the families of the seventy-three people he just slaughtered. He doesn't give a crap. He can't. And it's just as well for Arnold the Actor. Words of compassion would only confuse him. If a writer were to give him a scene like that in which he feels guilty and wants to talk to his priest the audience would run for the exits. Killers don't feel sorry. *The Terminator* and so many movies like it in its genre are about killing. Nothing else. Nobody at the studio expects you to go out for a late supper after the show with your date and her friends and discuss the moral of the story. There is no story. And there are no morals. Were there morals the movie wouldn't have been made.

Good drama is not about the thing. It is about how we feel about the thing.

In films that sucessfully confront morals, the story and the plot are carefully woven. It is easier in the very beginning to develop the story in broad strokes and the plot in broad strokes more or less separately. But once we start breaking down the broad strokes it is better to develop the specifics side by side. By doing that we can see the action and the emotional reaction working together in a scene. The method for doing this is discussed in the next chapter.

Again, this is like sketching the picture on the canvas first with bold broad strokes, and then as we refine our thinking and painting we work with line and color simultaneously. They become inseparable. One is the other and with the other is one. It's the only natural way to do things. We don't want to put down the line drawing first and color in the areas later as if it were a paint-by-the-numbers kit. We want to make sure that our lines and spaces go on in color together. Lines push color, color pushes lines, back and forth in concert, in expression. In creation. This is exactly what happens in screenwriting. The lines (the plot) try to confine the color and spaces (the emotional story), but the color and spaces cannot to be bound without its agreement. The struggle for statement ensues.

Episodic versus epigenetic structure

Here are my feelings about episode and epigenetic storytelling.

Soap opera is episodic. Soap opera contends with a gaggle of characters normally. It is impossible to connect the undercurrent of every subplot to all the others. There is a resultant style therefore that pushes the separate plots along at a parallel and compatible pace. First there is a scene with one desperate housewife and her husband painting their new baby's nursery. Then there is a scene in the house next door with that housewife and her husband threatening each other with knives. And then there is a scene in the house next to that with the housewife and the pool boy playing Marco Polo under the sheets. By the end of the hour each story/plot has moved along, albeit at a snail's pace.

A drama constructed epigenetically works very differently. Generally speaking this kind of drama focuses on a smaller group of central characters and everyone in the group is tied emotionally to someone or everyone in the group. Therefore, unlike the episodic structure where one family's actions do not necessarily directly affect the neighbor's, every action taken by one family in an epigenetic construction does affect its neighbors. This ultimately provides a unity of meaning. Woven into the subtext of each family's stories are common themes. And they are the ties that bind.

As an example, very different than the soap opera, we can consider *Wonder Boys* again. In that film everything that Michael Douglas did affected Tobey McGuire. And everything Tobey McGuire did affected Robert Downey Jr. And everything Robert Downey Jr. did affected Michael Douglas. And everything that Michael Douglas did as a result of what Robert Downey Jr. did affected Frances McDormand. And of course anything Frances McDormand did directly affected Michael Douglas and

Richard Thomas. And anything anybody did affected the nubile Katie Holmes. And so on.

Everything and everybody was emotionally commingled in the film, and everything the writers (screenwriter and novelist) developed was based on the fact that whatever happened in one scene could not have happened without the specific thing that happened in the scene before it.

This is not true in episodic structure where one scene in one house can act completely independent from anyone else's scene because anyone else's scene has no bearing on their lives. If you know what I mean.

In a drama such as *Wonder Boys* and so many of the others we've mentioned when the story is told epigenetically it creates the phenomenon of cumulative knowledge. What I mean by that is we (the writer and audience) can presume that since everyone is so tightly knit physically and emotionally some information travels between them off screen as well as onscreen. This eliminates a lot of redundant scenes.

In soap operas the sense of time standing still is a result of not being able to make this cumulative knowledge assumption. We see Sally tell Tom something. Then we see Tom tell Joe. Then we see Joe tell Mary. And then we see Mary tell someone else, *ad nauseum*. Because the spheres of influence in soap operas rarely overlap, no passing of information from one to the other can ever be assumed. So it has to be shown over and over again.

I don't want to dwell on soap writing. My point is to explain and encourage epigenetic structure over any other kind.

At the epicenter of epigenetics

In the middle of all this connecting and commingling is your protagonist. He somehow seems attached to everybody. John Book is a good example. His actions affect other people. He does not exist in a vacuum and the internal and external themes therefore are interconnected, too, because he is the connector.

As a morality play, John Book comes into a community and affects the whole community. He learns a lesson (the moral) and the community learns a lesson. Everyone is better off in one way or another for his having come through their lives. Or they are dead. This is an ideal set-up and the reason I suggest studying it is because if you can bring your outline structure around to be as well-constructed and clear as this one, you'd be off and running.

Because your protagonist is connected to characters who hatch in the plot as well as characters who hatch in the story, he affects their emotional state and they affect his. What is important to develop in each of his relationships is an emotional tone that can carry throughout the script. Strong characters, stronger than we meet in everyday life, are the staple of cinema. They are strong for a very good reason. They influence every scene they are in. The importance of that cannot be overstated. Your protagonist is the star of the movie. His story is either told about him or by him. In either case the "him" has to be felt in every scene. His presence should be the dominating one in every scene even if he's not dominating the action. The scene only exists because it has to do with him or is about him, so you must make it smell and feel like him.

This is not a design to put your star on a pedestal and create a monster whose dressing room trailer is bigger than your house. This is designed to create a consistent emotional tone throughout the film. His presence dominates. So his emotional tone should dominate. Clint Eastwood dominates the emotional tone of his movies. As does Woody Allen. In *Witness*, the place of Lancaster, Pennsylvania, dominates the tone because it represents the emotional truth the protagonist must find.

The tone is in the emotional truth. The emotional truth is in the details.

Leon and Mathilda in *The Professional* create their emotional truth as they go along. The very concept of the film is emotional truth. Each character is awakening. The act of awakening is in other terms a search for what is best. For what is right. For what is a dependable truth. Their story is about that search dressed up in a wonderfully cinematic plot of violence and corruption, both of which oppose truth.

In the details of their story, personal discoveries and admissions surface, albeit haltingly. But there is a world of information in every tiny detail. The details are enthralling and touching. They are the essence of intimacy. The story about their growth and growing attraction, an attraction they mistake as love, uses the tone of their epiphanies to emphasize their naiveté. This becomes the tone of the movie. It is a tone of innocence. Even her act of practicing to kill is completely innocent. That in itself is a remarkable tonal achievement. And his innocence is as clear as hers. He is safe and comfortable in his world of murder and mayhem. As soon as he lets love in his life he is no longer safe and comfortable. His life becomes more than the world of murder and mayhem. Love has its penalties.

In the shadows of the vapors of consequence

Creating relationships between your characters creates something else as well. It creates what I call a vapor of consequence. Not only do the protagonist and co-protagonist change little by little as a result of their encounters, but the world changes with them. It has to, don't you see? If the characters do not exist in a vacuum then whatever happens to expand them, also expands their universe.

Though it is frequently difficult for the characters to see the changes in themselves, it is not so for the world around them. Once the world around them feels the change, it changes as well. It cannot not change. It is instantly and automatically changed by the observation as it makes it.

The vapor of consequence spreads as the story widens, and this magical vapor casts a shadow over the field of the tale. Not unlike the reflex to a soft fog rolling in off the coast, the physical and emotional triggers we all possess activate an intuitive response to the vapors' pale shadow. It is usually a psychological pulling up of our collars around our necks and contemplating the shifts taking place within.

The people who access and absorb the quality of the shadow more readily than the protagonist and co-protagonist are the people sitting in the theater. This is the third and final connection. If the plot changes the characters, then the characters change the audience. Every successful film has that in common.

When certain films bridge the oceans and create a sensation on a global scale it is usually because the shadows of the vapors of consequence have moved us all to contemplate the changes possible within each of us. The great power of film, unlike the great power of literature, is its ability to present a common visual statement. Left with less to interpret than a great novel, the pictures of personal strength and victory revitalize a weary universe and unify it with hope.

A more thoughtful world is a better world. It is your job as a film writer to incite thoughtful contemplation. Or at least some chatter at the office water cooler.

Part 4

Building Blocks: Step-by-Step Construction

15

Card Tricks

Index cards have saved my life. No kidding. Index cards have changed the way I write, and the change has definitely been for the better. I'm one of those guys who is sort of organized. I'm not a complete slob and I'm not anal-retentive. I'm somewhere in between. The problem with being an almost organized guy is that I'm almost never organized. Writing a screenplay takes organization. I don't want to throw cold water on your enthusiasm, but it really does. And what kept me from being a better screenwriter was my aversion to, no, my anathema toward organizing art. For some reason I was convinced that the two, organization and art, were red states and blue states. I paid the price for a long time.

Whoever invented the index card has my eternal thanks. That Great Unknown Genius literally took the fear and frustration out of writing for me, because little, lined cards are the perfect tool for the almost-organized person. A deck of colorful cards and a ballpoint pen bound with a rubber band and I am ready. Carrying those things around even makes me *feel* like a writer. They have traveled with me all over the world. And everywhere I've been I've had the urge to erect a marble statue by the fountain in the town square dedicated to a great human being standing tall with his hand outstretched offering an index card to all who would want one.

I have been accused of having a big head from time to time. But I have never been accused of having a big brain.

When I begin work on a new screenplay I usually have all sorts of random ideas for scenes, and clues, and snappy lines of dialog. However I do not possess the kind of brain Stephen King has. I have run out of storage space. Not that I had much to begin with. So I need a place for all my great ideas.

Before I started using index cards I never knew where or how to begin putting down all these thoughts. Once I began using the cards my outlines took half the time to organize and they were twice as good when I was finished. Now I can't imagine attempting to write a screenplay without first getting out my deck of cards and making notes on them.

The number one asset sounds obvious now, but it was not obvious to me in the beginning. Using cards to write down my random ideas at least got the damn ideas down on paper in a neat little stack. No more crappy drink-stained cocktail napkins with smeared cryptic scribbling reeking of cheap Moselle. Suddenly I was Mr. Neat.

If one is good, two is better.

Every since I was a kid I held the firm belief that if one of anything was good, then two was better. We can figure out why later. If one scoop of ice cream was good, then two was better. If one Mickey Mantle trading card was good, finding a second one was better. By the time I hit college my theory had taken firm hold. If one beer was good, then two beers were better. And so on. When I started filling out my index cards with spectacular ideas I figured if one card was good, two was better.

I was keeping the company who printed them in business, but I worried I was denuding the forests of the Great Northwest. To say I had too many cards would be a lie. I had *way* too many cards. I wrote down every stupid thought that came into my mind because someone told me not to judge the ideas, just to write them down. So I did. I was advised that even though the thoughts might seem stupid at first, later on they could make a lot of sense. I have been waiting for some cards to make sense for over a decade. But most of the cards did make sense sooner than later. And I learned something else.

The cards are small for a reason.

I had a big problem in the beginning trying to write complete novellas on each card. That is clearly not the idea behind the cards. That is why the card is small. The point is to get the general idea for a scene down…not the whole scene. I am a slow learner. I was guilty of writing an entire opening scene on the front and back of a card once. The writing was so small I couldn't read most of it. There were a few things wrong with that approach.

First, I was going blind. Secondly, I was spending more time writing and reading my cards than I was writing the script. And finally and most important, the scenes on the cards were *never never never* good enough to use in a script. Scenes can only be written in a script when you are writing a script, basically. You have to be in the groove, in the moment, in the zone, or whatever. You have to be in the script. You can practice writing scenes. In fact I think that is a good practice. But don't expect those practice scenes to wind up in a script. The odds are impossibly steep. The danger of writing scenes out of context or out of the process is that we can fall in love with them and force them into a script. This is bad. Don't do it. Ever.

Many of the ideas for scenes that we write on cards change radically by the time we've translated them to an outline and then to a script. And many more are trashed. So don't do as I did, do as I say. Don't write scenes on your cards. Write the *headlines* of the scenes.

The crucial role of the index cards in the development process

Here is why cards are necessary in the development process:

We write a script working from a full outline.

We write a full outline working from a solid one-line outline.

We can't write a solid one-line outline working from a three-page treatment.

There is a gap.

The critical development stage between the three-page treatment and the one-line outline (or one-liner as it is called) is the index card stage. The index cards get us from the three-page treatment to our one-liner. Attempting to write a one-liner directly from the three-page treatment makes a hard job impossible.

So after we are happy with our three-page treatment we use it to start us off on our index card writing career.

One scene to a card.

Don't worry about the order of the scenes.

Take a look at your opening couple of paragraphs in your three-page treatment. You've already imagined many scenes for your first act. You had to reduce them into these few paragraphs to get to the core of the act. By doing that you created a much sharper focus dramatically. Now you are going to break down those paragraphs back into ideas for individual scenes with much greater clarity and flow.

One thing to remember while you are making out your cards is not to try to write them in sequence. This would be a frustrating waste of time at this stage. The immediate job is to put scenes on cards and note the salient points in them. Later on we arrange the cards on a bulletin board or spread them out on the floor to see how they lay out and what order pleases us most in terms of dramatic build. You'll see.

For now, just get the scenes down on cards.

While we are starting with the first act, there will be times when you will want to create a "sister card" for the second or third act prompted by what you are jotting down now. It may just be a reminder to somehow make a reference to this moment in the second act. There will also be times when you are working on cards for the second or third act and realize you had better tip a bit of information into an earlier act to forecast what you're putting in now so it won't seem as if it's coming out of nowhere. I always write which act I think the scene will go in on the top of the card and then put those cards together in separate stacks. That, too, can change.

Writing out your cards is not about structure. It's about putting everything down so you can see it in front of you. It's like storyboarding without the drawings, although I have been known to draw on cards if it helps.

As an illustration, the writers of *Witness* working on cards for the first act might have done something like the following.

Even though these particular cards are written in what seems like the order they will be in in the script, things could change at any time. Remember, when you have an idea for a scene or a note about a scene, just make

---

OPENING MONTAGE – NIGHT – PHILADELPHIA

A CROWDED BIG AMERICAN CITY.

Aerial shots and handheld subjective shots.

Sell the idea of the URBAN CRUSH OF HUMANITY and that NO ONE TALKS TO ANYONE ELSE.

IT'S AS IF EVERYONE IS IN HIS OWN WORLD.

This is anything but a serene and spiritual world.

INT. TRAIN STATION.

RACHEL and SAMUEL, an Amish mother and child, wait patiently for their train.

They are out of place. Rachel is uncomfortable with the crowds and chaos, but Samuel is fascinated.

There is an unsettling, almost ominous danger in a place like this for a couple of people like these two.

QUESTION: *How do we know this is their first time here?*

INT. MEN'S ROOM – GRAND CENTRAL STATION

Cold. Big.

SAMUEL comes into the room and is shocked by its size. He's never seen something like this before.

A MAN is washing at the sink. SAMUEL goes into a stall.

TWO BAD GUYS come in and MURDER the guy at the sink.

SAMUEL WITNESSES the MURDER. He hides without getting caught by the MURDERERS. Samuel SEES the MURDERER'S FACE, but the murderer DOES NOT see him.

AFTERMATH OF MURDER.

Police swarm the CRIME SCENE. They are consoling
Rachel and the boy Samuel.

DETECTIVE JOHN BOOK ARRIVES.

He questions Samuel gently. He tells Book he saw
the guy's face and Book asks him if he'd recognize him from a picture. Samuel thinks so.

Book TAKES THEM DOWNTOWN to go through the
mug shots. Over RACHEL'S OBJECTIONS.

the card and don't worry about where it belongs yet. This is important. If
you start editing yourself at this point you'll drive yourself crazy.

*In this example, an important question is raised
on the second card.*

The writers want to emphasize the complete difference in lifestyle
this environment is to Rachel and Samuel's home. How will the audience
know this, and also know this isn't something they do all the time? Samuel
could be curious simply because he's a kid and all kids are curious. Rachel
may be simply bored and put-off with the wait. But the writers want to say
more than that. They want to say that these are two people very much out
of their element, so it is more powerful later when Rachel insists on returning home rather than get involved in Book's investigation. The writers want
to show that the whole reason she lives in Lancaster is to avoid ever en-
countering this kind of violet event. In contrast, they want to show that
Book's attitude is that this is just another day at the office.

As I write my cards, a lot of questions like this one come to mind
and I jot them down on the card. I may not know the answer now, but I
know it's something I'm going to have to answer sooner or later.

In the example above, the writers may want to answer that question
with another card that shows where Rachel and Samuel are coming from,
physically and emotionally, and visually tell the audience how foreign
this train station and crime is to them. So maybe the writers change their
minds about the opening and instead imagine setting a sequence on their

Amish and farm under titles at the opening to show the contrast. The card might look something like this:

> Opening in AMISH COUNTRY.
>
> A FUNERAL. The COMMUNITY DRESSED IN TRADITIONAL AMISH CLOTHES. Then a gathering AT RACHEL'S FAMILY FARMHOUSE.
>
> We SEE the CULTURE and the PEOPLE. It is A GENTLE WORLD, SINCERE AND SWEET even at an emotional time as this.
>
> WE MEET RACHEL, SAMUEL, ELI, and the others. SET UP HER TRIP TO THE CITY (Maybe to a cousin's house or something?)

See? Isn't that great? Doesn't that make a whole lot of sense to you? I mean here you are writing the cards for your opening, you run into one of those nagging questions that drives you a little nuts. But because you are now armed with your fantastic deck of index cards you have a solution. Doesn't this make you want to run outside right now down to the town square and jump in the fountain and salute that sonofabitch?

Well almost. The above cards are what a normal card looks like.

But, we are not doing normal.

We are creating an *emotional structure* for our screenplay, and this card is worthless unless it contains *the emotional content* and *the emotional intent* of the scene. We are not creating a plot and then forcing an emotional story into it. We cannot develop an idea for a scene without knowing first and foremost what the emotional reason for its being is. Right? Right.

How, then, do we make our cards emotional?

We do the obvious. We turn the card over.

We write the emotional content and the emotional intent of the scene on the back of the card. The front of the card has the plot points. The back of the card has the story points. The two notions become inseparable from the very beginning, plot and story locked together. I can't emphasize enough how important it is to do this if you want to avoid the "muddle." The emotions of the characters in the scene are a little harder to reduce specifically to a couple of sentences, but give it time and you will get comfortable with it. Again, the emotional notes are reminders of what needs to be in the scene, so you may not know the solutions yet, but that's okay.

Back of Card Aftermath of Murder

It's important to convey in this scene that Samuel is intrigued by all the big city surroundings and by the activity of the police and other investigators.

Rachel is not just stunned by the events and repulsed by all the police work...MOST IMPORTANT she is worried about Samuel. SHE SEES THAT SAMUEL is more interested in the police work than he is freaked-out by what he saw in the men's room.

The last thing Rachel wants is her son becoming attracted to big city, modern life.

She wants to get the hell out of here, and when Book says he's taking them downtown, she is upset and very resistant.

Missing in action

For all the times when you've wondered what was missing in your script when the plot seemed to fall into place but the passion was missing, the answer is this: you can't stir the soul with a car chase. When you create any scene whether it's a police pursuit on the interstate or a heart-to-heart in the kitchen with a foot in the oatmeal, the emotional reasoning behind the scene has to be evident. When you develop the emotional current that sustains the action you are going to have a scene with heart and soul, and you are going to feel the passion.

Scene after scene you will build on those emotions until eventually even the smallest occurrences in the plot will have emotional impact. An emotional shorthand develops for you, and sensorial touchstones appear. By that I mean your audience will begin to react viscerally to things late in the script that were introduced in the beginning of the script through the emotions attached to them. And you will have them eating their popcorn out of the palm of your hand.

This is the missing development link.

As you can see, it's going to be a lot easier for us to create a one-line outline working from the stack of scene cards than it ever would be working directly from the three-page treatment.

NOT ALL GOOD IDEAS FIT

Arranging the deck. The bulletin board is your friend.

Once you have a your cards finished (I'm not sure you ever do finish) you will lay them out in the sequence that plays best for you dramatically and emotionally. I use a bulletin board divided into three acts. Armed with pushpins I put all the cards up for me to see and move them around until I like the flow *of the emotional story.* It's not unusual for me to play with the order of the scenes for quite a while. But not only that, there have been many times when I've noticed a beat missing; a scene or a clue or a tiny revelation that isn't in the cards. By placing them in sequence these kinds of discoveries occur routinely. You can see gaps and you can see redundancies.

It is easier to see how things fit, and what might be missing or might be unnecessary at this stage of development than at practically any other time. Sometimes, for example, I'll realize the content of one entire card can be reduced to a line of dialogue in another scene. So I add that note to the other scene and throw away the first card.

Once you have the cards in the order you like, it's time to write them down as a one-liner. You can refer to this one-liner that I developed from my cards for the script of *Indirection*. After you've studied it we are going to start constructing your one-liner but with a major difference. Your one-liner is going to be a two-liner that will reflect both sides of your cards. It is an Emotional Structure Two-line Outline. And it is worth its weight in gold.

Sample "One-Liner" Film Outline

Indirection
by Peter Dunne

ACT ONE

1. We meet RED PECK, sixteen, as she runs away from home in the middle of the night, leaving her middle-class life and her low class, divorced mother behind.

2. See MIDGE, nineteen, at a party in NYC. Gangs. Fight breaks out. Her brother is in the middle of it. She tries to save him, but can't. He's stabbed mortally.

3. Hospital. ER. Ambulance driver, SCOTT PECK, hauls Midge and her dying brother into the Emergency Ward. All business.

4. Red on the road. On a bus to NYC.

5. Midge buries her brother. Police want her to tell them who killed her brother. She won't cooperate. Wants to get her own revenge. Cops tell her she's crazy. She should be watching her back because the same guy's probably going to kill her next. Cop gives her his card telling her to think it over and call him any time, day or night. A beat later and a kid secretly slips Midge a message that the killer is looking for her before he goes back to his own turf in Philadelphia's Little Cuba.

6. Red arrives in NYC Grand Central Station.

7. Scott gets call from MOTHER telling about Red running away. Very tense conversation. Scott and Mother blaming each other for not taking care of Red. Scott realizes he's got to go after her.

8. Red and Midge in Grand Central. Midge and her street bum pals steal what they have to in order to survive. Midge follows Red into a shop

and makes small talk with her. Asks her where she's going. Red tells her she's headed to Disney World. Midge picks her pocket while they talk.

9.   Scott in Grand Central looking for Red. Shows her picture to a million people. Finally SHOP OWNER says he saw Midge with Red's wallet after Red was in the store buying magazines. Points out Midge. Scott takes off after Midge.

10.   Foot chase through the Station and down into the bowels of the subway below.

11.   Red almost runs right into the gang guys who killed her brother. Just like the cops said, they're looking for her. She's scared. Runs.

12.   Scott finally finds her living in the underground tunnels where all the runaway and homeless kids live. Big Scene. He sees Red's wallet and could kill Midge for making it worse for his sister. She knows where Red is heading but she won't tell Scott until he's willing to strike a deal. He's got to take her with him out of town. She'll help him find his sister. He doesn't want any part of her, but knows he has to find his sister. Red says his sister needs him, and he needs Midge. It's simple. Begrudgingly, he makes the deal. She smiles. They're off to Disney World. END OF THEIR ACT ONE

13.   Red, on the train. Realizes she's broke, steals a sleeping man's wallet but is caught by a drunk college kid heading to Florida on Spring Break. He drags her into the bathroom and offers her a deal: His silence can be bought for a little sex. As he forces himself on her, she catches him off-guard and drops him in pain with a quick knee to his groin. She drops the stolen wallet and takes his, instead. She gets off the train as it pulls into a station and runs into the night.

END OF RED'S ACT ONE.

ACT TWO

14. Morning. Parkway diner and gas station. Midge and Scott at breakfast. He remarks about her appetite, her clothes, her everything. She tells him to fuck off. She doesn't want his opinion or his sympathy. Nonetheless, he strongly suggests they wash up while they're there. He buys some cheesy tourist t-shirt and shorts for her to change into, and leads her to the ladies' room. They argue constantly. When she comes out to the car all cleaned up, we see for the first time how beautiful she truly is. Scott is a bit stunned. She's embarrassed.

15. Morning. Red wakes up in Washington, DC. She heads off into the city in awe.

16. Parkway. Scott tries to tell Midge how to read the map they're using. She's insulted at the way he talks to her. He tries to get her to open up about who she is, etc, but she clams up. Who she is is too painful for her to talk about.

17. Washington, DC. Red taking in the sights as a tourist. Engages in dialog with a Vietnam vet in front of the memorial. An emotional lesson for her.

18. Scott and Midge at train station in Rocky Mount, North Carolina, looking in train which has stopped to load and unload passengers. Red *should* be on this train, but is not. As they search, they run into a cop and the fraternity brother who is charging Red with assault and robbery. They learn she got off in D.C.

19. Red comes across a huge political rally (pro-choice/pro-life) and gets sucked into it...the power of the emotions behind the politics. The rally gets out of hand. People overrun the police. Fights break out. Red gets smacked on the head and trampled.

20.   Emergency room. Doctors stitch her head up, but Red can no longer remember who she is. She is kept in the police/hospital lock-up ward.

21.   On the road back to D.C. Midge and Scott have a huge argument over brother/sister relationships and responsibilities. Scott can't figure out where all of Midge's anger is coming from. She's a mystery to him.

22.   Night. Red is in hospital checking out the names on the clipboards hanging on each bed in her ward. She "tries on" names to see how they fit her. She comes to her bed and sees "Jane Doe." She goes to window, looks out at city, wonders if anyone is looking for her.

23.   Highway. Night. Cop pulls Midge over (they take turns driving now) for speeding. Gives her a ticket and a warning when she admits they've been driving day and night looking for Scott's sister. He tells them they either pull into the nearest motel and rest before they drive anymore, or he'll give them a bed in the city jail.

24.   Crappy motel. Scott's pissed they're losing time because of her. They're both tired and dirty. He showers. She showers. They share the same bed. They talk a little bit. Face away from each other as far apart as they can without falling off the bed. She says something nice to him (reacting to his passion for his sister) like tomorrow will be a better day. They'll find her.

25.   Hospital. Night. Everyone in the ward's asleep. See Red having a terrible nightmare of the guy on the train trying to molest her. She's tossing and turning and struggling in her sleep.

26.   Smash cut to: Scott being beaten up by Midge who is having her own nightmare, screaming her brother's name, trying to stop him from being brutally stabbed. Scott wakes her. She's shaken. Won't talk about it. Won't let him in to her world.

27.   Morning. Police station. Scott and Midge know the police are looking for Red so they go there first to see if they have found her. They tell them they think they have...she's in a hospital, and they found the wallet of the guy on the train in Red's possession.

28.   Hospital. They check the ward but the doctors tell them that the Jane Doe died last night of a massive brain hemorrhage. They need to identify the body downstairs in the morgue.

29.   Morgue. The body is finally brought to the room and they pull back the sheet. It's not Red.

30.   Midge goes to the ward and looks around. Sees there's been a mix-up in the clipboards on the beds. The "Jane Doe" isn't the one who died. One of the other patients tells Midge Red took off last night, scared as hell, traded her ring for this patient's bus ticket out of town.

31.   Bus Station. Information where the bus is headed and how many hours behind they are. Scott and Midge head out after Red again.

32.   They catch up with the bus finally, at a bus station. But Red isn't on it. THIS IS A BIG SCENE. Scott rages, frustrated and frightened, that this is all a waste of time and that he never should have let Midge lead him on this wild goose chase. That they'll never find her. Midge has had enough of his bitching and moaning, and says a brother would never give up until he finds her. He berates her for constantly inferring that he's a lousy big brother and that he's fucked up somehow. He tells her she obviously has a problem with her brother and she should settle it with him instead of taking her anger out on him. She tells him he doesn't know what he's talking about. He tells her he thinks he does, and relates the bits and pieces of her nightmare, of her calling out her brother's name; trying to stop him from

getting killed. She tries to run away from the argument. He won't let her. He chases her and confronts her, telling her to forgive her brother for getting killed, for leaving her alone. It's the only way she'll ever love him again. She breaks down and he holds her in his arms. THEY HAVE A NEW RELATIONSHIP AS A RESULT OF THIS SCENE. This is probably going to be my half-way point in the script.

33.   We find Red, meanwhile, riding in the front seat of a Wal-mart truck, having hitched a ride in the middle of nowhere.

34.   Scott and Midge go back to the bus. A passenger tells them that Red got off at a rest stop and hitched a ride on a Wal-mart truck heading east.

35.   Suddenly they're staring at the biggest truck distribution center in the world, as a seemingly endless stream of Wal-mart trucks load up for the road. Which truck could have seen Red? It's like a giant shell game.

36.   On the road, the Wal-mart driver pulls over and says it's time for his nap (regulations). Red gets out and starts to take a walk...thinks about hitching another ride rather than wait for this guy. Suddenly the driver joins her on the abandoned stretch of roadside, offering to walk with her in case she runs into trouble. She says there's no one around to make trouble. He grins stupidly.

37.   At the Wal-mart distribution center Scott and Midge work with the facility manager to determine which trucks were at the spot at the time Red got a ride. Two trucks were headed east at that time, one to north Jersey, one to the shore. One of the two is the truck they're after, but the dispatcher hasn't been able to reach either driver yet because they're on rest break. What to do? Midge studies the map. Philadelphia is staring

her right in the face. It's in direct route to Jersey. She hatches a plan and decides that they should head to Philly so they don't lose more ground. When they get there, they'll call back to this guy and see if he's reached the drivers, then they'll know whether to head north or south from that point. Scott hesitates, but Midge persists and pushes him out the door.

38.   At a roadside, in a cornfield, we find Red, barely conscious in a heap. She struggles to get to her feet, but her legs fail her. She crumbles, weeping, in pain.

39.   On the road, Scott and Midge speed toward Philly. Play a scene here where Scott is worried that Red will wind up dead like Midge's brother. He blames himself for not being around for Red when she needed him. Midge tells him to get down off the cross. No one forced Red to run away from home. It wasn't his fault. He tries to talk about it but she cuts him off saying a brother and being a parent aren't the same thing. He says sometimes in families like his the line is pretty fucking blurred. He feels shitty.

40.   Farm field. Red is found by a handful of Amish farmers. Barely coherent, not knowing who she is or where she is, she tries to fight them off, but they carry her to safety.

41.   Scott and Midge reach Philly. They call the Walmart guy who says none of his drivers claims to have picked her up. Scott is stunned. Midge grabs the phone and gives the guy an ultimatum: either he calls them back at the suchandsuch hotel (she sees it across the street) with the names and social security numbers of the all the drivers heading east that day, or she'll call the FBI and tell them he's harboring a child molester.

42.   In the hotel. Scott doesn't understand what

the hell she's doing, that he doesn't even know where the fuck he is anymore. She says he hasn't known where he is for a long, long time. He's about to burst waiting. Finally the call comes from the Wal-mart guy with the names and SSN's. Scott can't imagine what she's going to do with them. She pulls out a cop's card from the scene in the cemetery and dials the number. She makes a deal with the cop. She'll testify as a witness and help the police if he'll help her with some information now. She gives him the SSN's and asks him to call her back at this number if any-one of these guys has a record. Deal. Then this turns into A HUGE SCENE FOR THE CHARAC-TERS OF MIDGE AND SCOTT. He blows up be-cause he has no idea what she's doing. She tells him that if one of the drivers has a record, then he's the one they'll go after because he's the one most likely lying. Record? You mean criminal record? She nods, they have to wait a couple of hours for the cop's phone call. He can't wait! He starts to crack and finally he says what he was trying to say in a round about way in the car earlier. He ran away from home, too. And now he's the role model for his kid sister, because he's been pretending that he's been doing okay, but really he's been a failure. His life's been shit. And now he realizes he can't run away from some things. If he had had the balls to stay home and tough it out, and not abandon Red, she never would have needed to run away now. If she dies, it's going to be his fault. He breaks down. She tells him he's wrong. That he did what he had to in order to save himself from an untenable situ-ation, and that what he did was an inspiration to his sister to save her life, too. His fury and guilt turn to sorrow, and her compassion and strength lead to an immensely intimate moment.

One that neither has shared before. And all the confusion and fear turns to safety and passion. They comfort one another, falling into each other's arms, and make love. Finally. (Their relationship continues to deepen.)

43.   Meanwhile, back at the farm, Red is washed and dried and fed and taken care of by a large Amish family. The family doctor is there to examine Red and talks to the parents privately. She's been molested, and she's suffering from traumatic amnesia. The parents will take care of her, but the doctor says he'll have to report her to the police and social services. They ask him not to act too hastily since they've heard about the social services as being nothing but a dead-end. The parents go inside and put Red to bed with the rest of the kids.

44.   Scott sleeps in the afterglow. Midge leaves a note on the dresser and splits.

45.   In a series of scenes, Midge works her way through the streets of Philly's Cuba District looking for her brother's killer, a guy named Rico. From alleys to parties, all the places and kids remind her of the crappy life she left behind under the streets of Manhattan. There is a universality about the kid culture. A safety, even at its most dangerous. She connects with a kid who knows where Rico might be.

46.   The phone wakes Scott in the hotel room. It's the NYC cop. Scott sees the note she left behind saying she's gone for some air, be back soon. Cop tells him one of the names on the list has a long record, that he's out on parole but hasn't checked in with his parole officer in a long time. Scott's almost afraid to ask what the guy served time for. Cop says, fucking a twelve-year old. Scott freaks; doesn't know where Midge is. He turns the paper note over and sees what she's been

carrying since the funeral. It says: Rico, Philly Cuba. Now the cop freaks. He tells Scott he's got to find her in a hurry before Rico kills her.

47.   Midge works her way through a crack house with her newfound friend on the search for Rico. This atmosphere is familiar. The atmosphere she left behind in NYC.

48.   Scott drives through the streets looking for Little Cuba. When he asks for help he doesn't get a lot. Generally, young people are afraid to talk to him.

49.   Midge arrives at a big party where a lot of drug deals are going down. She sees some of Rico's friends. She's getting close. She's getting tense.

50.   Scott talks to a HOOKER on the street. Pays her a lot of money to lead him to Rico.

51.   At the party Midge gets herself in deeper, flirting with guys and drugs. She steals a hypodermic needle and tucks it in her waistband.

52.   The Hooker brings Scott up to the front of the shitty apartment building where the party is taking place. Scott will never get in on his own. He gives the Hooker more money to be his "date" and take him in.

53.   In the apartment upstairs the heavyweights come out of a backroom meeting and join in the party for a few minutes. Midge sees Rico and her heart skips a beat. She's scared shitless of what she's thinking of doing.

54.   Downstairs, Scott and the Hooker wait for the elevator nervously. Other "partygoers" look at Scott like he's from another planet. The eye him suspiciously.

55.   Upstairs Rico and the guys decide to get out of there with all the money they're holding. They'll feel a lot better once they get it all safely home. They head for the elevator. Midge is nowhere in sight.

56. Downstairs everyone sees the elevator light blink on. It's coming down. They are visibly relieved. Scott is sweating bullets because he has no idea what he's got to do to get Midge out of here.

57. In the elevator. Rico among all the men. Suddenly feels a sting in his groin, looks down, surprise, Midge is standing next to him holding the syringe plunged into his leg. Some guys pull guns. She tells them to back off. This is personal. She tells them that's his femoral artery, and that's air in the syringe. One push of the thumb and he's dead. Everyone backs off. Then the elevator comes to a stop.

58. Lobby. The small crowd, including Scott, stand there as the doors spring open and ALL HELL BREAKS LOOSE. People scream and run in every direction. Rico tries to get away and Midge twists the syringe and breaks it off in his leg as he screams in agony and limps away. Shots ring out. A girl is hit directly in the back a couple of times and thrown into Midge against the back wall of the car. The dead weight of the girl knocks Midge to the floor. She's covered by the dead girl and her blood and guts. Scott comes rushing in as the dust settles. Checks the girl. She's dead. Checks Midge. Alive but wounded and crying in anger and frustration.

59. Pre-dawn on the farm. Red and the other children walk in a single file to the barns with their lanterns to milk the cows. Red begins to allow herself to relax in this safe atmosphere.

60. Dawn in the Philadelphia hotel where Midge and Scott face each other. Midge confesses to Scott that back in NYC she thought she could help him find his sister and get to Rico at the same time. She never meant to screw up his chances to find his sister. She talks about her brother. He was her hero.

He was her only hope. And she was the one who ran away from her home. She was the hard-ass. She opens up completely to him, as she has never opened up to anyone else in her life. She admits this, saying she never even said this kind of thing to her brother. This has got to be a gut-wrenching scene. Scott has to feel her pain and understand her and accept her motive in order for them to be able to move on. He tells her she doesn't have to be the tough guy anymore. (Their relationship has now gone to a deeper level.)

61.   Farm. Later. Red helps set the lunch table outside with the other girls. They let her ring the chow bell. The men and boys drop their tools in the fields and come running. Red smiles.

62.   Truck stop diner. Wal-mart Driver comes out, gets in his truck, and drives away.

63.   On the road. He almost screams when he sees Midge in his rearview mirror peering out from the sleeper compartment behind him. She asks if he'll give her a ride. He leers and tells her he'll give her the best ride she's ever had. She grins and ducks back into the sleeper cabin. He pulls over. Scott pulls in behind him. The driver turns off the engine and his door swings open. Scott reaches in and pulls him down to the ground and sits on him, pressing a tire iron against his throat, choking him. Scott would like to kill him, but he needs him to tell him where he dropped off his sister. He tells them. They hog tie him to his truck and call the police.

64.   Intercut the next two sequences:

Main Street, Strasburg, Pennsylvania. Armed with snapshots of Red, Scott and Midge scour the shops in this quaint town asking if anyone has seen her. Midge is showing the picture to a Nurse in a doctor's office when the Doctor comes out of an examining room and notices the picture. He's the one who treated Red.

Meanwhile, the Truck Driver slowly working, working, working the ropes that bind him. Finally he manages to free himself. Starts his truck and drives away.

65.   Red works with a couple of kids stacking bales of hay in the hayloft. She's working hard and enjoying it.

66.   We now intercut all the following action to create an urgency and danger. As Red works, we see the Wal-mart truck come to the edge of the field near where she was dumped. The driver gets out and heads into the field, sees the farmhouse and heads toward it. In the loft Red takes a break and looks out the big double-bay doors. She sees the Wal-mart truck in the distance and freaks. She runs away screaming, leaving the others scared and confused. They run to get their father and mother. Meanwhile Scott, Midge, and the Doctor come roaring down the road and spot the parked truck. They jump out and run into the cornfields calling for Red. Now we see the Driver running, Red running, Scott running, Midge running. The cops show up at the parked truck and car. They jump out, pull their weapons, and run into the cornfields, too. Many cuts building to Red running right into the Driver. He grabs her and tells her to keep quiet and everything will be all right. Scott smashes onto the scene and starts beating the guy. The cops burst onto the scene and pull Scott off the Driver. They don't know who's who. Suddenly all the farmers burst through the rows of corn with their pitchforks, surrounding everybody. They tell the cops and everyone else to leave their land now. The Truck Driver uses this distraction to make a break for it. The cops give chase and fire their weapons. They chase and shoot and chase and shoot. Finally they cut him down. He crashes to the

ground grabbing his shot-up legs. Scott scoops Red up in his arms. She stares at him as if he were a complete stranger. He assures her everything's going to be all right. Suddenly the cornstalks rattle and burst open again. The cops draw their weapons and aim. Midge stumbles through them into the opening, totally out of breath. She sees that Red is safe and tries to smile, but winces instead. We see blood pouring from a gun shot wound in her side, shot by a stray police bullet. She looks to Scott and passes out.

END OF ACT TWO.

ACT THREE

67. Farmhouse. The Doctor patches up Midge in one of the upper bedrooms. She looks out the window and sees Scott and Red on a hill in the distance.

68. On the hill. This is the big scene between Scott and Red. It is a long scene in which Scott tries to jog Red's memory of their life together. It is a touching, tentative scene filled with tender observations about how people get to the places they get to. Red listens patiently, then tells him she doesn't recall much, and for right now at least, she isn't going to return with him. He's really shocked. She says she has no reason to go back to a place she hated so much she risked her life to leave, whether she remembers it or not. This family has offered her a safe place to stay and she's going to accept their generosity. Scott can stop trying to get her to remember the past. She's not interested in who she was; she's looking for the girl she can become. He's crushed. He was a big part of the past she now wants to forget about it. She tells him to settle instead for being a big part of her future. How's he supposed to do that,

he asks. By letting go of her, she tells him. He understands, but he's going to call her every week and check on how she's doing anyway. That's about as much letting go as he can handle now.

69.   Midge approaches them. She needs to talk to Red alone. Scott leaves them. In this scene Midge apologizes for stealing her money and being the cause of all her troubles. Red listens very carefully, but there's something else going on in her little mind. She looks around at all the spectacular natural beauty and serenity and says that she's never been more comfortable or more at peace in her life. If being here safe and sound is a result of something Midge did to her that Red can't remember, then Midge doesn't owe Red an apology. Instead, Red owes Midge a huge thanks. Midge smiles and looks around. Red is right. This is such a beautiful place. Red looks Midge in the eye and says, It sure as hell beats Disney World. She walks back toward the farmhouse. Midge is STUNNED.

70.   They all say goodbye. Scott thanks the family for taking care of Red and they exchange phone numbers. He'll be calling a lot. Red kisses him goodbye.

71.   Scott and Midge drive away. Midge is now aware that Red is faking her amnesia. Scott doesn't have a clue. He rattles on about how sooner or later his sister will start remembering all the good times they had together and she'll want to come back home. Midge just nods endearingly. There's something about him, even when he's totally wrong, that she's fallen in love with. She humors him. Then she asks if that's where they're headed. Home. Scott shrugs and says something Red said got him thinking. When he told her that sooner or later everyone runs away from home, she asked him sooner or later

does everyone go back? Midge asks Scott what his answer was. He says he didn't have an answer for her then, but he has an answer for himself now. He can't go back to New York City. At least not to the way it was. It was that bad, Midge asks. It was without you, he says. Oh, she says.

72.   The car drives down the long country road. Red stands on the front porch of the farmhouse alone, watching Scott's car disappear in the distance. After a long beat, she smiles and goes into the house.

THE END

16

The One-Liner Becomes the Two-Liner

The one-liner for most screenplays is almost exclusively a plot one-liner. There are usually not many real indications detailing the most important part of the film, which is the emotional story.

Of course it's quite possible to write a script from a one-line outline. Hype and excitement can be drawn from it, but clearly it will lack passion. And we will know little about what's going on inside each character.

We must write our scenes from an emotional point-of-view.

If we don't write with the emotions of scenes guiding us, the audience won't have anything to grab onto. In my script, a kid running away from home means nothing to the viewers unless they feel her suffering and her fear and identify with it. I want the audience to be more than interested in my story; I want to be them involved. I want them engrossed and feeling the things my characters are feeling.

That being the case, I have to tell them know how to feel by letting them know in what emotional turmoil my characters find themselves. Watching a girl, Red, sneak out of the house late at night with her backpack doesn't tell them if she's a delinquent or if she's a victim trapped in an intolerable situation. The audience would feel one way about her as a delinquent, and another way were she an abused child, for example. So I have to make it clear in the scene which she is, delinquent or victim, and I have to do this by expressing her emotional state-of-mind through her behavior. Her actions therefore are not random, they are manifestations of her psychological plight. Therefore, I must know who my character is and what events occurred that shaped her into the person she is from the moment I introduce her to you. I can't make it up as I go along.

**We can't just have characters doing
things because it's convenient.**

There have to be strong, internal reasons for their behavior. The stronger the better. We can't just say, in this case, that Red is bored with life in the suburbs and wants to find some excitement somewhere else. That's not good enough. A bored character who would risk horrifying her family by selfishly seeking pleasure is not the kind of character we're going to root for. We want the audience to care about Red. If the audience doesn't care about Red, then the whole film will fall on its face. There would be no tension because there would be no interest.

The first ten pages of Act One have to do more than merely introduce the characters and their situations. The first ten pages have to involve the audience emotionally right off the bat. In order for me to do that, I have to incorporate the emotional content I've written on the back of each card into my one-line outline. This transforms it from a one-liner to a two-liner.

Working from a two-liner insures that I will be dealing with the emotions in the scene as I write it. Following is a glance at the process of transforming a one-liner into a two-liner.

ACT ONE

1. We meet Red Peck, sixteen, as she runs away from home in the middle of the night, leaving her middle-class life and her low class, divorced mother behind.

    ES (Emotional Structure)—We want to show that Red is scared and heartbroken. She doesn't want to run away, but she has no other option. Her life is lonely and she is ignored and unwanted by her mother. Her mother drinks too much and sleeps with any man that walks through the door. Red can't watch her do it anymore. Question: How do we show this visually?

So you can see here that I'm trying to build sympathy for the character of Red. I want to tell the story of a young girl who, like so many of us, has been abandoned emotionally even while living in the nicest of homes. I have to get that sense of abandonment across to the audience. I decided that in the script I would have her packing her bag and sneaking out of the house past her mother's bedroom where she hears her in the throes of a torrid sexual encounter with a house painter.

As Red heads down the stairs and through the house we see the mother's clothes all over the place and the painter's overalls, shoes, and shirt. I have to get across the point that they are behaving as if Red were not alive. This is a form of child abuse and it is the cause for myriad problems later in the child's life.

As I introduce the other major character, the street girl, Midge, in the next sequence I have to show where she is emotionally, too. In the middle of the chaotic drug and booze drenched party described in the plot line it's hard to see anything but her attitude. And this is a problem. I must be able to see her emotional side somehow, at the same time I want to create a character who hides her emotions. The Emotional Structure notes in my two-liner, transferred from the back side of my note card, don't solve the problem in this case, but they help keep me honest about remembering that this problem still has to be solved when I write the scene.

> 2. See Midge, nineteen, at a party in NYC. Young adults having a good time. Lots of drugs and drinking. A fight breaks out. Her brother is in the middle of it. She tries to save him, but can't. He's stabbed mortally.

> **ES—Midge is tough and cool on the outside. Almost too cool... too tough. You get the clear impression she is an angry kid, but at this point it's hard to tell what that anger is based on. She's a runaway living on the streets and in the subway tunnels. The time on the streets has not been kind to her. She slips into these parties every now and then not to party but to see her older brother whom she idolizes and who stills lives at home with their mother. Make sure this is clear!**

That's the emotional note I gave myself. The big problem, and you may find it to be true in your opening, was that I didn't want to overload my opening sequence with a truckload of exposition and risk slowing down the excitement. It turned out that I wrestled with this for quite a while. But that was a good thing. I knew the problem existed and I didn't avoid finding a solution. Were I to have pushed ahead in the script without addressing it, I would have made a big mistake. Further, the mistake would have complicated things later on (problems grow) and I wouldn't have known where things went wrong or how to fix it.

If you come across a problem with your plot or story you must solve it then and there or make a big note about it so you don't lose track of it. When you write your outline and script you will have a thousand things on your mind and it will be easy to forget things. Make notes as you go along to insure that important points won't be lost. It's the difference between a script that works and one that does not.

And now I take my third card and write it down in the one-liner and add the emotional content from the back of the card to make it a two-liner. Another problem pops up.

> 3. Hospital. ER. Ambulance driver, Scott Peck, hauls Midge and her dying brother into the Emergency Ward. All business. Bloody business.

> **ES—This is where Midge's story crosses into Scott's story. Need to show that Scott is cool under fire and handles a bloody situation with calmness and humor, and that his coolness is not a facade as Midge's is. I want to see his emotional response to yet another kid dying on the streets. This is critical.**

I made this note "CRITICAL" because later on when Scott learns that his sister Red has run away, the first thing he imagines is her coming into an emergency room this way.

The Order of Things

As the index cards transform into a two-liner, the order of your scenes will have a different "feel." I don't know why, it just does. Pay attention to this. Your instincts are usually right. And here is why.

I was uncertain that I would maintain the order of these opening scenes. Sometimes one order creates a better build than a different order might. Although I felt comfortable with the plot order, *I didn't feel comfortable with the story order.*

I realized I had to solve the *emotional questions* on the cards before I would be sure that the order was the best one for me.

I decided that the underlying theme for my film, as portrayed by my characters, would be one of loneliness and disenfranchisement. No matter if one girl lives in a house in Muncie, Indiana, and another in the tunnels under the streets of New York City, their loneliness and disconnection to a loving world was the same.

I knew I had to express this subtly so that there would be a visceral connection for the audience to make. I also had to show that Scott was disconnected, even though he *seemed* to be handling it better than the two girls were, and he seemed to be on his way to reconnecting to a caring environment.

I needed an Emotional Structure to do this.

The Magical River that is Emotional Structure

I began to notice a bigger problem as I wrote the introductory scenes for my three leading characters. I wanted to do more than express each one's emotional state. I wanted to do more than cross-pollinate their plot lines. I wanted to connect their emotional states. I wanted an emotional flow from scene to scene between them and I wanted that emotional flow to gradually build. As each character's emotional journey progressed I wanted an emotional progression between all three of them to emerge. This would be my emotional structure. As their emotional union intensified the film's power would be created.

So my search was on for the Emotional Solutions.

I decided my biggest problem was smoothing out the difference in emotional intensity between Red's bedroom in Muncie and Midge's drunken party in New York. Were I to cut back and forth between the two it would be halting and confusing, and lack any rhythm. If I started with Red leaving her house and then cut to Midge at the wild party I would have to stay at the party until the fight breaks and her brother gets stabbed.

At that point I knew I could not go back to Red on a Greyhound bus to keep her story alive, then come back to Midge and her dying brother being rushed into the emergency room by Scott. It would all feel episodic, like a television show rather than a film. Once I started Midge's story at the party, I knew I had to stay with it until the hospital scene with Scott. If I did that, then I could connect Scott's emotions to the next scene that would be the scene of his sister running away, thus connecting them.

In real estate it's location, location, location.

In screenwriting it's connection, connection, connection.

So I decided to try opening the film at the party in the city apartment. Then I ran directly into the problem of where Midge was coming from, physically and emotionally. If I opened the film with her at the party there was no way of knowing that she was a kid living on the streets, unlike most of the others who had homes. This was important to state because it says so much about her. Fortunately a fellow writer who was familiar with my problem suggested the obvious. (It is great to have a trusted friend who is also a writer for he or she will always see the obvious when you can't.) It was a simple solution: start the film showing Midge living in the tunnels under the city, then take her to the party. That way I start Midge's story at "home" and see the condition of her life, just as I will start Red's story at "home" and see her conditions. The change worked wonderfully.

The Emotional Structure was taking shape. And it was taking shape because I remained aware of it at all times. And I remained aware of it at all times because of those fantastic index cards and their little backsides, on which is revealed the heart and soul of storytelling.

As you work on your two-liner now, keep a sharp eye for the Magical River that is Emotional Structure in your story. It's there. It's up to you to find it.

17

Creating an Emotional Outline

Writing a full-blown outline from your two-liner is more than an expansion of what you've already developed.

Once again take a look at what you're doing that others are not doing in this process. You are developing an emotionally complex story. If all you were to do at this stage is expand the two-liner into a full outline you very well could disconnect from all the hard thinking you've done thus far. That is why you must think of this next logical step not as an expansion, but rather as an advancement of your ideas.

Just as your two-sided index cards were a radical departure from the card method others use, and just as your one-liner became a two-liner because of your new card system, so too must your full outline become a radical departure from past methods. By expressing your full outline as an advancement of your themes and ideas, not just as a magnification of plot points, it becomes a denser and more meaningful working outline, and succeeds as a radically improved writing tool. Far from being a mechanical step in the development process, this is an artistic step of the first order.

This is the critical "thoughtful" step in your process of screenplay writing.

And the thinking is inward directed.

You must take your time creating this vital document. It should reflect a great deal about you personally, both in your thinking as a storyteller and your philosophic energy as an advocate of your film's theme.

Thoughtfulness is the byword in this process. When I am drafting the outline for a scene in which my character is running away from home, I have to be in her room with her. I cannot sketch out the scene objectively. This scene is not in the drama for its objectivity. This scene is there strictly on the basis of its subjective nature. It is a highly charged scene and it is the very first overt statement on what will develop as the film's prominent theme. It is so important to get right that I must force myself not to rush it.

The tendency to rush this development step is understandable. On the surface it almost doesn't seem necessary. In fact, I know writers who go from their one-liner to their script with confidence. I can only tell you that doing that is an invitation to create a shallow and static script. Think of all the cultivating that is jumped over. Like our analogy to painting a picture, this is the point at which we apply complex forms and bold colors to the sketch. We see the entire canvas as a painting for the first time. All the brush strokes are put down in concert. We refine the organization of ideas and theme by seeing them transcend the sketch and become a completely different form of art. In no less a way the outline is an expression of another form of the art of your screenplay.

In applying this colorful and thoughtful information we are deepening the intelligence of the idea. We are not dressing it up; we are intensifying its beauty and validating its purpose.

If I want to write about the dismaying circumstances in which a child finds herself seeking compensation for the love denied by her dislocated family in the darkest of places, I must take a long and critical look at every scene to make sure that statement is being advanced.

How do I do that? First and foremost I have to keep the goal in mind, not so much intellectually, but viscerally. I have to get in the emotional space I put my characters in and sit there with them. In this case I have to sit down on the bed next to the girl, Red, who is packing her backpack while her mother is in the next room fucking the house painter. This is a monumental moment in her life. I have to feel that. I have to understand that with my gut. She is scared and angry like she's never before been and I have to be scared and angry with her. And in a way, I have to be angry for her. I have to make sure that I help her pack that backpack with the things that are important to her. And I have to help her pass her fucking mother's room and down the steps littered with panties and bra, and out the front door. I have to feel the night air push against her skin, and against her life. It is cold and dark and completely unfriendly air. It is air difficult to breathe.

I have to carry her heart because I know it's broken. Broken? Hell, it's shattered. She is fifteen and on the outside looking in. How can her life ever be the same again? How will her young heart ever repair? Will this harden her? Will her search be painful or joyous? When did she become "in the way" at home? When did she stop mattering to her mother? Will she ever matter to her mother again? Will she ever matter to anyone? I get angry just thinking about these things. I promise myself I will be her defender and that I will stay emotionally present for her.

You can see what I mean when I say the outline is not a simple expansion of the one-liner. During this phase you and I will become more committed to our film's message. Our deepening commitment assures us that we won't become bored, or complacent, rather that we will grow with our idea. This is the great value in Emotional Structure. We learn by our writing.

What are you willing to learn?

Sound like a strange question? It really is not so strange. What you are willing to learn depends on what you are willing to reveal. What you reveal is as much what you don't know as what you know. How much you don't feel and how much you do feel. How much you care. How much you are willing to risk.

Think of your idea now. Think of it in terms of your protagonist's deep emotional state. What's going on inside his or her head these days? Not about her job and not about his kids. About the gap inside. About the disappointments of the past. About the dreams unfulfilled. We all carry them. Some more graciously than others. If your protagonist is like most people she is gracious and patient. Maybe even willing at this point to say that not all dreams can come true. It is not overt suffering. It is not playing victim. It is just the way it is.

But most of us commingle acquiescence with blame. Many of us give up on too many things when really most of what we give up on should be pursued to the gates of heaven. We tend not to give up selectively. We tend to give up completely. Many things contribute to this, most prominently childhood experiences.

So what are you willing to reveal about you that you are going to find in your hero? What is it in your hero you will love because it is you? We write what we know about. We write what we know to be true. What we know to be true are those things we have experienced. Place your heroine and her dilemma in any part of the world you want. Give her any skin color. Give her an exotic name and drop-dead good looks, or rip out all her teeth. It doesn't matter. She is still you. She is the literary expression of your DNA. She cares as you care. She is capable of loving and being loved as you are. She is lonely at times and cries about it. She is scared sometimes and cries about it. She is as human as human gets. And she needs your love more than she needs anything else or anybody else in the world.

Can you give it to her? Can you reveal yourself to her? For that is where the truth lies. And it is truth that bears trust, that thing which is the foundation for all love. Can you give her all of that? Because if you think you can then you have to give her life in your script. And your truth will be told through her.

Your truth is her mantle. What the world will see of this character is a glimpse of your soul. You must decide now, if you are going to be a

WRITING MEANS LISTENING.

writer, that you will not be afraid to tell on yourself. It does not matter how people react to your truth. It matters how you feel after you've done it. It is your reaction that validates you. You tell your truth without shame and without excuses. Truth has no shame and has no excuse. It simply is what it is. It is the best of human qualities. It is the bridge between heaven and earth, so to speak. All truth relies on an innate willingness to risk emotional vulnerability. Internal spiritual openness invites blessings beyond conscious desires. In your script this will all lead to an ending, a spiritual/soulful emergence into a space and state the likes of which your protagonist never dreamt possible. That is the reward. That is the resolution. It is a gift from the universe for honesty.

But this is what it takes. It does not take intellectualizing. It does not take commentary. You cannot bluff your way through it. And why would you want to? It takes being honest and self-revealing. And if you can be that kind of a writer you will be blessed. Because truth is always blessed. I assure you that if your dream is to write, then your dream will come true…if you can seek the truth and tell it.

Back to the magical river

Experience has taught me to take a look at the first two or three scenes in my two-liner as a group before I start writing them out in outline form. I do this because I want to maintain an overview of the picture's opening in regard to its emotional impact. I don't want to get caught up trying to dazzle everyone with a spectacular opening and be disappointed by it later because it isn't connected to the rest of the picture. The first few scenes express something of the film's theme. They must be connected emotionally. This is the wellspring of The Magic River, the emotional current streaming through the film. By considering the first few scenes as a group I can specifically begin the design of the stream.

My first three scenes in *Indirection* were not emotionally connected. The scenes were emotional in and of themselves, but their emotions didn't link up as a singular expression. Each scene or sequence introduced one of the three central characters but they were not building on each other. The concern I had was that the opening would seem episodic instead of epigenetic. Take a look at my two-liner.

Indirection

Act One

1. We meet RED PECK, sixteen, as she runs away from home in the middle of the night, leaving her middle-class life and her low class, divorced mother behind.

I want to see how tormented Red is and how heartbreaking her decision is for her to have made. I want to see her have to choose between things to take with her... her dearest things. She can hear her mother screwing a guy in the next room. She leaves and it is gut-wrenching.

2. See MIDGE, nineteen, at a party in NYC. Gangs. Fight breaks out. Her brother is in the middle of it. She tries to save him, but can't. He's stabbed mortally.

A tough exterior, but she's really at this party to see her brother because she is alone in the world. Every kid sister needs her big brother even if it's just to be near him for a little while.

3. Hospital. ER. Ambulance driver, SCOTT PECK, hauls Midge and her dying brother into the Emergency Ward. All business.

Scott is confident, but I need to connect him to what's happened to Midge somehow, probably by making an observation about kids who live on the streets.

4. Red on the road. On a bus to NYC.

Red is exhilarated but isolated. While others on the bus enjoy the travel experience she is clearly ill-at-ease. Second thoughts, perhaps? Or is she distancing herself to protect herself? Don't forget how hard this was for her to do and how angry she is at her mother. Acting tough, but scared shitless inside.

5. Midge buries her brother. Police want her to tell them who killed her brother. She won't cooperate. Wants to get her own revenge. Cops tell her she's crazy. She should be watching her back because the same guy's probably going to kill her next. Cop gives her his card telling her to think it over and call him any time, day or night.

The sense of loss is overwhelming. She is still in shock. No amount of kind words can alleviate her grief.

6. Red arrives in NYC Grand Central Station.

This is the emotional equivalent of the Country Mouse in the Big City. She is using all of her defense mechanisms to keep the world at a distance. The longer she's away from home the angrier she is deep inside at her mother. Maybe show her hesitation somehow (a call to her brother?)

First we see a girl packing and leaving her Indiana home. Then we see a girl at a crazy party halfway across the country in New York. Then we meet a guy who drives an ambulance in New York. Then we go back to the runaway girl on the road. Then we go back to the girl in New York at her brother's funeral. Then we go back to the runaway girl arriving in New York. Bouncy-bouncy. Back and forth. Bad film.

The search for an emotional common denominator

I know I can tie this all together with clever transitions from one scene to another to create the verisimilitude of emotional balance, but that's not the answer. The challenge is to keep the same emotional values going *within* each scene. Certainly it will help to create a level of urgency in each character's story that is compatible with the others. That, in this case, is easy to do with the two girls' stories, but the brother's story isn't there yet. It will get there soon enough, however, so I can live with that. But it needs more.

What I finally decide I can trust as an emotional common denominator is their youthful and careless risk-taking. All three characters are clearly operating on the premise that there is no tomorrow. Today is what matters. Tomorrow can be taken care of tomorrow. The runaway girl,

Red, has no idea what tomorrow will bring. She only knows that today is unacceptable and she's got to move on. Midge, suffering the loss of her brother, the only person that ever mattered to her, cares only about revenge and the sooner the better. Scott, who feels like he's living like a king driving an ambulance and dating a nurse, believes he's the shits and tomorrow will only be better.

Their common trait is the belief that living for today is good enough. Worrying about bank accounts and retirement is for adults. They neither trust any of the adults in their lives, nor wish to emulate them. It is a youthful rebelliousness, but it is a dangerous one, and that is the thing I will hang my hat on. I can create a strong emotional connection between them with it, and keep them on the same wavelength.

Exponential emotion

Unfortunately, what happens now is that the emotional connection between the scenes demands greater plot finesse. I can solve the emotional stream but it really does not solve the problem of the "bouncy-bouncies." For now, though, I'll build my outline on the basis of the two-liner to see how it feels. I don't remember ever writing an outline that I haven't rewritten heavily before going to script, so I expect the same thing will happen this time.

Here is the first rendition of the outline:

Indirection
by Peter Dunne

1. INT. PECK HOUSE—RED'S BEDROOM—MUNCIE, IND.—NIGHT

We meet RED PECK, 16, in her bedroom as she packs her bag to run away. We hear her MOTHER making love to someone in the next room. The sounds repulse and anger Red. She zips her backpack and heads down the hall past her mother's room. The intense and vulgar orgasm her mother seems to be having sends Red running down the stairs and out the door.

2. INT. NEW YORK CITY APARTMENT—NIGHT

A wild party in full swing. We meet MIDGE DELISA, 18, streetwise and tough as she works her way through the different rooms jammed with people, drugs, and alcohol. This is the world of lost and forgotten teenagers. She looks around for her older brother, LONNIE, and sees him dancing with YVONNE, the beautiful girlfriend of RICO, the meanest, sickest drug dealer on the East Coast. Midge suddenly panics when she sees Rico come in through the front door, angry and dangerous. He sees Lonnie dancing with Yvonne and heads straight to them. People get out of the way. Midge tries to intercept him. But all she winds up doing is getting in the way of Rico's knife as he stabs Lonnie again and again in the chest, pinning Midge's hand to it.

3. INT. HOSPITAL EMERGENCY WARD—NIGHT

We meet SCOTT PECK as he jumps out of the ambulance and helps wheel in the bodies of Lonnie on one stretcher and Midge strapped down on another. Lonnie is not moving. Midge is screaming her head off. Scott tries calming her down, but her response is to spit in his face and scream even louder. They give her a shot to knock her out while they go to work on her wounded hand.

4. EXT./INT. GREYHOUND BUS—NIGHT

Red Peck is on the road to freedom.

5. INT. HOSPITAL MORGUE—NIGHT

Midge has to identify her brother Lonnie's body.

It kills her. A COP wants her to play ball with them and finger Rico. They know it was him, but they need her for an eyewitness. She won't make a deal with the cops. She says she's going to get her own revenge. The cop warns her that she could be the next one on a slab in this room if Rico gets to her before she gets to him. She says she's not scared. Too bad, the cop says, because you should be very scared of Rico.

6. EXT. CEMETERY—DAY

Midge has to watch the burial of her brother from a distance; afraid that Rico or his buddies might be looking for her. A friend slips her a note with Rico's address in Philadelphia where he'll likely be going back to soon now that the cops are putting the heat on him.

7. INT. GRAND CENTRAL STATION—DAY

Red Peck arrives in NYC. She buys a train ticket to Florida, then goes to a phone booth to call her brother. Line's busy, so she starts to leave a message.

8. INT. SCOTT'S APARTMENT—DAY

The line is busy because Scott is on the phone with his mother. They yell at each other. This fairly depicts their relationship, which is horrible. She called to tell him that Red has run away. He blames her for being a shitty mother. There is no love lost. When he hangs up his message light is blinking. He listens to Red's call from Grand Central saying goodbye for a while. She's going to hit the road to freedom. Don't worry about her (but he hears the worry and fear in her voice). He pulls a photo of Red and him out of its frame and runs out the door.

9. EXT. UNDERGROUND TUNNELS—GRAND CENTRAL STATION—DAY

This is the underground world of the young and disenfranchised people of New York. It's a dead end. Crawl spaces, tunnels, and wide open two-story cavities where the subway builders did their work. Midge has lived here since she was kicked out of her house almost a year ago. It is an unbelievably horrible place, but a very real place. Midge heads down a tunnel toward the terminal.

10. INT. GRAND CENTRAL—DAY

Midge and her pals mill around the main floor of Grand Central, picking pockets and generally looking for money or food to steal. Their path crosses with Red Peck's as she buys some snacks in a shop. They see all the cash she has in her wallet. Midge chats with her, finds out she's headed to Disney World, wishes her luck. When Red leaves we see that Midge has Red's wallet with all her money.

Scott comes into Grand Central looking desperately for Red. He sees Midge buying stuff with a lot of money and recognizes Red's wallet. He tries to grab it; she runs and he chases her through the station and down onto the subway platforms below. Midge leaves Scott in the dust. As she runs from Scott she almost runs right into Rico and the guys who killed her brother. They're looking for her, just like the cops said they would. Suddenly Midge is scared. She ducks down onto the tracks and heads into a tunnel.

11. INT. SUBWAY PLATFORM

Scott jogs this way and that, looking for Midge. He lost her. Then he catches sight of a couple of other kids heading down into a tunnel. He sucks it up and follows them at a distance, hoping they'll lead him to her.

12. INT. TUNNELS

Scott is horrified at the conditions he encounters as he searches through this underground world. He can't imagine anyone living here like this. He finally finds Midge's hovel and pounces on her, furious over what she's done.

13. INT. MIDGE'S SUBTERRANEAN CRYPT

This is a converted washroom used by the construction workers years ago, dank and squalid, but it is all Midge has. There's an old mattress on the floor and some other shit strewn around. Candles she steals light the room.

Scott bursts in while she's going through Red's wallet, counting the money. AND THEY HAVE A HUGE SCENE.

We learn a lot about each of them here. Scott is desperate to find his sister before she gets killed. He says she's not like Midge and the rest of the girls, that Midge and her friends are losers. Midge says, take a look around because we all started out the same way your sister did... she's no different than any one of us... she's just like us. This pisses him off even more. He takes his sister's wallet and looks through it for any hint of where she was headed.

Midge is desperate, too. She doesn't want to be found by Rico. She needs to get the hell out of sight for a while. She looks at the paper her friend slipped her at the cemetery with Rico's Philadelphia address on it. She tells Scott he'll never find Red on his own. Midge knows the streets and knows what Red's going through. She can think like his sister, and she can go into places he can't. She offers a deal. She'll help him find her, but he's got to take her with him. He doesn't want to make the deal. He doesn't know her, he doesn't like her, and he doesn't want to have to take care of her on the road. She can't believe what she's hearing. She'll be the one to take care of him, she says. He'll get completely lost out there. He says he'll buy a map. She says there aren't any road maps for the trip he's about to take. He says no way. She blows up at him. What kind of a brother is he anyway? It's time he worried about his sister more than he worried about himself. She tells him he's just like all the rest. Acting like an asshole like all these other kids' families have acted, unwilling to help before it's too late. She says, look around because it's too late for a lot of people already. He hates hearing what she says.

She pushes one more time. His sister needs him, he needs Midge, Midge needs to get out of town. It's simple. When they find Red they will go their separate ways, not owing the other anything. He looks around at all the abandoned, screwed-up kids. Very reluctantly, he makes the deal. They head out of the underground into the big bad world, one more ambivalent and nervous than the other.

THIS IS THE END OF SCOTT AND MIDGE'S ACT ONE.

14. INT. TRAIN—LATE AT NIGHT

Red, sitting alone, now realizes she's been robbed. As a bunch of fraternity brothers party all around her on their way to Florida for Spring Break, she wanders through the cars looking for an answer. Then she sees it: A sleeping man, his jacket off to one side, with a wallet bulging from it. She looks around, steals the wallet, and goes for the door to the next car. She's caught leaving the car by a horny and drunk fraternity brother. He drags her into the bathroom and tries to force a deal on her: his silence for some sex. As he presses her, she reaches down and grabs his zipper and pulls it up with all her might. He goes into shock. There is nothing as painful as having a zipper closed on your scrotum. He falls to the floor paralyzed in agony, weeping. She drops the stolen wallet and takes this guy's instead and runs out. As the train pulls into a station, she gets off and runs into the night.

THIS IS THE END OF RED'S ACT ONE.

Once it gets going it moves pretty well, but I'm still concerned with the opening. I know I'm going to rework it a few more times to smooth it out and get the most out of it. What I want to impart here is the amount of serious thought you will put into your emotional outline. I urge you to take your time with it and to challenge your structure with your eyes shut as you watch the projection of your film in your mind. Feel it. Use your gut. It's the best damn tool a writer has.

Part 5

Writing the Script

18

Writing the Script—Act One

A good way to approach your screenplay is with the knowledge that you will be tempted to rewrite your opening soon and often. Rewriting your first act before you write your second and third act is a very bad habit. Don't form it.

Also, you should be aware that once you finish your screenplay you will definitely rewrite it. Rewriting your script is a vital part of the process. It does not mean the first draft is lousy. It means it's a first draft. Every good script and certainly every great script has gone through many revisions.

Therefore, it bears repeating: don't rewrite the first act before you finish the entire script. Once you finish the script you will rewrite it anyway, but by that time you will rewrite it with a great deal more knowledge and a healthier, more positive approach.

As you begin your script, I suggest you take it in parts. They will come together, you will see, because your outline is already together. The reasons are twofold. First, it's easier on the heart and brain. Focusing on the first twenty-five pages and the job they must do is a lot easier than constantly imagining the entire script and getting depressed at the amount of work ahead. Working on an act at a time creates a peace of mind because the segments are not overwhelming. And secondly, each segment really demands its own particular attention from you. Acts One, Two, and Three are very different emotionally and it is better to write from that particular emotion while you're in it. We also maintain a keener awareness of the page count as we write each act.

We will break down the acts into segments that are easy to see and write. Dealing with a few pages at a time is more rational and certainly more productive.

I will continue to use my story of the runaway girl in *Indirection* as an example since you have already seen it take shape from a three-page concept to an outline. Now we will take it through the script stage an act at a time. Meanwhile, you overlay your outline over mine, and overlay your script over mine. You will see how your plot and story lay out so easily and clearly this way.

I want you to use the charts from the earlier chapters as a guide, and I want you to always approach each act with an overview toward its responsibilities and goals. You will be pleasantly surprised to see how much of this work you've already done!

Act One—Life as It Was

Here we go. Put your outline on your desk in front of you and take a look at the first couple of scenes up to the point where your "opening" happens. By "opening" I mean the opening piece of action that wakes everybody up. In *Witness* the opening action was the murder in the men's room. In *Leon: The Professional* it was the slaughter in Mathilda's apartment. In *The Thomas Crown Affair* it was the heist of a masterpiece from the museum. In *Casablanca* it was the round-up of usual suspects and the shooting of one of them. This is the piece of action that often involves one of our central characters and many times brings two or more of them together in its aftermath as a consequence. This is the case in *Witness* when Book meets Rachel at the scene of the crime, *The Professional* when Mathilda rushes to Leon's door for safety, and *The Thomas Crown Affair* when Faye Dunaway meets and challenges Steve McQueen (or Rene Russo suspects and challenges Pierce Brosnan).

In my script the opening action is the murder of Midge's brother at the party by another gang member. This action ultimately brings Midge together with Scott in the hospital's emergency room. I wanted to set a very specific intensity early on and state that life and death existed in the world of my characters. The murder served the purpose of creating a motive for Midge, that of revenge that would later take her near her own death while she betrayed Scott. And it also served the purpose of adding validity to the subtext in Red's runaway story that she was alone and about to enter a dangerous world.

Check now to see if your opening action serves purposes such as these. We don't want to have an action opening just for the sake of action alone. Whatever your opening action is, it should be substantial enough to kick off your protagonist's plot or story, and it should be memorable enough to refer back to much later on. Remember we said earlier that most good scripts have a cyclical nature to them. The beginning can become the end and the end can become the beginning.

Does your action in the opening set up the intensity of your story? Does it set in motion the meeting of your central characters sooner than later? Good.

Now remember that the action doesn't have to be on page one. The murder in the men's room came after the tone of the Amish countryside in Lancaster, Pennsylvania was strongly established. It was a one-two punch. I like openings like that and I tried to manufacture one in my script but it didn't work (or I couldn't make it work) so I changed it. I wanted to open up with a Red in a quieter sequence in Muncie, Indiana, and then go to the craziness in New York with Midge and the murder at the party. But it was a false set-up. The reason I say that is because it didn't have an organic relationship or build. It felt forced. It felt tacked-on, as if the scene in Muncie were an afterthought. So my opening changed from the outline to the script.

For several reasons it made better sense to open my script in Midge's home rather than Red's home. First, it established that Midge lived on the streets, actually under them, in squalor, and that she was one of many who young people did.

This is an actual fact. I was astonished to learn that children of the night live in the subway tunnels of New York City with the rats and detritus of the city. I was more than astonished. I was pissed. Are we that callous and uncivilized that we would permit that to happen? Can we live with that? I don't care whose children they are. They are all of our children. What have we come to? Every time I pictured those kids underground with no hope I wanted to scream. I wanted to cry. I actually did cry while I wrote about them. And I wanted my opening in that wasteland, and an especially important scene later in the first act when Scott hunts down Midge underground and sees how she lives and how his sister may live as a runaway, to be as emotional as I could possibly portray it.

This is life as it is for Midge. This is how I will start her story.

The job of the first ten pages

The scenes in your first ten pages have very specific jobs to do. They must reflect how passionate you are about your idea.

That doesn't mean you need a "cause." This isn't the place for preaching on the soapbox, but it does mean an immediate expression of your passion and your emotional commitment to your film. If you want to excite your audience and grab their interest (and you do) then you have to be excited, too. Let your passion show through. But you are never allowed to use exclamation points in your script!!!!! Never!!!!

Your vision speaks for itself.

The first scene or sequence must establish your point of view about the world in which we find your characters. It will be a point of view that sustains your intellect and logic as a storyteller. If you are in love with your characters and their world, show it.

Look at the way Woody Allen expresses his love of New York City in his film—*Manhattan,* for example. The elegant black and white chiaroscuro rendering of its skylines, the majesty of a symphonic score to embrace its culture, the madly intellectual denizens hustling and bustling up and down its avenues, all add up to his love letter to his hometown. But, wisely, it is more than mere homage. He is making certain that we understand his city viscerally because his city is as important a character in his movie as any actor or actress. And he treats it with the respect and dignity he would give to any of those artists. His passion speaks through his vision. Notice how Sophia Coppola cherishes her characters in the opening scenes of *Lost in Translation*. Her affection for them bleeds into our consciousness. The same could be said for the craft and sophisticated opening sequence in *The Thomas Crown Affair* which represents and reflects the craftiness and sophistication of its lead characters.

As you introduce your characters you are also introducing yourself and your voice. They must be synergetic.

This point goes back to the logic we discussed regarding your writing about the things you know. You have to know what you're writing about, of course, and you have to know your feelings about the subject as well. And you have to be able to express those feelings as fully as you express your knowledge. They are equally important.

Your point of view reveals more than your knowledge of your subject, it reveals your experience with it.

Your point of view is transparent. It tells us how deeply you care about your subject. Your audience will only go as far as you feel, not as far as you tell them to feel. We go back to honesty. In your opening, don't try to b.s. the audience with something superficial. Feel what you're writing and they will feel it. And feel it by experience when possible.

So many of my students have wanted to write about a person, man or woman, who, jilted by a lover takes off for a distant land to try to forget about the lover and to find himself or herself. It's a very popular film notion. I am reminded of *Under the Tuscan Sun* as a fairly recent and successful example. It tells me that a great number of my students have been dumped by their lovers. If you, too, want to write about a person flying off to places unknown on the rebound, I hope to God (and I wish you no ill) that you've at least experienced being dumped. I hope you know the pain and the feeling of loss. It is a desperate feeling. It can be frightening. If you have experienced these desperate, frightening, deeply sad emotions then you can and should write about them. If you have not, then you should try to write of them from compassion. We established this before, but I reiterate it now because in the opening of your film everyone will be able to tell if you have suffered or if you are bullshitting. The difference between the scenes one would write who has experienced heartbreak compared to those written by one who hasn't experienced it will be the difference between good writing and mediocre writing.

My outline showed that the film would open in Red's bedroom in Muncie, Indiana, and then go to Midge in New York City at a party. I was hoping to introduce the two girls and somehow connect them, but it really was disconnected physically and emotionally.

Here's how that would have looked and felt like. I hated the way it bounced back and forth. Take a look at it.

Indirection
by Peter Dunne

FADE IN:
TITLE CARD: **MUNCIE, INDIANA**

EXT. PECK HOUSE—MIDNIGHT

An older house undergoing painting and repair. Dropcloths and ladders clutter the front porch. The house is dark and still except for the sounds of a couple making love inside.

INT. RED PECK'S BEDROOM—NIGHT

Moonlight illuminates the small room as ELIZABETH "RED" PECK, a freckled-faced, fifteen-year-old red-head, silently jams clothes into her backpack. The sounds of sex coming from an adjoining room clearly unnerve her. Confused and in a hurry, she packs and unpacks a sweater for the third time.

TITLE CARD: **NEW YORK CITY**

EXT. CITY STREETS—RAIN—NIGHT

The masses walk the streets, anonymous in the city's loud and garish slickness.

INT. NEW YORK WALK-UP APARTMENT—LIVING ROOM—NIGHT

Kids from those streets. Black/Brown/White. Partying. Hustling. Dancing. Drinking. Sweating. Letting loose. Letting go of their shit. It's hot, and it's LOUD. MIDGE DELISA, striking, street wise, part Latin, part unknown, part teenager, part used up, cruises the room stuffing her pockets with whatever she can steal. She is a survivor on turf where survival is against the odds.

BATHROOM

Jammed with users and abusers. Every party has its pharmacy. Name it, it's here. A tab, a toot, a chip, a stick, a needle in your arm or anywhere else, it feels good. Two fully clothed people in the bathtub; entangled; wasted. Midge drifts in, sticky fingers itching, looking for cash or drugs.

INT. Red PECK'S BEDROOM—MUNCIE, INDIANA—NIGHT

The sounds of sex in the room next door grow louder and more intense. Red lifts her backpack to test its weight, takes out a book, tosses it, and zips it back up. Hefts it again. Better. She looks around the room, sees her jewelry box and goes to it. She scoops out everything, filling her pockets.

INT. NEW YORK WALK-UP APARTMENT—KITCHEN—NIGHT

Mobbed. Booze to satisfy a thirst, not a palate. Anything in a gallon jug. The glasses are big. The floor is sticky. Trey, a nasty reprobate, shoves a TIGHT GIRL with both hands. Midge passes by and hears.

> TREY
> It's your eyes drive me up, Baby, don't you know. Ain't just your body. There's more to you than that. I see that.

> MIDGE
> Jesus, Trey.

> TREY
>
> Fuck you say.

> MIDGE
>
> Fuck I say. You see Lonnie?

> TREY
>
> I'm in the middle of something big here.
> Find your own brother.

INT. PECK HOUSE—HALLWAY AND LANDING—
CONTINUOUS

Red comes out of her room and heads for the stairs,
stopping momentarily at her mother's bedroom door.
We see her tears and her anger for the first time. The
grunting and grinding build as her mother wails in the
throes of an hysteric and vulgar orgasm. Cursing. Begging. Demanding. Repulsed, Red slips down the stairs.

EXT. PECK HOUSE—ACROSS THE STREET—MID-
NIGHT

Red stares back at her house, no longer able to hear
her mother. Backpack over one shoulder, she pulls
her collar up against the wind and heads off into an
unsure world in search of some kind of peace she
can no longer find at home.

INT. NEW YORK WALK-UP APARTMENT—LIVING
ROOM—NIGHT

Midge drifts into the room passing a couch
overstuffed with groping couples. A GIRL IN HEAT
lap-dances on her BOYFRIEND, who is either in a
coma or heaven. Boney, a traveler in the lost world
with Midge, slinks by. You'd never know Boney was
a girl. Boney's bony. And Boney's strung-out.

BONEY

Midgy, Midgy, Midgy dance with me.

MIDGE

Man, Boney, you gotta eat.

So you see what I mean. It bounces all over the place. The cross-cutting is confusing and gets in the way of the flow of the story. The whole device of going back and forth becomes obtrusive. A good thing to remember when you are trying something like this is that if it's obvious, it's not working. The construction should for the most part be hidden. So I simplified my opening.

Taking my friend's advice I changed it to open instead in Midge's hovel under the streets of New York City and to see her leaving her "home" and going to the party where her brother would be murdered in front of her. I held off introducing Red packing and leaving Muncie until we meet her brother Scott in the emergency room first. Remember, too, that I wanted Midge and Scott to meet as adversaries first (Midge is co-antagonist before becoming co-protagonist) because I wanted them to feel forced to be on the road together, knowing ultimately they would fall in love. Here's how the script looked:

Indirection
by Peter Dunne

FADE IN:
INT. ABANDONED UNDERGROUND WASHROOM—
NIGHT

A concrete chamber crumbling with age, built fifty years ago for the subway construction crews. A young girl sits amid the rubble and ties her shoes.

She is Midge DELISA. Striking, street wise. Part Mediterranean, part unknown. Part youthful, part used up. A survivor on turf where survival is against the odds. And this subterranean sanctuary of rusted piping and rat shit is her home.

INT. SUBTERRANEAN TUNNELS—GRAND CENTRAL STATION

Midge comes out of her crypt and makes her way through the clammy darkness of the subway caverns, past small pockets of semi-conscious, drug-addled young people huddled in hate, toward a riot of echoes and sparks in remote tunnels.

INT. SUBTERRANEAN TUNNELS—CONTINUOUS

Midge drops onto the catwalk at the mouth of an arching, tiled tunnel guided by habit and the glint of a distant station's florescence streaking off the steel rails below.

INT. GRAND CENTRAL—SUBTERRANEAN SUBWAY STATION

The unforgiving blue-green electric glow bleaches life from a swarming public, ebbing and flowing in a trance of precondition and pity. Human beings avoiding human contact.

Midge appears at the end of the tunnel and climbs a rebar ladder onto the platform without notice. She moves through the masses with a trained eye and undetectable contact, and heads up the stairs.

INT. GRAND CENTRAL—MAIN FLOOR—NIGHT

An awesome place. As graceful as it is haunting. As dignified as it is degrading. As crowded as it is lonely.

Midge pushes through the sea of humanity, brushing against the overburdened and distracted commuters with purpose. Her hands move faster than her feet. Squeezing, searching, poaching, picking. Here and gone before notice. She is a study in criminal grace. She makes her way to an exit.

EXT. GRAND CENTRAL STATION—RAIN—NIGHT

A New York kind of night. The Storm and the City are natural enemies. Traffic's worse. People are worse. The dirt washes around, but never away. Midge, collar up against the wind and the world-at-large, crosses an intersection and heads down a darker side street.

EXT. DARKER SIDE STREET—RAIN—NIGHT

Moving quickly, Midge rifles through her take, keeping the money and throwing the wallets away in a trail behind her.

INT. NEW YORK WALK-UP APARTMENT—LIVING ROOM—NIGHT

Kids from those streets. Black/Brown/White. Partying. Hustling. Dancing. Drinking. Sweating. Letting loose. Letting go of their shit. It's hot in here, and it's LOUD.

Midge comes in, brushes off the storm, pushes her hair off her face, and we see her beauty for the first time. A cool intelligence protecting a bankrupt heart. She lights a cigarette and heads into the crush looking for anything that isn't nailed down.

HALLWAY—BATHROOM STEEL CAGE DOOR

Jammed with users and abusers lined up to buy a thrill. LUIS, an armed guard, keeps the line moving. Name it, it's here. A tab, a toot, a chip, a stick, a needle in your arm or anywhere else it feels good.

Fully clothed people on the floor; entangled; wasted.

KITCHEN—NIGHT

Mobbed. Booze to satisfy a thirst, not a palate. Anything in a gallon jug. The glasses are big. The floor is sticky. Trey, a nasty reprobate, nibbles on a TIGHT GIRL'S long brown neck as Midge passes by.

> MIDGE
> Hey, Trey.
> *(he grunts)*
> You see Lonnie?

He pushes her away. She moves on.

LIVING ROOM—NIGHT

Midge drifts past a couch overstuffed with groping couples. A GIRL IN HEAT lap-dances on her BOYFRIEND, who is either in a coma or heaven. Boney, a traveler in the lost world with Midge slinks by. You'd never know Boney was a girl. Boney's bony. And Boney's strung-out.

> BONEY
> Midgy, Midgy, dance with me.

> MIDGE
> Man, Boney, you gotta eat. Seriously, go in the kitchen and find something.

> BONEY
> No appetite. This shit kills it.

> MIDGE
> Shit's killing more than your appetite. You see Lonnie?

> BONEY
> Who hasn't?

Midge follows Boney's glance across the room where her brother LONNIE boogies with a breathtaking blonde, YVONNE.

> MIDGE
> What's he doing?

> BONEY
> What every guy wishes he had the balls to do.

Midge watches Lonnie and Yvonne dance the dance of lust. Tighter. Hotter.

> MIDGE
> Balls will never replace brains.

On the couch, every measured rise gives way to a quivered fall, as the Girl In Heat presses down hard on her Boyfriend.

The crowd builds as more people arrive, including RICO CANTORES. Big and hostile, he heads for the bathroom drugstore. The guard, Luis, nods to Rico as he arrives, pushes people at the mesh window aside and signals the guys inside the room.

Beyond dancing now, Yvonne crushes her hot open mouth against Lonnie's face. Hungry. Chewing him like a last meal. Eyes. Chin. Lips.

A briefcase is handed out the cage window. Rico grabs it and moves toward the exit when he catches sight of Yvonne and Lonnie. He twitches involuntarily, then without hesitation, shoves people out of his way and moves toward Yvonne. The commotion draws everyone's attention, including Midge's.

MIDGE

    Shit.

The Girl In Heat shuts her eyes, and clenches her teeth. It's happening. She screams in satisfaction. Her Boyfriend screams. Midge screams.

MIDGE

    Lonnie! Lonnie!

Rico pulls out a huge knife. At the sight of it, all hell breaks loose. People scatter in every direction. Becoming aware of the noise around them finally, Yvonne and Lonnie pull apart. By the time they do, Rico is on top of them, seething with anger. Lonnie is completely defenseless.

Midge explodes through the hysteria and tries to pull Lonnie away, but the downward thrust of Rico's knife is too fast. THE BLADE PUNCTURES Midge'S HAND as it plunges deep into Lonnie's chest.

Rico stabs him again and again. And each time he does, Midge's hand, skewered on the blade, swings with it. She cannot stop her hand. Lonnie cannot stop dying.

With a final, vicious arc, Rico drives the knife into Lonnie and runs. Midge collapses to the floor under the weight of her brother, her hand still pinned to his convulsing body. She wails inconsolably.

INT. ER—NIGHT

A gurney carrying Lonnie's body pushes through the chaos. Not far behind, AN EMT and the Ambulance Driver, SCOTT PECK, struggle to hold onto Midge.

Lonnie's gurney is wheeled into one bay, and Midge is dragged into another. Scott helps the Nurse, JAMIE, strap Midge down. Midge screams at him. He ignores her. She SPITS in his face.

> SCOTT
> Great. Thanks. Why do they always do that?
> I just deliver them.

Nurse Jamie gives Midge a shot to knock her out.

> NURSE JAMIE
> I think it has something to do with want-
> ing to kill the messenger. What happened?

> SCOTT
> Friday night happened. You party. You fight. You stab somebody.

> NURSE JAMIE
> No one ever heard of pin the tail on the donkey?

Midge fades quickly as the drugs take hold Nurse Jamie examines her wound.

> SCOTT
> Don't look now, Dorothy, but you're not in Kansas anymore. In New York you pin the tail on anybody who pisses you off.

She looks around at all the wounded bodies in the ER.

> NURSE JAMIE
> That's a lot of pissed-off people.

> SCOTT
> (re: Midge) Pissed-off and young people.

TITLE CARD: **MUNCIE, INDIANA**

EXT. PECK HOUSE—PRE-DAWN

An older house undergoing painting and repair. Dropcloths and ladders clutter the front porch. The house is dark and still except for the sounds of a couple making love inside.

INT. RED PECK'S BEDROOM—CONTINUOUS

Elizabeth "Red" Peck, a pissed-off, fifteen-year-old redhead, jams clothes into her backpack. The sounds of sex coming from the adjoining room clearly unnerve her. She lifts her backpack to test its weight, takes out a book, tosses it, and zips it back up. She looks around and sees her jewelry box. She scoops out everything, filling her pockets.

INT. PECK HOUSE—HALLWAY AND LANDING—CONTINUOUS

Red heads for the stairs, stopping momentarily at her mother's partially open bedroom door. She sees her mother in the throes of an hysteric and vulgar orgasm. Cursing. Begging. Demanding. Repulsed, Red slips down the stairs.

LIVING ROOM AND BOTTOM OF STAIRS—CONTINUOUS

Red steps over her mother's clothes and those of the house painter. Shoes, socks, overalls. Her anger builds as she kicks the things in disgust. She hears the jingle of keys in the overalls' pocket. She takes them and studies them.

EXT. PECK HOUSE—PRE-DAWN LIGHT

Red turns the key in the ignition and the Painter's truck starts up. She stares at the house, bites her lip nervously, and slowly drives away. She drifts too close to a parked car, and scrapes it. Overcorrecting her steering, she weaves into a couple of trash cans, taking them out. She keeps on going, even though she doesn't know where she's going, on an unsure search for the happiness she can no longer find at home.

I like how all of this felt. It has a much cleaner flow and it is a reminder of a very important lesson. Simple is often better. This is doubly true at the opening of your film. We already know we have so many things to introduce within ten pages that making it more difficult to grasp by putting it in a complicated structure is risky.

Each of my three central characters has his or her own set of problems. As each personal story progresses we discover that though the problems have manifested in different ways, all three sets of problems are virtually the same.

We spoke, too, of an action being a pebble thrown in the pond and watching the ripples reach the shores of other characters' lives. This certainly happens here. When Red runs away it directly affects her brother, Scott. When Scott goes after her he confronts Midge as the last person to have seen her. Midge doesn't give a crap about Red but she does need to get out of town before the guy who killed her brother kills her.

The rest of the first eight or ten pages or so flesh out the problem for Midge (that her life is in danger) and the problem for Scott (he learns that Red has run away from home and he has to try to find her). These pages also introduce other characters and begin the set-up of the bigger problem that will end Act One on around page twenty-five.

The job of the second ten pages

In the second ten pages of Act One the central characters come together. Each person's set of problems gets worse and conflict rules the day. During these scenes we see that the "old" way of handling things does not work for the characters anymore. Midge, who goes back to picking pockets and scamming people, runs into Red who stands up to her and won't be threatened. But Red's ways don't work either because as tough as she is in self-defense Midge still manages to pick her pocket. Meanwhile Scott's life takes a turn when he has to drop everything and go after Red. When he confronts Midge and chases after her in the subways he discovers he is no match for her. She gets away from him easily. However she almost runs right into the arms of the guy who killed her brother and is looking for her. The threat on her life is staring her in the face.

Midge's problem worsens, Scott's problem worsens, and Red's has worsened when she looks for her wallet and finds it missing.

In the scenes that follow I also want to show that Midge has isolated herself from her family and so therefore she cannot go back to her family for help and safety. I play this scene at the burial of her brother. This limits her options when she realizes she has to hide or get out of town.

I also want to see Red's life become further complicated by an action she takes as a result of being broke. Her trip is starting to turn into a nightmare.

Scott, as well, realizes he has very few ways of coping with his problem.

So the second eight to ten pages of the first act show a worsening of problems, the fact that the old way of doing things isn't exactly working, the protagonist and co-antagonist clash, and the risk or danger is heightened.

NOTES

You will see my notes in the margins. The sequence with Scott on a lunch break in his ambulance bothers me. It makes Scott seem glib. I'm thinking of changing the scene in the next draft to one in which we see him working and going home to get the message that Red has run away from home. I want to keep his character harder edged. When you see this happen in your script make notes as I have, but you cannot rewrite it until you've finished the rest of the script.

Indirection—*continued*

INT. HOSPITAL—MORGUE—DAY

A tech holds a clipboard as Midge struggles to sign a death certificate with her bandaged hand. She shakes with pain and anger. He gives her a copy, along with a bag containing Lonnie's personal items and leaves her standing at the slab where Lonnie lies. A man enters and crosses directly to her. A badge dangles from his pocket. He's NYPD Det. Devlin.

> DEVLIN
> Midge Delisa?

> MIDGE
> This is a bad time.

> DEVLIN
> I'm sorry. But the sooner we talk the better.

She turns away. He goes to the other side of the slab and faces her over Lonnie's dead body.

> DEVLIN
> We need a statement.

> MIDGE
> Fuck off. How's that for a statement?

> DEVLIN
> We know it was Rico Cantores. He's not from around here. You can help.

> MIDGE
> Don't worry. I'm going to help.

> DEVLIN

With you as a witness, we get him off the streets for good.

> MIDGE

As a witness, my life would be over. I'd never live to testify. You know that.

> DEVLIN

We can protect you.

> MIDGE

I can protect myself.

> DEVLIN

These vaults are stuffed with people who thought the same thing you're thinking right now. That you can do my job. That you can get him first.

> MIDGE

Doesn't say much for how you do your job, does it? My odds are better without you.

> DEVLIN
> (in her face)

You want odds? For every body Rico sends down here, he kills a dozen more on the streets that we never find. And the odds are you're next, because even if you don't testify, he can't afford to have you around as a potential witness. Sooner or later he's going to find you.

This scene has two purposes. First we see Midge mourn the death of her brother (**story**) and secondly we put pressure on her to watch her back because she may be the next one who is killed (**plot**).

This gives her the motivation she needs to hook up with the protagonist, Scott.

> MIDGE
>
> I'm praying he does. I'll be waiting for him.

> DEVLIN
>
> You won't stand a chance, honey. You're not in his league.

> MIDGE
>
> You're not scaring me.

> DEVLIN
>
> That's too bad, because you should be scared. You should be watching your back day and night. *(puts card down)* You're angry, but you're going to need more than anger to get the job done. You're going to need help. And I'm it. Think about what I'm saying. Then call me. Twenty-four seven. You call; I'm there.

He leaves. She stares at Lonnie. Alone. Scared.

EXT. INDIANAPOLIS, INDIANA—CITY STREET— DAWN

The Painter's truck, worse for the wear, weaves down the street and comes to a stop in front of a bus station. Red turns off the engine and gets out with her backpack. She heads into the building, dropping the keys in a garbage can.

INT. GREYHOUND BUS STATION—DAWN

Hoosiers, Fighting Irish, and other college kids heading off for spring break. Red is swept up in the commotion. She goes to the ticket window.

                    CASHIER
Where to?

                     RED
Where's Spring Break?

                    CASHIER
Aren't you a little young for that?

A Hoosier tight end, Boxer, moves in on her and the window.

                    BOXER
You take this piece of crap bus to New York, then get a train to Florida.

                     RED
            (nods to Cashier)
Cool.

                    CASHIER
Cool?

                     RED
New York. One way.

                    CASHIER
            (shakes head)
Indianapolis—New York. No return.

The Cashier rings up the ticket. Red waits; determined.

EXT. EAST RIVER, N.Y.—PARKED AMBULANCE—DAY

Gray. Damp. Noisy. Gulls spin and squawk.

INT. AMBULANCE—CONTINUOUS

Scott and Nurse Jamie do lunch and watch the gulls.

> SCOTT
> I see them and I think they're crazy. But
> I'm just like them.

> NURSE JAMIE
> Free as a bird?

> SCOTT
> Going in circles. Endlessly.

> NURSE JAMIE
> They go around in circles to gain
> altitude. Like you. You're on your
> way up.

He looks at her. He has to smile.

> SCOTT
> You're hopeless. I've worked my
> way up to a part-time ambulance
> driver.

> NURSE JAMIE
> Don't forget how much work that was. There
> were times I wasn't sure you'd make it.

> SCOTT
> I don't believe that for a minute.

He leans over and kisses her.

INT. BUS—DAY

Speeding down the highway. Spring break is well un-

Sometimes my cards fool me.

I thought I needed to show my protagonist in a relaxed mode, but I was wrong. Now that I see the scenes in context with the intense scenes before them, they seem too light. I want to show my protagonist as someone with an "edge" or depth.

I'm going to re-do this in the next draft.

der way. Red sits apart from the others, secretly counting her money in her wallet. She looks at a picture she carries. It's of her sitting on her brother's lap, singing into his stethoscope. The brother is Scott. She closes her eyes and takes a deep breath.

INT. PECK HOUSE—RED'S BEDROOM—DAY

Red's mother, Mary Anne, sits on Red's bed staring blankly into space. She holds Red's empty jewelry box.

INT. AMBULANCE—EAST RIVER, N.Y.—DAY

Scott and Nurse Jamie are now stretched out in the back of the ambulance, making out. Suddenly her NEXTEL screeches to life, shattering their reverie.

> ER
> Jamie! You there? Jamie!

> NURSE
> JAMIE
> Jamie.

> ER
> You know where Scott is? He's not responding.

> Same note here as before. I don't want Scott to look like a Lothario. That would have nothing to do with my story. I'm not even sure he knows what love is until he meets Midge. I'm definitely going to change this in my next draft.

She looks down to her hand deep inside his pants.

> NURSE JAMIE
> Wanna bet?

> ER
> What?

> NURSE JAMIE
>
> I said I bet I can find him.

> ER
>
> Because he's got an emergency. His mother called.

> SCOTT
>
> That's not an emergency, that's a miracle.

> ER
>
> Said it was urgent.

> NURSE JAMIE
>
> I'll let him know.

She clicks off. He takes the Nextel and tosses it.

> NURSE JAMIE
>
> You're not going to call?

He embraces her again.

> SCOTT
>
> One emergency at a time.

EXT. CEMETERY—LONNIE'S FUNERAL—DAY

A small group of MOURNERS. Old and young, clutched around a woman in black. She is Lonnie's and Midge's MOTHER and she is bitter and embattled. As the PRIEST drones on, the Mother scans the scene beyond the group. She catches something.

EXT. CEMETERY—NEARBY KNOLL—CONTINUOUS

Hiding in a stand of elms, Midge scans the crowd for Rico. Her eyes catch her mother's eyes. There is distance in their connection. Not in yards or years, but in the sadness and disappointment that separates mothers and daughters. Her mother turns away in rejection.

EXT. CEMETERY—FROM A CAR—CONTINUOUS

Det. Devlin watches Midge watch her mother.

EXT. CEMETERY—NEARBY KNOLL—CONTINUOUS

A twig snaps behind Midge. She spins. It's Boney, her friend from the party, who hands Midge A NOTE on YELLOW PAPER and slips away. The note reads: RICO C. HABANA TOWN PHILLY.

EXT. NEW YORK CITY STREETS—DAY

Midge walks. Dead inside. Eyes swollen and unfocused. She crosses the street with a thousand other people, moving without moving.

INT. GRAND CENTRAL STATION—DAY

Midge comes into the huge main concourse. As she drifts around, several OTHER KIDS, her friends, collect around her tentatively. They know what she's just been through. One by one they touch her. Their sign of affection. Their limit of emotion. She acknowledges them.

EXT. GRAND CENTRAL STATION—BUS PLATFORM— DAY

People mill around, bored. Crowds pour out of the interstate buses and head downstairs to the grand terminal below.

INT. GRAND CENTRAL STATION—MAIN TERMI-
NAL—STREET LEVEL

Midge and her Friends prowl around, checking everything out, looking for a way to survive. They pan-
handle; they pick-pocket. Midge sees Red hunched
in a phone booth talking on the phone as Boxer, the
tight end from Indiana, passes by the booth and waves
his train ticket at Red.

INT. PECK HOUSE—KITCHEN—DAY

Mary Anne, Red and Scott's mother, talks on the
phone.

> MARY ANNE
> If you'd stop yelling, I can explain.

> SCOTT
> You can't explain, Mom. What you did is
> beyond explanation. You're beyond expla-
> nation. Your daughter runs away and you
> wait two days before you tell anyone. What
> is that?

> MARY ANNE
> We thought it was better to wait.

INTERCUT WITH:

INT. SCOTT PECK'S SUB-STREET LEVEL APART-
MENT—DAY

Scott paces in a circle around his low rent place.

> SCOTT
> We?

MARY ANNE

Warren and me. We figured Red's just pissed-off, and that she'll get scared and hungry and come home.

SCOTT

Warren?

MARY ANNE

A friend. He's...painting the house.

SCOTT

You get your family counseling from a fucking house painter!

MARY ANNE

Well you don't have to be a genius to figure out a fifteen-year-old, you know. They're all idiots.

SCOTT

She's allowed to be an idiot. You're not. Those are the rules.

MARY ANNE

The rules suck.

> **Hiding early clues.**
>
> Scott and his mother have no relationship. He instantly blames her for forcing Red out of the house.
>
> **When he calls her a lousy parent she reminds him that he wasn't much better as a brother.**
>
> This hurts and tips off something of his past that he doesn't want to look at. **I want to make this point stronger in the next draft.**

SCOTT

No. You know what sucks, Mom? You being a parent.

MARY ANNE

Kind of like you being a brother.

>   SCOTT
>   (stung)
>   Call the police.

He hangs up and stares at a framed picture, the same one Red has, with Red singing into his stethoscope, sitting in the ambulance. Then for the first time he notices the message light blinking on the machine. He punches the button.

>   RED'S VOICE
>   Hey, Scott. It's your little sister passing through Grand Central Station.

>   SCOTT
>   Thank God.

>   RED'S VOICE
>   I totally maxxed-out on Mom's soft porn drama. She's in heat over Warren the Housepainter. You should hear them all night long. I will never, ever, have sex.

>   SCOTT
>   Shit.

>   RED'S VOICE
>   So, I bought a one-way ticket to independence. I'm waiting for the train now. Hell, I'm fifteen. Time I did something with my life, right? I mean, we both knew that sooner or later I'd need to do this.

>   SCOTT
>   Shit.

>   RED'S VOICE
>   So don't worry about me, because you know

how much I've grown up lately. *(very un-grownup)* Okay... well... I love you...

Nothing but dial tone. Scott cringes; angry and anxious.

INT. GRAND CENTRAL—MAGAZINE AND SNACK STORE—DAY

Red carries a magazine to the counter. Midge and her buddies follow her closely, making things tense. Red takes a bulky wallet out of her backpack and pays. They see her money.

                    MIDGE
        Wanna play a game?

                    RED
        Does it involve you going away?

                    MIDGE
        I call it "Destinations."

                    RED
        How clever.

                MAGAZINE MAN
        Stop bothering my customers. Get outta
        here.

Red takes her change and leaves. Midge and her pals follow.

                    MIDGE
        It works this way, I try to guess where
        you're going and you tell me when I'm
        right.

> **For story purposes** this scene shows the kind of characters these two young women are. Tough, smart, and stubborn.
>
> **For plot purposes** it serves the purpose of plot by the action Midge takes at its end.

                    RED
          I'll spare you the mental an-
          guish.

                    MIDGE
          No. No. I like this game. Let's
          see. I'd say you're not head-
          ing North because you don't
          have any ski hat or gloves or
          stuff like that.

                    RED
          Incredible. I can see you're re-
          ally good at this. You've probably already
          guessed I'm not heading East because I have
          a ticket for a train not a boat.

Midge pulls Red's ticket out of her hand.

                    MIDGE
          The Florida Limited. South!

                    RED
               (grabs ticket)
          What a great game. You should give your-
          self a prize.

                    MIDGE
          She's going to Disney World.

                    RED
          Hardly.

                    MIDGE
          Everybody wants to go there. It's the Magic
          Kingdom.

                    RED
          Really? And I thought this was the Magic
          Kingdom.

> MIDGE
>
> This is reality.

> RED
>
> Reality's what you left behind.

> MIDGE
>
> Yeah? What are you leaving behind?

> RED
>
> Besides you? Not much.

Red pushes past them and rushes for her train. Midge turns to her friends and holds up Red's bulky wallet.

> MIDGE
>
> That's what she thinks.

So now Midge has definitely complicated Red's life. I wanted to show what kind of people these two young girls were more than anything else in this scene. Each in her individual way is fearless and smart. Each demands respect. We have seen, too, that Scott's rather comfortable world is about to become a lot less so.

The job of the third ten pages

In the final eight to ten pages of the first act we escalate everyone's problem once again and send them all off on a journey they didn't bargain for.

This is the point at the end of act one when the first big commitment takes place. The reluctant hero begins a journey he thinks he can manage. He will learn in the second act that he cannot manage it at all. Here's how the protagonist and the co-antagonist meet and strike a deal based on a challenge. This is not unlike Book having to stay with Rachel, or Leon opening the door for Mathilda, or Ilsa walking in the front door of Rick's Cafe American. Things will never be the same.

Indirection—*continued*

INT. GRAND CENTRAL—MAGAZINE AND SNACK
STORE—DAY

Midge and friends are at the counter with a mountain of shit.

                    MIDGE
          On me.

                    MAGAZINE MAN
          With what? Your good looks?

Midge waves a few 20's. The Magazine Man rings the
sale up.

                    MAGAZINE MAN
          Forty-seven twenty.

He takes the cash and gives her the change. She stuffs
it in the wallet. He recognizes it immediately.

                    MAGAZINE MAN
          That's not your wallet.

                    MIDGE
          What?

                    MAGAZINE MAN
          It's that girl's. You jacked it.

                    MIDGE
              (on the move)
          You're crazy, you know that? I could sue
          you for saying shit like that.

> MAGAZINE MAN
>
> You can sue me from jail, you little shit. I'm calling the cops.

INT. GRAND CENTRAL—MAIN TERMINAL—STREET LEVEL

A weary Porter faces Scott, hands him back the picture.

> PORTER
>
> No.

> SCOTT
>
> You sure?

> PORTER
>
> Try the ticket booths.

> SCOTT
>
> I did. Every one.

> PORTER
>
> Try the food.

> SCOTT
>
> The food.

INT. FLORIDA LIMITED—DAY

Spring break madness. The Fraternity Brothers rock and roll. Red sits on the fringes ransacking her backpack for her wallet. She realizes she was picked. She looks around, totally pissed. Boxer, drunk, waves. She flips him off.

INT. GRAND CENTRAL STATION—LADIES ROOM

Midge and her buddies clean up at the sinks, sated from their pounds of snack food. Midge dries her hands, and studies the hand that was crippled by Rico's knife.

INT. GRAND CENTRAL—MAIN FLOOR

The gang comes out of the ladies room and wanders off in different directions. Midge spots something across the way.

Magazine Man is in front of his store with Scott, who is still holding the picture of Red. Magazine Man sees Midge and points her out to Scott. Scott heads toward Midge. Midge doesn't wait around. She runs like hell.

This is her territory and she covers it like a cat. She toys with him. He, on the other hand, though fast, is out of control. People scatter, yelling angrily at him as he collides with everything and every person in sight.

INT. GRAND CENTRAL—SUBTERRANEAN SUBWAY STATION

Midge races down a flight of stairs, over obstacles, under stiles, as if people were getting out of her way and purposely stepping into his. She disappears around a corner.

INT. SUBWAY PLATFORM—GRAND CENTRAL

Scott comes down the stairs and races around the corner. Looks left, looks right. Crowds of people cram onto the train cars as the doors close. He runs alongside the cars, looking in the windows for Midge. She's nowhere in sight. The train picks up speed and leaves him behind. He flops on a bench and catches his breath.

From a phone booth not more than thirty feet away we discover Midge watching him. No way he'd ever catch her. She smiles in smug satisfaction and turns around and freezes.

> Keep the pressure on every character.

Not more than thirty feet in the other direction stand Rico and his gang of slugs. Detective Devlin was right. Her heart pounds. She turns away from them and watches them in the glass reflection as they move away from her. Ahead of her, Scott wanders; hunting still.

Another train pulls into the station. Scott watches it. A couple of Midge'S BUDDIES come down the stairs. He pulls back and watches them through the crowd. They approach the last car in the train. He follows them, pushing his way through the crowd, hoping they'll lead him to Midge.

He gets to the last car as the doors start to close. He can't see the kids. He jumps in the last car and looks around. The kids are nowhere to been seen. He panics, pries the door open and jumps back out onto the platform as the train pulls away.

He looks one way. The other. Nothing.

Suddenly something catches his eye. In the tunnel. Midge's Buddies are silhouetted on the tracks, heading deep into the belly of the beast.

INT. FLORIDA LIMITED—NIGHT

Red makes her way down the aisle of a car. Everyone is asleep. She passes a HEAVY MAN, head back and snoring. His jacket is folded next to him. She stops. Desperate.

> Red is forced to take a risk but it just makes things worse.

Holding her breath, she reaches down and slowly unfolds it, exposing the inside breast pocket bulging with a wallet. She hesitates, then takes the wallet and walks away to the end of the car. She grabs the handle on the door. Just as she does, another hand clamps down on hers. It's Boxer, the Frat Boy she flipped-off earlier.

> BOXER
> Uh ohh. Did we just get into trouble?

EXT. TRAIN CAR PLATFORM—NIGHT

Boxer bullies Red onto the platform between two cars. The wind and noise howl. He roughs her up.

> BOXER
> You rip people off?

> RED
> I'm broke. I just need a few dollars. I'll pay him back.

> BOXER
> You'll pay him back. Right.

> RED
> I swear. I'll send him the money when I get home.

He "frisks" her like a cop; really just copping a feel.

> BOXER
>
> I think we should talk to a cop. How many other wallets you take, huh? You got more?

She's humiliated and frightened.

> RED
>
> There's no more. Honest. No more.

> BOXER
>
> I don't know. I mean, how do I know?

> RED
>
> You can trust me. Honest.

Boxer studies her. Making her sweat.

> BOXER
>
> We'll see if I can trust you.

INT. SUBTERRANEAN TUNNELS—GRAND CENTRAL STATION

An unimaginable underworld, this is not only the subway system, this is the vascular system of a city on life support. Clogged, decaying, in pain.

SMALL TUNNEL

Scott moves through the dark and chilling tunnel. He climbs onto a treacherous ledge above the tracks that run with a yellow acrid stream of waste. He rubs along the slippery wall, gagging on the stench.

This is the statement about the living conditions Midge and other kids endure. Seeing it through Scott's eyes makes it organic.

TRAIN TRACKS BENEATH HIM

He tightropes the narrow shelf, occasionally losing his footing on the slime, grabbing onto the rusting stubs of rebar to keep from falling. A train approaches.

Panicked, he presses himself into the wall and shuts his eyes, bracing for the impact.

A SPEEDING TRAIN

ROARS BY, not more than a foot from him. The NOISE AND CRASH OF HOT AIR frighten him out of his skin. He screams back at the train at the top of his lungs. Screaming for his life.

The train passes. Scott moves quickly out of the tunnel and into an open area. It is a sight unlike he's ever seen.

WIDER ANGLE—SUBTERRANEAN CAVERNS AND TUNNELS

A living nightmare. A ghostly, gaping, two-story cavity laced with a spider web spun of concrete and steel spanning the confluence of access tunnels and rancid crawl spaces oozing with conduits and slime, made barely breathable by huge, noisy ducts blowing the burned electric air of locomotives into endless cycles of dust.

These are the labyrinthine bowels of New York City. The suburb of her disenfranchised where, incredibly, the crannies and crypts are home to the children of the street. Where they eat and sleep. Where they too often die.

Oblivious to Scott and the underscore of SHRIEK-ING BRAKES AND BLINDING BLUE SPARKS, a teen-age couple takes flight from the madness, and make love in their cardboard shelter.

Scott passes other kids chattering incoherently, shar-ing drugs around a small fire. Someone far off is sing-ing. Someone else is crying. He moves slowly, over-whelmed and sickened by the reality that this place actually exists.

INT. ABANDONED SUBTERRANEAN WASHROOM—NEARBY

A broken utility sink on one wall and a fetid mat-tress on the floor. The room is cold and dark except for the glimmer of stolen candles.

Midge sits in the low light counting the money from Red's wallet, studying a picture of Red and Scott. It reminds her of her own brother Lonnie. She pulls out THE YELLOW NOTE and stares at the name: RICO. She remembers Det. Devlin's warning and shudders.

> Keep the threat on her life alive with the yellow note.

DEVLIN (V.O.)
The odds are, you're next.

Suddenly a shadow falls across the note and her heart stops.

A MAN'S VOICE
Love what you've done to the place.

His silhouette fills the doorway. She springs to her feet. He pushes her back down and crouches next to her.

MIDGE
Jesus! Who the fuck are you?

SCOTT
Forget me. That magazine guy upstairs...

MIDGE
That magazine guy is crazy.

He sees Red's wallet, and he's instantly enraged.

MIDGE
That's mine. I found it. Finders keepers.

SCOTT
(shaking) Shut up. Just shut the fuck up.
If you hurt my sister...

MIDGE
I didn't hurt anybody.

SCOTT
You took this from her. That's hurting her.
She's fifteen and scared. And now, thanks
to you, she's broke.

MIDGE
Welcome to the club.

SCOTT
I don't want her in your fucking club! I
don't want her on the same planet as you.
What I want is a straight answer. When
did you see her? Where was she going?
You might be the only person who knows.

MIDGE
Well then that's bad news for you, because I
don't give shit to guys girls run away from.

SCOTT
She's not running away from me. Christ.
She loves me.

MIDGE
Where have I heard that before?

SCOTT
And I love her.

MIDGE
People used to "love" me, too.

SCOTT
What is it with you?

MIDGE
They'd go, "What are you doing, Midge?"
"What's wrong with you?" "Come home.
Come home." Like they were going to fix
me or something.

SCOTT
Obviously you didn't let them.

MIDGE
They were the ones who broke me.

SCOTT
You think I broke my sis-
ter?

MIDGE
I saw her. Somebody broke
her. It really doesn't matter who.

> Cleverly, the protagonist is
> not allowed to go back. She
> forces him to go forward with
> her dialog.
>
> Scott really doesn't want to
> hear Midge tell him in essence
> that sooner or later his sister will
> live in a place like this.

SCOTT

It matters to me. She matters to me. More
than anyone. If I don't find her fast, I
may never find her at all. She can't survive out there alone. She's not like you.

MIDGE

(in his face) She's just like me.

He's stunned by the remark. He shakes his head in
denial, repelled by the possibility. He looks around
at these bizarre and tragic surroundings.

SCOTT

There's got to be something. There is, right?
Money, right? Just tell me how much. You
need food. You need new clothes. I can get
the money for that. Whatever you need.

MIDGE

I don't want your money. And I don't want
your fucking sympathy.

SCOTT

What do you want? There's got to be something.

She stares at the yellow note in her hand.

SCOTT

Just name it.
She stares. She thinks.

SCOTT

Anything.

And thinks. And she stares. Then turns to him slowly.

                    MIDGE
Anything.

                    SCOTT
Anything.

                    MIDGE
I give you what you want. You give me what
I want.

                    SCOTT
Name it.

                    MIDGE
I've got to get out of town.

                    SCOTT
Let's go buy the ticket.

                    MIDGE
Uh unh. No bus or train. No public trans-
portation. I'll go with you.

                    SCOTT
What?

                    MIDGE
And I'll help you find her.

                    SCOTT
Forget it.
                    MIDGE
You said 'anything.'

                    SCOTT
That's not what I meant.

                    MIDGE
        You won't find her on your own. You don't
        know where to begin.

                    SCOTT
        I'll buy a map.

                    MIDGE
        They don't sell maps for the kind of trip
        you're going to take.

                    SCOTT
        I'm resourceful.

                    MIDGE
        I don't give a shit if you're an eagle scout.
        Right now your sister's life is at stake, and
        I'm the one with the merit badge in street
        life.

She approaches him seriously. No wise-cracking.

                    MIDGE
        You may not want to hear this, but your
        sister and I have more in common than
        you think.

He can't believe this. He turns away.

                    MIDGE
        I've been where she's been. I understand
        how she feels. I can think like she thinks.
        I can go places you can't go.

She watches him watching the other kids share their
dope, then throws the knock-out punch somberly.
She leans in close and practically whispers the bad
news.

> MIDGE

Every one of us here... We all started where your sister did.

The idea scares him.

> MIDGE

Your sister needs you. You need me. I need to get out of town. It's simple.

He turns to her slowly.

> MIDGE

When we find her, you go your way, I go mine. End of story.

> SCOTT

You know where she's headed?

This drives the point home. An agreement with the Devil of sorts.

Midge is desperate to get out of town and sees a way to do it. She delivers the knock-out blow. He knows she's right but really doesn't want her to tell him what to do. They finally agree to take the journey together neither one wants to take.

This is the end of their Act One story.

> MIDGE

You got a car? With a car we can beat her there.

> SCOTT

Beat her where?

> MIDGE

The Magic Kingdom.

INT. TRAIN LAVATORY—NIGHT

Not exactly the Magic Kingdom. Boxer pins Red against the wall, her blouse half open. She resists the best she can.

                    BOXER
          Relax.

                    RED
          You're hurting me.

                    BOXER
          I don't want to hurt you. And I don't want
          to turn you in. I want to trust you. Can I
          trust you?

                    RED
          You can trust me.

He reaches down and unzips his fly. Red's heart races.

                    BOXER
          Can I trust you with this?

He smiles stupidly, forcing her down. Scared and repulsed, she slides down the wall and reaches between
his legs. Then with one movement, she jumps back
up yanking his zipper with all her might, closing it
on him.

                    RED
          Trust this.

His face lights up in agony. He unzips himself but
only tears more skin. He never sees Red's knee come
up full force into his groin. He crumbles to the floor.

                    RED
          (tight; angry) Why couldn't you leave me
          alone?

The train's brakes squeal. She buttons her blouse,
runs her fingers through her hair, then quickly puts

the Heavy Man's wallet in Boxer's pants, and takes
his.

EXT. TRAIN STATION — NIGHT

Red works her way through the crowd, frightened,
getting as far away as she can.

EXT. STATION—Red'S POV

She sees the Heavy Man through the window angrily
waving his jacket at the Porter.

EXT. STATION—NIGHT

Red turns and runs out of the train station and into
the night.

This is the Act One end for Red's plot and story. She is forced on a
journey she does not want to take. Now everyone's lot has been cast. All of
the characters are set out on a journey they will never forget.

The new journey is about to begin for Scott and Midge as protagonist and co-antagonist/co-protagonist. And for Red her planned one-way
trip to a good time was quickly becoming the trip from hell.

Now to try your scene work. With each scene you write from your
outline consider the depth of the emotions you are working with. Not just
your characters' emotions, but yours as well. Remember that just because
this is the start of your script doesn't mean it's the start of their lives. You
may be starting your guy off waiting for the bus, but remember he's had a
lot on his mind ever since he woke up and noticed his wife dabbing perfume in the cleavage of her miracle bra on her way out to her chanting
class. Life is complicated, so bring all those unspoken complications to
each moment you write about.

Although you work on one scene at a time you will keep an eye on
the scenes surrounding it. Concern yourself with the flow of things, as I
had to in the opening of my script. It's a feeling you'll get. Trust it. Each
scene you write will leave an emotional residue or shadow. Pay attention
to the things that lurk in your shadows.

Your act should end around page twenty-five or so. Don't go past page thirty to reach your goal of starting your protagonist's journey, for that would be too far into the film.

The plan for Act Two will be for your protagonist's journey to become more complicated. In my Act Two I plan to see Red's days go from bad to worse. She is a small girl in a terribly cruel world and her luck runs out. For Midge and Scott I plan on seeing each of their "strengths" being challenged as they chase after Red, and for their relationship to turn to a love story... slowly. They will find new strengths in each other as they get honest with each other. They will face their fears together.

We do not live our lives in a straight line.

No matter how sure we are of ourselves, and no matter how well we know ourselves, and no matter how clear our direction in life may be, some things can't be foreseen. Your second act must be filled with the unforeseen.

19

Writing the Script—Act Two, Part One

Act Two
Part One: Life Torn Apart

You have heard me talk a great deal about the middle of your script becoming the "muddle." Well here we are at the middle. This is the belly of the beast and the next fifty to sixty pages separate the boys from the men and the girls from the women. Or as an insensitive boob in California once said, it separates the girlymen from the men.

Once again the sanest approach is to break down this large act into emotional sections, because this is the emotional center of your film's theme.

This is the journey through the heart of the matter.

Some points I keep in mind that help me a great deal might also help you. I look at Act Two in halves. The first half of the act shows the protagonist and co-antagonist begrudgingly working on a mutual goal. They get on each other's nerves and they certainly *don't trust each other*. They want to get past the job they have to do together so they can get on with their individual agendas.

The goal of the first half of the second act is to create situations for them in which they argue and fight while they pursue their mutual goal. Each time one imposes upon the other his or her way of doing things, it should backfire or fall short or even fail completely. The reason for this is that with each stumbling or failure a constructive humbling occurs. With each occurrence a character flaw or a fear is exposed. Every time a fear is exposed the chance to get over it appears with the help of the other. Bit by bit one will discover more about what makes the other guy tick, and that what *is* making him tick is kind of nice.

Now take that a step further. The more one sees and understands the other guy, the more one is able to influence and be a part of the other's life. And as a consequence, the more one's own life is affirmed. The more this happens, the more one seeks further affirmation. It is a life-fulfilling attraction. That is why one likes what he or she sees in the other. The more they argue with each other, the more they are falling for each other because of the revelations within each encounter.

This is the challenge of the emotional structure of the first half of the second act. Find it in your work and stick to it.

In *Indirection* the challenge of finding Red, their mutual goal, beats Scott and Midge up. This is the dynamic I chose to create in the first half of the second act. As my protagonist and co-antagonist (who gradually turns co-protagonist) face their task and truly struggle, they become more desperate to succeed. They bang their heads together hard enough to force themselves to "come clean" with each other. As they open up, a sense of mutual trust forms. And the more they trust, the more they open up. They don't always open up in a sweet and pleasant way, sometimes it's opening up with a barrage of expletives. But anger is just an expression of fear anyway, and within that expression the other can find the "opening up." When they trust each other enough to open up to each other they have reached a critical emotional moment in their relationship.

> **Check your first half of Act Two to make sure you have a continuous emotional build, the effect of which drives your plot. This is the key to your emotional structure. It bears repeating.**

The combination of fighting the common foe and of battling with each other exhausts protagonist and co-protagonist and makes them vulnerable. Don't forget you didn't start out with superhuman beings. You started out with characters who were flawed and doing their best just to survive. And remember the great value in vulnerability is that it makes a person teachable. When your protagonist becomes vulnerable, either out of exhaustion or injury or uncontrolled anger, the co-antagonist/co-protagonist will pick up on it and force the protagonist to deal with what's really underneath the pain or anger. The more they force the opening up of each other, the more they begin to trust each other.

There is another element you want to make sure to keep an eye on. If either one of them wants to call it quits and go home, the other one will not let him go. They force one another to carry on.

During these pages you have to keep the plot threat alive. In my script I do it by returning to Red's runaway story where we see her getting into deeper and deeper trouble. This reminds the audience that there is a great deal at stake for Scott and Midge, and that they are racing the clock before it runs out on Red.

In *Witness* there are many little scenes dispersed throughout the second act showing the bad cops back in Philadelphia getting closer to finding Book's location. This keeps Book, Rachel, and the audience aware of the ticking bomb. Make sure your "danger" is always evident. And make sure that things get a lot worse for your hero before they get better.

A war on two fronts

Make these first twenty-five pages of the second act engage your protagonist and co-protagonist in two battles. The first battle is for them to solve their mutual problem before it's too late. Time is the enemy. The second battle is the personal battle in which they are engaged. Here, Truth is the enemy. Both wars are deadly.

Shifting the balance

The balance of these battles shifts during the course of the first half of the second act. At first the first battle—the plot—is the primary motivation for their actions and the primary cause of disagreement. This balance must begin to shift later in the first half of the act as their personal discoveries divert their focus. By the time they reach the midpoint of the second act we will see them struggle less with the question of how to succeed, and more with their feelings for each other that have risen out of the first battle.

The tent pole scene

At the midpoint of Act Two I create what I call a tent pole scene. It signals the shift in the story from an action adventure to a love story, or vice versa. The first half of the second act is powered by the action: the plot. The plot creates the emotional turmoil that gives birth to the story. The second half of the second act is empowered by their emotions: the story.

It happens in *Witness* when Book and Rachel's story turns from wanting him to leave the farm, to wanting him to stay for the rest of his life. All of the important developments in the second half of the second act in their story have to do with their personal feelings as the plot slides into the background.

In *Body Heat* in a moment of passion William Hurt agrees to kill Kathleen Turner's husband. This is the tent pole scene for them. It turns a love story (or lust story, really) into a murder mystery. And, though each has the tools for lust, neither has the tools for murder. They must struggle to find them if they are to succeed.

In *The Thomas Crown Affair* remake the opposite happens. A crime story turns to a love story when Rene Russo and Pierce Brosnan succumb to the temptations of an affair like moths to the flame, thinking they can still outsmart each other. But do they have the emotional tools to do this? That is the question for the second half of Act Two for them.

In *The Professional* Leon and Mathilda fall in love and their story changes from murder to something much darker and far more complicated. In matters of love neither one of them is a professional. Without the right tools they are inviting absolute disaster.

In *Indirection* my tent pole scene occurs in the ladies room at the Greyhound bus terminal when Scott and Midge have a huge fight. He ultimately demands that Midge take a hard look at what she's doing. He tells her she has to stop pretending to be a helpless little girl. He tells her that she is a beautiful, albeit aggravating, woman and that she has nothing to hide or be afraid of. But she has much to hide, and she admits to him how scared she is and how lost she feels. At this moment he realizes what a difficult admission that is for her to make. He must treat it and her with care. Rather than ridicule her he tells her he understands, and that he will protect her and if she is lost he will help her find herself no matter what it takes. This is the turning point in their relationship. They bond emotionally. *And from this point on their story changes.* But they don't have the tools for this. They know how to fight but they don't know how to love. This is the challenge of their second half of Act Two. They must develop the tools to succeed in a loving relationship.

You must make sure of your tent pole scene. If you don't have one you love, you better find one fast because you need it now.

Meanwhile, here is the first half of my second act. It leads up to Scott and Midge's tent pole scene at the Greyhound Bus station. They travel the emotional road from bickering and sniping, to cautious attraction. First I make it harder for them to work together and then I scare them together to elevate their emotions and make them vulnerable. Once they are vulnerable they are able to teach each other something of value. This then becomes the basis for their falling in love and turns the film in a different direction. In their case an inwardly direction.

Indirection – *continued* – The Second Act

INT. SCOTT'S RATTY VW—JERSEY TURNPIKE—
NIGHT

Speeding south. Midge soaks in the passing landscape.
It's been a long time since she's been outside of New
York.

> SCOTT
> We'll push straight through. Catch the train
> in Rocky Mount by morning.

She plays with a lever next to the seat and suddenly
it reclines in a thud, surprising her. She adjusts herself. Closes her eyes. He wonders how crazy this idea
is.

CLOSE ON RED—MORNING

She sleeps curled-up in a ball against a concrete wall.
The hum of traffic rumbles nearby.

CLOSE-UP—GROUND LEVEL—SPEEDING TRAFFIC

Cars and trucks roar by.

CLOSE ON RED—CONTINUOUS

The concrete wall vibrates with the weight of the

speeding trucks and cars, shaking her awake. She looks around, tries to orient herself. She looks up.

EXT. ARLINGTON MEMORIAL BRIDGE—DAY

The bridge spans the Potomac River, connecting Arlington National Cemetery to the Lincoln Memorial and the National Mall. Morning rush hour traffic packs the bridge.

EXT. UNDER THE BRIDGE—CONTINUOUS

Red comes out from under the huge structure into the park, and heads up the rise.

EXT. LINCOLN MEMORIAL—CONTINUOUS

Red comes around the Memorial and is awestruck by the sight in front of her.

The National Mall and all of Washington, D.C. gloriously backlit by the sunrise. It is a breathtaking view. She is overwhelmed by the city's beauty.

EXT. PARKWAY GAS STATION & COFFEE SHOP—VIRGINIA—DAY

Sun streaks across Scott's VW in the parking lot.

INT. RESTAURANT—CONTINUOUS

Scott exits a phone booth and heads for the table. Midge is eating her second breakfast. He sits across from her, checking his watch. The Waitress approaches.

> SCOTT
> Amtrak's on schedule. So are we.

> WAITRESS
> More coffee?

> MIDGE
> Yeah.

> SCOTT
> Just a check.

Midge holds her cup up with her bandaged hand. Gets a refill.

> SCOTT
> That's a lot of caffeine.

She looks up at him slowly, not liking his judgment. He stares back at her, not caring.

> SCOTT
> When was the last time you had a decent meal?

> MIDGE
> Don't do this. Don't start asking those stupid questions.

> SCOTT
> That mean I can't ask what you did to your hand?

She drinks her coffee. He regroups.

> SCOTT
> We might as well take advantage of the washrooms here. Clean up. Put on some fresh clothes.

These are "clashing" scenes which allow your protagonist and co-protagonist to antagonize each other. They do not know or trust one another. These scenes help us disclose exposition in a lively and organic fashion.

Keep your "clashing" scenes smart and direct. You don't want your characters to be whining or annoying.

Your protagonist should fight to maintain the upper hand and control of the situation. He will lose his grip eventually.

> MIDGE
> (looks at hers)
> What's wrong with these?

INT. GAS STATION GIFT SHOP—CONTINUOUS

Strictly tourist stuff. Scott pays at the register as the CLERK jams a bunch of things into a bag. Midge is insulted.

> MIDGE
> This is ridiculous.

BY THE WASHROOMS—CONTINUOUS

Midge holds the bag of stuff at the Ladies' Room door.

> SCOTT
> Have fun. I'll meet you outside.

She shuts the door in his face.

EXT. PARKWAY GAS STATION & COFFEE SHOP—VIR-GINIA—DAY

More people around now filling up. Scott has the top down and sits behind the wheel checking out a map.

ANOTHER ANGLE

Midge comes out and adjusts her Ray Bans against the morning sun and self-consciously crosses the ser-vice islands to the VW. EVERY head turns.
Her long, wet, black hair is combed straight back. Her over-sized Williamsburg T-shirt is tucked into her baggy shorts. Anyone else would look like the tour-ist from hell. But Midge is far from anyone else. She looks sensational.

SCOTT'S VW—CONTINUOUS

Scott traces a route on the map with his finger. Midge throws her old things in the back and climbs in.

> MIDGE
> I feel stupid.

Scott's dumbfounded. He needn't be a prodigy to see there is a woman under those clothes, not a teenager. Something she's been working very hard to conceal.

INT. VW—PARKWAY – LATER – DAY

Scott checks his watch and glances over at Midge who looks at the map, but seems confused.

> SCOTT
> See it? Interstate 21. It's sort of bigger than the rest. About two inches above Rocky Mount.

She looks at him, not appreciating his condescension.

> SCOTT
> How old are you?

> MIDGE
> Old enough to read a map.

> SCOTT
> That's not what I meant. I mean you look older than I thought you were.

> MIDGE
> Oh. That's better.

Debate as Dialog

Midge tries to keep her emotional distance. She is sarcastic instead of truthful.

Scott doesn't do much better. As wise-ass as each can be, neither one is good at respectful conversation. There is a lot of exposition in this scene about Midge but it works nicely in the form of a debate rather than a dissertation.

SCOTT
I don't mean *old old*. I mean older in a nice way.

She shakes her head; goes back to the map.

SCOTT
Take your skin.

MIDGE
What about my skin?

SCOTT
I thought it was dirt.

MIDGE
What?

SCOTT
Your complexion. How dark it is. I thought it was dirt. But it wasn't.

MIDGE
Jesus.

SCOTT
What I mean is the color of your skin is... It's not white and it's not black. It's kind of amazing. What are you anyway?

MIDGE
What am I?

SCOTT
Your ancestry.

                MIDGE
We don't have ancestries in the Bronx. We
have breeds.

                SCOTT
That's funny.

                MIDGE
The hell it is.

                SCOTT
It's nothing to get upset about. We're all
from somewhere.

She looks out at the countryside, remembering how
bad her "somewhere" was.

                SCOTT
It was a simple question.

                MIDGE
Simple questions have simple answers.

They drive in silence. She looks up in the sky.

AN ANTIQUE BIPLANE

Suspended in the air. Next to it a WWII Fighter floats
without a sound.

INT. NATIONAL AIR AND SPACE MUSEUM—DAY

Red looks up at the flying machines suspended above
the tourists, captivated by the energy and expanse of
the displays.

EXT. WASHINGTON MONUMENT—DAY

Red pins herself against the wall, staring straight up its side. A marble rocket piercing the bright blue sky.

EXT. VIETNAM VETERANS' MEMORIAL—DAY

Red walks the length of this spectacular homage, shocked by its power. Its polished face of marble reflects not only her, but everything America stands for. She tries to absorb all the emotional details confronting her. The flowers and flags, the mothers and fathers, the candles and snapshots, the girlfriends and babies, the Purple Hearts, and the Vets in wheelchairs quietly praying; quietly crying.

Red finds a place to sit on the grass not far from A MAN who also sits contemplating the memorial.

> MAN
> Incredible, isn't it?

> RED
> How does it do that? How does a thing ...this marble thing, make me feel so... strongly... so... much?

> MAN
> I think that's the secret of Democracy.

EXT. TRAIN STATION—ROCKY MOUNT, N.C.—DAY

The Florida Limited. People climb on and off. Porters carry bags. Scott trots alongside the train, looking in the windows. Midge stays with him.

> MIDGE
> You sure this is the train?

SCOTT

I'm sure this is the train we've been chasing. Are you sure this is the train she took?

MIDGE

I'm sure.

SCOTT

Good. I can't wait to get my hands on her.

Midge jumps in front of him, stopping him.

MIDGE

What is that shit?

SCOTT

What shit?

Once again the plot is driving their action to find the train and get on it to look for Red, **but the emotions their actions bring up are the subtext of all their conversations.**

This builds their emotional story while the plot moves along quite nicely.

Here, too, Midge and Scott argue over brother-sister relationships.

MIDGE

You-can't-wait-to-get-your-hands-on-her-shit.

SCOTT

Jesus wept. A lecture.

MIDGE

You give her that crap and she'll just run away again.

SCOTT

How many times do I have to say this She's not running away from me.

MIDGE

You're in such denial.

> SCOTT
>
> Can we discuss your take on child psychol-
> ogy after we find her? We have five min-
> utes. You go this way. I'll go that way. Here.

He hands her the photograph from her wallet. He
has the same photo from his apartment.

INT. TRAIN CAR

Scott comes through quickly.

INT. ANOTHER CAR—CONTINUOUS

Midge comes through calmly.

INT. ANOTHER CAR—CONTINUOUS

Scott comes through. Scanning. Anxious.

INT. ANOTHER CAR—CONTINUOUS

Midge comes through. Still calm.

INT. ANOTHER CAR—CONTINUOUS

Some very tired people try to ignore Scott as he approaches.

> SCOTT
>
> I hate to bother you but I'm supposed to
> meet my little sister here and I can't find
> her. Could you tell me if you've seen her?

INT. ANOTHER CAR—CONTINUOUS

Midge comes through and stops in her tracks.

INT. ANOTHER CAR—CONTINUOUS

Scott is squatting next to two little kids who are looking at the picture of Red and nodding.

                    SCOTT
            Yeah? You saw her?

Then they shake their heads "no."

                    SCOTT
            No? You didn't see her?

Then they nod "yes" again. He wants to kill them.
Then he notices a crowd gathering around him. It's
Midge with a Conductor, A Cop,
Boxer, and SEVERAL FRATER-
NITY BROTHERS.

                    MIDGE
            We've got help.

Scott stands, suddenly very worried.

                    COP
            You have some I.D.?

                    SCOTT
            What's going on?

Scott takes out his driver's license.

                    COP
            Your sister's wanted for
            questioning. Suspicion of
            robbery.

This scene combines the
plot and the story and results
in a heightening of just what
is at stake.

The danger facing Red is
rubbed in Scott's face and he
is furious.

This moves the plot well
because they learn they have
to turn around and head back
to where they were and it
moves the story along with its
emotional reactions.

All of this is tied into the
next beat between Scott and
Midge which reminds us why
Red is in trouble in the first
place.

**Everything, plot and story,
works together.**

SCOTT
A train robbery?

BOXER
What do you mean suspicion? There's no
suspicion. There's fact. She robbed me.

MIDGE
Can you believe this?

COP
This young man says your sister jumped
him, knocked him unconscious, and stole
his wallet.

Scott takes in Boxer's size.

SCOTT
Then you're looking for the wrong person.
My sister's five foot two and weighs maybe
ninety pounds.

BOXER
(embarrassed)
She caught me off guard.

SCOTT
Off guard?

COP
According to the complaint, your sister
lured him into the lavatory to have sex with
him. It was during that time that she...

Scott's reaction is quick. He lunges at Boxer's throat.

SCOTT
You motherfucker...

Scott pounds him, punctuating his speech with his fists.

> SCOTT
> You... scum... fucking... bag...

Everybody jumps in to break it up. Friends hold Boxer. The Cop and Conductor hold Scott.

> SCOTT
> You don't buy that, do you?

> COP
> I'm not buying anything until we find your sister.

> CONDUCTOR
> At least now we have her picture to send to Washington.

> MIDGE
> Washington?

> COP
> D.C. That's where she got off.

The train lurches forward. The Conductor checks his watch.

> CONDUCTOR
> Speaking of getting off.

The Cop hands Scott back his license.

> COP
> We'll be in touch with you, Mr. Peck. Fair warning. Sister or no sister. You aid and abet her; you're as guilty as she is.

> SCOTT

She's not guilty of anything.

The crowd breaks up. Scott and Boxer exchange glares.

EXT. TRAIN STATION—ROCKY MOUNT, N.C.—DAY

Scott practically drags Midge off the train and into the station.

> MIDGE

We have to get back up to D.C.

> SCOTT

There's something else first.

> MIDGE

I know, I know. If she robbed that guy, it was because I robbed her first and she was broke.

> SCOTT

Forget that. *(gives her keys)* This stops in Raleigh next. Meet me there.

> MIDGE

What?

Start attaching your co-antagonist to your protagonist now so that she becomes a co-protagonist, albeit still with some reservations.

She is guilty. She is sorry. And she is expressing her concern for his welfare for the first time. It is the first indication that she cares about him.

This will be expressed in another, angrier way in their next sequence.

> SCOTT

Don't tell me you can't drive.

> MIDGE

I can drive. I'm a great driver.

SCOTT
Jesus, don't try to be great, okay? Just try
to get there in one piece.

The train lurches again. They study each other.

MIDGE
This is stupid. You don't have time for this.

SCOTT
I don't? You believe that guy?

MIDGE
He's huge. He'll kill you.

The train rolls and he runs for it. She calls out a
warning.

MIDGE
Whatever you do, don't fight fair!

EXT. STREET—WASHINGTON, D.C.—DAY

Red comes down the street and sees a crowd of pro-
testers in front of a small building. She nears a
woman, Sharon, who's carrying a "pro-choice" poster.

RED
What's going on?

SHARON
A bunch of pro-lifers are threatening the
clinic again.

RED
Clinic? (reads her poster) Oh. Clinic.

EXT. CLINIC—DAY

As they come upon the scene Red is face-to-face with a real live hostile and dangerous clash of pro-life and pro-choice fanatics. Mob mentality anger.

On one side, the pro-choicers stand in front of the clinic, arms linked together. On the other side, behind a police barricade, the pro-lifers raise their signs and fists. AN ENORMOUS WOMAN holds a BLOOD-SPATTERED BABY high in the air.

> Always reveal something emotional about your characters in every scene no matter what it's about. Plot and story in every scene.
>
> Some insight into Red's feeling about home and motherhood. (story)
>
> I now plan on making Red's life even more miserable. This reminds the audience of the time frame Scott and Midge have to deal with. (plot)

ENORMOUS WOMAN
Murderers! Baby Killers!

Red is shocked by the sight.

RED
Man, that doll looks like a real baby she's waving around.

SHARON
That is a real baby. This is a real fight. Pick your side.

RED
How do you know which side is right?

SHARON
Can't decide?

RED
My mother's pro-life. She calls me her "little mistake."

> SHARON
> Then I guess you should be happy you're alive.

> RED
> I *should* be.

Things start getting out of hand. People throw things at each other. The Mounted Police shove the mob back. The mob shoves the police back.

Red gets swept up right into the middle of it, pushed from behind by the throng, poked in the stomach by the cops. It gets louder and scarier and completely beyond her control.

Someone hits a cop from behind, sending him reeling. The mob overruns his position. Sharon tries to pull Red out of harm's way. Sticks and stones and broken bones. The Enormous Woman with the Bloody Baby steps up behind them and slaps Red on the back of the head with a homemade blackjack. She goes down in a heap. EVERYTHING GOES BLACK.

INT. D.C. HOSPITAL—EMERGENCY WARD—NIGHT

An assembly line of people being mended, screaming for drugs, or bandages, or Mommy.

Two D.C. Cops flirt with a PRETTY CANDY STRIPER. Red sits on a bed behind them, where a NURSE and a Doctor finish wrapping her head. As they leave, they pass the cops.

> DOCTOR
> We'll have to keep her overnight. She's still in never-never land. You find any i.d. on her?

> D.C. COP #1
> We found a wallet stuffed in her shorts,
> but it wasn't hers.

> D.C. COP #2
> We have to ask her some questions.

> DOCTOR
> Go very easy.

RED'S HOSPITAL BED—CONTINUOUS

The cops approach her.

> D.C. COP #1
> Hi.

> RED
> Hey.

> D.C. COP #2
> How are you feeling? You took
> quite a hit.

> RED
> Did you see it? Was I with you?

The cops trade looks.

> D.C. COP #1
> No. You weren't with us. You
> were in the middle of the brawl.

> RED
> Oh.

> The worsening situation for the "target" creates an equally increasing pressure on the protagonist to find it. They must always be tied together.
>
> Red's journey has just taken a terrible turn in the wrong direction. Not only is she alone in the world, she is now suffering from amnesia. She can't go home even if she wanted to because she doesn't know where home is.

> D.C. COP #2
> We have to ask some questions, okay?

<pre>
                    RED
        Sure.

                  D.C. COP #1
        Let's start with your name.
</pre>

CAMERA PUSHES IN on Red's face. She doesn't have
a clue.

At this point we can see that we are maintaining everything in the direction we said we wanted to in the first half of Act Two. Scott and Midge are constantly fighting over which way is the best way, his or hers. And Red's life just got a whole lot more complicated now that she's suffering from amnesia. If you take a look at the chart for "The Muddle" you will see that this is about the point where your characters begin to suffer loss and they have their route altered. Their lives are not one hundred percent controlled by them any longer. This is a very big issue.

One of the key points to remember is that each of these characters, and each of your characters will fight forever to hold onto his or her own control. Each character feels very certain about who he or she is and how they want to live their lives. Just like you and just like me, we think we know what's best for us. We think we know who we are and we like it that way. We don't want someone coming along and telling us we need to change. But that is what's happening to our characters. One of the reasons many characters want to give up and go home is because they don't want to change. Most people fear change. But we can create obstacles and accidents in their lives that force them to accept change.

Remember what Artemis Ward once said, "It ain't the things you don't know that gets you into trouble. It's the things you know for sure that just ain't so."

Your job as the writer is to constantly challenge their thinking. When they think they should zig, make them zag. That way they will have to rely on their intuition to get them back on track or to get themselves out of trouble. It will be in the spontaneity of the action that the lessons are learned. It is a new level of risk taking for your protagonist and his co-protagonist. Check to make sure that you are on this path.

What you are doing, in essence, is breaking them down before you build them back up as stronger and better people. The fact that there is a witness to their breakdown is humiliating at first, but it ultimately is only a healthy humbling. And the witnessing creates the bonding well worth the humbling. I guess that's why I feel it's healthy. It is an involuntary act of intimacy. And it gets as its reward a return of intimacy. Each time this happens in your story their relationship becomes stronger.

EXT. TRAIN STATION—RALEIGH, N.C.—DUSK

This is one of those genteel, Southern buildings. Midge is parked out front with the top down and her feet up. A train is at the station. Something catches her eye.

AT THE FRONT OF THE STATION

It's Scott coming out of the building, heading her way. He's limping and he has an anxious look on his face.

Midge is on full alert. She sits up and starts the car.

As Scott gets closer he walks with more urgency. His bloody nose and puffy eye are now visible.

AT THE FRONT OF THE STATION

The doors swing open again and a very badly beaten Boxer and the ENTIRE FRATERNITY come rushing out.

PARKING LOT

Scott is weakening. He looks over his shoulder and stumbles.

Midge jumps out and runs over to him, helping him to the car. But she is not sympathetic. She is angry.

           MIDGE
You had to do it, didn't you?

           SCOTT
It was great.

           MIDGE
You fought fair.

           SCOTT
It was really great.

           MIDGE
Shut up and get in.

> **Story and action interwoven.**
>
> Midge lets him have it because this is the kind of risky behavior that cost her brother Lonnie his life. Scott has no idea what's eating her. All of this will make sense to him later when he puts two and two together.

She pushes him over the door. He tumbles into the back seat, ass over tea kettle. She clambers for the wheel.

           MIDGE
What is it with you? What is the big deal about acting tough?

PARKING LOT

The Fraternity charges, yelling a sort of Greek war whoop.

           MIDGE
You think what you did was brave? Let me tell you what it really was.

Midge aims directly at them and floors it. Tires screech.

           MIDGE
It was bullshit. It was testosterone at its worst. And it gets you killed.

People dive everywhere like the parting of the sea.

EXT. CENTRAL AVENUE—RALEIGH—CONTINUOUS

Midge wheels out into traffic, her anger building. Scott tries to sit up and grasp what's got her so pissed-off.

> MIDGE
> Which you may think is cool, but which is so not cool you'll never know, and which won't help your sister one bit. What do you think she's going to say when they lower you into the ground? That she loves you more because you died for her? *(very angry)* She'll hate you for dying! Because being your sister can be the most important thing in her life! And when you're stupid enough to get killed, you take that away from her.

Scott may be puzzled by this speech now but he will put it together later and call her on her crap. She will do the same with him.

The real benefit of this protagonist and co-protagonist relationship is their ability to act as truth sayers to each other.

She leans on the horn, passing an old truck.

> MIDGE
> Then you're not a little sister anymore. You're not anything anymore. *(gritted teeth)* I gotta tell you, I didn't come along for this kind of shit.

Scott sits in stunned silence.

INT. LADIES ROOM—CITY HOSPITAL WARD—NIGHT

Red, in a hospital gown, stares at herself at the basin mirror. On one side of her, a Tiny Woman washes fingerprinting ink off her hands. On the other side, a Hooker fights with the "push" in her push-up bra.

> TINY WOMAN
> She sure likes looking at herself. Looking that much isn't right.

Red traces her features with a finger.

> TINY WOMAN
> You don't see me looking at myself all the time.

> HOOKER
> You're too short to look at yourself.

> TINY WOMAN
> You look at yourself like that and you turn to salt.

> HOOKER
> What? You don't turn into salt for looking at yourself. You turn into salt for looking at a city.

> RED
> What's your name?

> TINY WOMAN
> My name?

> RED
> I need a name.

Red has watched the Hooker, then looks down inside her own gown at her breasts, and examines them.

HOOKER
I got lots of names.

TINY WOMAN
Then give her one of yours, because she
can't have mine.

Red bends over, looks underneath her gown.

RED
A name for a redhead.

INT. HOSPITAL WARD—NIGHT

Everyone's asleep. Red walks along the long row of
beds. At the foot of every bed is a CLIPBOARD with
the patient's I.D. and condition. Red takes a clipboard
as she passes a bed.

RED
Sally Burnett. Sally. Sal.

She passes the next bed, takes that clipboard and
leaves the other. She walks on.

RED
Betty Lou Bender. Betty Lou. Betty.

She reaches the next bed, and takes the next board.

RED
Marissa Martinez. With red hair? I don't
think so.

She reaches her bed and reads her clipboard.

RED
How can I be a Jane Doe?

She goes to the next bed, and the next clipboard.

> RED
>
> I'm not stupid. I can figure this out. I've
> got to remember something.

She moves over to the barred window and looks out
at the city.

> RED
>
> Somebody out there must miss me.

EXT. WASHINGTON, D.C.—NIGHT

The city glistens. We become aware of police radio
static.

> SCOTT
>
> I can't believe this is happening.

INT. SCOTT'S VW—PULLED OVER—HIGHWAY—
NIGHT

Midge sits at the wheel. The city is in the background.
As are wildly colorful, spinning lights of a highway
patrol car.

> MIDGE
>
> Let me ask you something. As an ambu-
> lance driver, can't you give yourself some-
> thing to chill the fuck out?

EXT. HIGHWAY—HIGHWAY PATROL CAR—NIGHT

The Highway Patrol Car is parked behind Scott's VW.
The Highway Patrolman finishes writing up a ticket,
then walks back to Midge's window. He hands her
the prize.

HIGHWAY PATROLMAN
This is your warrant, Miss Delisa. You can
pay it in person or mail it in from New
York. Sign here.

MIDGE
Thanks.

She signs.

HIGHWAY PATROLMAN
Have you been celebrating, Miss Delisa?

MIDGE
Celebrating?

She looks at him, confused. He holds her license up
to her.

MIDGE
It's today?

HIGHWAY PATROLMAN
What's got you in such a hurry you forgot
a day like today?

SCOTT
Actually, I can explain, officer...

HIGHWAY PATROLMAN
I didn't ask you. I asked her.

MIDGE
His kid sister's a runaway. We think she's
in D.C. now.

HIGHWAY PATROLMAN
How long have you been chasing her?

MIDGE
Since last night.

HIGHWAY PATROLMAN
Straight? No sleep?

She shakes her head "no." He leans in.

HIGHWAY PATROLMAN
Okay, here's what we're going to do. Since you people are tourists here, I'm going to point out a few of the our local attractions. *(pointing North)* You see those lights on the horizon over there? That's Washington, D.C. The West Wing. George W. The Supreme Court. *The City Jail. (Scott dies)* Now, you see those lovely pink neon lights right over here? That's a motel. Granted, it's not listed in the Historical Registry, but it's not Bubba's Playhouse, either.

They all stare at the crappy pink glow in the distance.

> Circumstances—the effect of the plot on their actions—create yet another turn in their journey. **Make things quickly spin out of your protagonist's control.**
>
> In this case they will be forced to spend the night together in the Pink Motel. Much can happen during the night at the Pink Motel.
>
> **Find your Pink Motel.**

HIGHWAY PA-
TROLMAN
It's your choice where you want to spend the night, folks. Either way, sister or no sister, no one's driving anymore 'til the sun comes up.

MIDGE
I love pink.

HIGHWAY PATROLMAN
Good answer. Happy Birthday.

They nod "good night." She puts the car in gear, and pulls away slowly, heading for the pink lights.

INT. PINK MOTEL—NIGHT

Scott and Midge stand in the middle of a small, dingy room.

SCOTT
And a cell is worse, how?

MIDGE
(looks around)
We need a plan for the morning. We can't just walk into Washington and expect to trip over you sister.

> Their bickering continues throughout this scene but it is really an expression of their fear. Neither one is experienced in what is about to happen to them tonight.
>
> **Your journey must continue to force your characters to face those things that make them uncomfortable or afraid.**

SCOTT
I know that. I have a plan. You take the bed, I'll take the couch...

There is no couch.

SCOTT
...the floor.

MIDGE
There's enough bed. You have a plan?

SCOTT
You mind if I sleep on this side? I can't sleep on that side.

> MIDGE

Your plan?

She goes in the bathroom; turns on the light and heat lamp.

> SCOTT

My plan. We check the train station right away while people's memories are fresh. You go ahead and shower first. Then all the youth hostels. Then all the hospitals.

> MIDGE

We should start at the police station. You shower first.

> SCOTT

The police? We're trying to avoid them, remember? We're trying to find Red first.

> MIDGE

Maybe they already found her. We'd be pretty stupid running around looking for someone who's in custody.

> SCOTT

She hasn't been caught. I know that. You don't want to shower first?

> MIDGE

Knock yourself out.

> SCOTT

Great. I'm ripe.

He grabs his overnight bag and goes into the bathroom. She goes to the bed and sits on it and bounces. Then lies flat on her back and savors the feel. She hasn't felt a bed like this in a long time. She picks up the TV remote control.

DISSOLVE TO

INT. BATHROOM

Scott has showered and is shaving at the sink. He checks his swollen eye, then smiles.

> SCOTT
> I know...I know...but you should see him.

He thinks about Red, and his smile fades.

> SCOTT
> Be careful, Red. Give me a chance to catch up.

INT. MOTEL ROOM

Midge is trying to fathom an episode of "The Apprentice." Scott comes out wearing his surgical scrub pants.

> SCOTT
> I feel human again. Here's my scrub shirt. I use them for pj's... if you want to sleep in it.

She takes the shirt and looks at it. She hasn't slept in anything but street clothes in a long, long time.

> SCOTT
> What?

> MIDGE
> Nothing.

She goes into the bathroom. Scott picks up the remote and flips stations. He stops at Paris Hilton.

INT. BATHROOM

Midge is in the tub. She gently washes her arms and shoulders. Then her neck. Then, tentatively, the rest of her body underwater. It's as if she's surprised it's still there. She cannot remember the last time she has been this intimate with her own body. She closes her eyes and rests.

INT. MOTEL ROOM

Scott paces. He can't settle down. The TV drones on as he grabs the phone book and flips through it, looking for an address. He checks his watch and looks over at the bathroom.

INT. BATHROOM—ANOTHER TIME—ANOTHER PLACE

A TUB FULL OF BUBBLES. A beautiful, LITTLE Midge, age four, sits in it facing LITTLE LONNIE, age six. They play with a sponge birthday cake. Little Lonnie dollops soap suds on each candle tip, as if they were the candles' flames. She draws in a huge breath, ready to blow them out, but he stops her.

LITTLE LONNIE
Not yet! I have to sing first!

And he sings an animated version of Happy Birthday as she holds her breath for all she's worth. Finally he finishes the song and she lets the soap suds "flames" have it with all her might. Bubbles fly everywhere.

LITTLE MIDGE
Birthday!!! Birthday!!!! Birthday!!!!!!

SCOTT
Midge? Midge?

INT. BATHROOM

Midge snaps out of it. Sits up in her tub.

SCOTT
You okay in there?

MIDGE
Yeah. Fine.

> I want to do a couple of things in this bath scene.
>
> First, I want to see that the experience of a bath is something she has not had since she left home. And second, being reminded that it was her birthday brings back a memory of her beloved brother whom she now misses terribly.

But she's not fine. She unravels the soaked bandage on her hand, and stares at her stitches. Fascinated. Saddened.

INT. MOTEL ROOM

Bored, Scott sees the plastic bag from the gas station with Midge's things in it. He checks it out, going through her old clothes. They smell. He puts them back, disgusted.

INT. BATHROOM

The water spins down the drain in a whirlpool. Next to the tub Midge's towel drops to her bare feet. As the camera PANS UP her legs, the hem of Scott's shirt drops into frame.

She stands in Scott's shirt, self-consciously assessing herself in the mirror, as if the pretty girl she sees isn't really her. Isn't really pretty.

> MIDGE

You're not White. You're not Black. What are you, anyway?

INT. MOTEL ROOM

The bathroom door opens, silhouetting Midge in its frame. Scott can only stare. She may not be White; she may not be Black; but what she is, is breathtaking. She turns out the bathroom light, walks to her side of the bed, and sits down softly. Their conversation is awkward.

> SCOTT

Nice bath?

> MIDGE

I guess. *(sees notes)* What's that?

> SCOTT

Addresses. Police station. Youth hostels.

> MIDGE

Good.

> SCOTT

Yeah. We'll start early, okay? I always get up early. It's the doctor in me.

> MIDGE

Right.

He hits the remote control and the TV goes black, dropping the room into the ambient light of the parking lot lights outside. After a long pause Midge lies down tentatively.

A sweet note that she cares. Her awareness of her own caring is something new.

> MIDGE
> It wouldn't be so bad if they caught her,
> you know. At least she'd be safe. And you'd
> be there for her.

They each crowd his or her edge of the bed, facing away from one another. Facing their own mixed feelings instead.

INT. HOSPITAL WARD—CORRIDOR—NIGHT

All is quiet. A MAN mops the floors.

NURSES STATION

The NIGHT NURSE is half-watching a late night movie on her tiny TV, and half-reading a PEOPLE magazine.

INT. HOSPITAL WARD—NIGHT

The familiar row of beds. Red is in the foreground. She sleeps fitfully, tossing and turning wildly.

INT. TRAIN LAVATORY—NIGHT—FLASHBACK

Boxer has Red pinned against the wall, molesting her. She fights him off with all her strength.

INT. HOSPITAL WARD—NIGHT

Red's face clenches in anger. She's covered with sweat, growling and struggling with every ounce of courage.

FIST SLAMS VIOLENTLY DOWN

INT. MOTEL ROOM—NIGHT

Midge's fist is slamming Scott in the chest. He wakes in shock and tries to defend himself.

> MIDGE
> No! No! Lonnie!

> SCOTT
> What the?!

Midge is in the throes of her own terrible nightmare. She swings her arm in stiff arcs, screaming painfully, as if her hand were at the end of a puppet string.

> MIDGE
> Stop! You're killing him! Lonnie! You're killing Lonnie! Nooo!

Scott rolls on top of her and pins her to the bed.

> SCOTT
> Hey, Midge! Wake up! Wake up!

Midge "comes to" and breaks free and takes another swing at him. He catches her hand just inches from his face.

> MIDGE
> Let go of me! Get off of me!

> SCOTT
> Hold on! Will you hold on!

> MIDGE
> Let go, dammit! What are you doing?

> SCOTT
> I'm not doing anything. You, on the other hand, have been beating the crap out of me.

> MIDGE

What?

He releases her gently, noticing the stitches on her hand.

> SCOTT
> You were screaming and punching.

She pulls her hand away, and moves away.

> SCOTT
> It was one hell of a dream.

> MIDGE
> It wasn't just a dream.

INT. HOSPITAL WARD—NIGHT

Red sits in her bed, shaking uncontrollably. Panicked.

> MIDGE (V.O.)
> Dreams are things that *don't* happen.

> The device of carrying an action from Red's scene into Scott's scene is especially cinematic and ties the two stories and plots together visually.
>
> This creates the epigenetic flow we aim for, rather than the episodic static flow.

We have now reached another critical point in our emotional structure.

What we don't want to happen now is for this clever bickering to go on forever. Discipline and restraint are key here. We don't let them get too comfortable. They still have a way to go before they commit to each other emotionally, so we have to tax them a few more times. We use the plot to do this. We want to stir things up again and raise the ante. The secret to the combination of plot and story at this point is this the plot problems you devise (roadblocks, broken legs, old lovers, etc.) must create not just greater physical risk but more importantly greater emotional consequence. The only purpose of the plot device is to up the emotional costs. Make the consequences of their responses to the physical challenges more serious. Don't lose sight of this in this section or you will drift from the middle to the muddle.

By the end of the next ten pages or so—three or four good scenes—we want each one to hit the wall and either blow up or give up or both. It will be at that point where they will confess their fears and desires and commit to staying together until the bitter end. This then turns the story in a whole new direction, one that is about their relationship. The action/murder mystery story turns to a love story just as we had planned all along.

We should take a look at our second act chart and see where we are. You will notice that in the plot (those notes above the line) things get worse. In the story (notes below the line) there is tremendous emotional turmoil as a result. See if that's where you are now. Add twists and turns or roadblocks or broken legs or a smelly foot in the stew if you must, but do something in your plot now to take their anxiety to the next higher level.

Your new goal will be to bring them to your "tent pole" scene where they can finally trust each other.

The "tent pole" scene must cause them to be honest with each other in a deeper, more intimate fashion. This brings them closer together, but it also illuminates a deeper complexity. Though they are learning to trust one another, they are not quite sure how to learn to trust their own instincts—that is, their feelings toward one another. Trusting a person, and trusting how you feel about a person are two completely different facets of the love emotion. Their reflective values create distinctly unique strengths. The trust they have for each other may become the basis of their love, and consequently their love story. But the lack of trust they have in their ability to love can be ruinous if not dealt with soon. Another way of thinking of this is that their feelings of love scare them as much as they excite them. This is understandable because there has been a lack of love in their lives in which they could put their trust. This ambivalence is another complication we'll throw at them later as they adjust to the comfort of their love.

Here is the next sequence that leads to my "tent pole" scene. I raise the anxiety level for them by making them aware of the "life-and-death" nature Red's crisis.

Indirection – *continued* – The Second Act

EXT. PINK MOTEL—MORNING—ESTABLISHING

The Pink Motel doesn't look any sexier in the morning than it did in the neon night. It's still early. Still quiet.

INT. PINK MOTEL—MORNING

Still quiet in here, too. They are asleep.

Sunlight filters through the well-worn drapes, casting bands of peach across Midge's cheeks. Scott's face is buried in Midge's beautiful, pitch black hair.

She is coiled in a fetal position, inside the semi-circle of his larger fetal position, her back against his chest. Two small feet. Two larger ones. Tied in a knot.

Midge's scarred hand, slender, fragile, changed forever, holds the strong arm Scott has wrapped around her.

Her soft eyes open sleepily. Happily. Then close softly again. Then they SNAP OPEN again when she realizes they are sleeping in an embrace. She tries to glance behind her without moving her head. It doesn't work. She looks down.

Scott's hand is innocently cupping her exposed breast. Midge feels the blood rush to her face. And everywhere else. She tries to steal another look at him. He's sound asleep.

WIDER

Midge looks down again, and holds her breath. She gently places her hand on top of his and begins to remove it. Then stops. And puts it back and holds it on her breast. She closes her eyes for a second. A long, long second.

ON SCOTT

Still completely out of it.

ON MIDGE

She opens her eyes, then finally, slowly lifts his hand and slips out of his caress, and out of bed. She holds her breath, and her breast as well, as she studies him. He is beautiful. Bare from the hips up. Serene. Edible.

CLOSE UP OF MIDGE AT THE BATHROOM SINK

Splashes cold water on her face.

CLOSE UP OF SCOTT

He wakes slowly. Rolls over. No Midge.

> **Beat One**
>
> This is a critical romantic reflection for her. It demonstrates her desire without having to face any consequences yet. His turn comes shortly.

EXT. PINK MOTEL—MORNING

Midge sits on the car sipping a cup of vending machine coffee. Scott opens the drapes in the motel window behind her, and takes her in.

INT. MOTEL ROOM—CONTINUOUS

He stares at her. Beautiful. Mysterious.

> **Beat Two**
>
> Scott's tells us that he is attracted to her. Their love is developing and we create a rooting interest.

SCOTT
What do people do to people?

INT. POLICE STATION—DETECTIVE'S AREA—DAY

Scott and Midge are seated in front of a beat-up desk covered with wire baskets and folders. An equally beat-up Detective Rose rummages around a few feet away, quarreling with himself.

DET. ROSE
I just had it. This is so frustrating.

Scott and Midge stare at each other. Deep in thought.

DET. ROSE
Finally.

He comes back to his desk.

> **Beat Three**
>
> Now they give each other the look and in the gentlest of ways express a softening and an accepting. Their feelings are complicated and naturally a little tentative. We, the audience, are now with them in their attempt to figure love out.

DET. ROSE
Well, no positive I.D. has been made, but we're waiting to talk to a Jane Doe in city hospital. Could be your sister.

SCOTT
In the hospital?

DET. ROSE
That guy from the train, William Boxer, his wallet was found in her possession. That doesn't make her guilty, of course, but it does make her our only suspect.

MIDGE
What's wrong with her?

DET. ROSE
She and a lot of other people were hurt in
some kind of riot outside an abortion clinic.

SCOTT
Abortion clinic? Can we see her?

DET. ROSE
I'd like nothing more.

INT. HOSPITAL WARD—NURSES
STATION—DAY

The place is bustling. Scott, Midge,
and Det. Rose wait patiently. The
Day Nurse, Holly, approaches
them grimly.

HOLLY
I'm afraid you're going to
have to see the doctor, Pete.

DET. ROSE
Give me a break, Holly.

HOLLY
Sorry. He says he wants to talk to you and
the family first.

DET. ROSE
They may not even be her family.

HOLLY
He's waiting in his office.

> The plot thickens and
> pulls them in deeper. The
> commitment gets tougher to
> keep for your characters.
>
> The news just gets worse
> for them. And I say "them"
> on purpose because they are
> both emotionally involved
> in Red's welfare now.

INT. DOCTOR'S OFFICE—CONTINUOUS

Scott, Midge, and Det. Rose face DR. Stinson across his desk.

DOCTOR STINSON
The patient you're asking to see, one we know only as Jane Doe, expired during the night.

Scott feels his knees flex. Midge grabs his arm.

MIDGE
Expired?

DOCTOR STINSON
Would you like to sit down?

Scott waves him off, and tries to breathe again.

DOCTOR STINSON
According to yesterday's admission records, her head wound was so severe that she didn't know who she was or where she came from. She was completely amnesic.

SCOTT
Jesus.

DOCTOR STINSON
Apparently she suffered a cerebral hemorrhage in her sleep. Her body has been moved downstairs to the morgue.

> **Step by step things get a lot worse before they are going to get better.**
>
> The bad news keeps coming. Scott's truly scared. Midge steps forward to take the punch for him as a sign that she's in this with him. Her reaction is the result of the plot forcing an emotional response to the life and death nature of the plot.
>
> **Pull your protagonist and co-protagonist together by this point, too.**

DET. ROSE

(gently) It would help if one of you would make an identification for us. For the record.

MIDGE

I can do that.

SCOTT

No. I will. I want to see my sister.

INT. MORGUE—DAY

Scott, Midge, and Det. Rose are led into an ante room by an Attendant. The room is completely empty. And cold.

ATTENDANT

Be right back.

They can hear him whistling in the other room. After a minute, he comes back in, wheeling a corpse on a gurney.

ATTENDANT

Have you ever done this before?

It is a ludicrous question. Midge looks at him in disbelief.

ATTENDANT

I just want you to be prepared.

SCOTT

Just do it.

The Attendant pulls the sheet away from the face.

Scott and Midge look down. Detective Rose watches them for a reaction.

ON SCOTT

Staring. Not knowing how to react. Then, tears come.

> SCOTT
> Dear God.

THE FACE OF THE CORPSE

The WOMAN is a stranger.

> SCOTT
> It's not her.

INT. HOSPITAL WARD—DAY

Scott, Midge, and Det. Rose come out of the elevator onto the main floor. They head for the exit.

> SCOTT
> Where do we go from here?

> MIDGE
> Ladies' room. Meet you outside.

Midge carefully doubles back to Nurse Holly.

> MIDGE
> Holly? Did our...sister leave any personal belongings?

> HOLLY
> There wouldn't be anything here. All personal items are sent to the Police Property Room.

MIDGE
Can I take a last look anyway?

HOLLY
(sympathetic)
Ward B, right over there.

INT. HOSPITAL WARD—DAY

Midge comes in and looks down the row of beds. Some empty. Some occupied. One stripped bare. She goes to it.

Midge looks around the stripped bed, then sits on a rumpled bed next to it, thinking. A PATIENT watches her.

The protagonist is stunned by this turn of events but the co-protagonist is not. Keep your co-protagonist more "on-point" through this next section than the protagonist. It is logical because the protagonist is suffering emotionally at a deeper level than his co-protagonist. **The co-protagonist won't let the protagonist give up and go home. She finds a reason to keep on going.**

MARISSA
She died last night.

MIDGE
Yeah. (goes to her) Have you been here long? (looks at name) Betty Lou?

MARISSA
Since yesterday. And my name's Marissa.

BETTY LOU
I'm Betty Lou.

Midge goes to the next bed, and reads Betty Lou's chart.

The co-protagonist takes a strong part in the solution. Make sure yours has a chance to do this, too.

It serves the plot, but more importantly it deepens her commitment to her relationship with the protagonist. Make your co-protagonist clever.

> MIDGE
> Then who's Sally Burnett?

> SALLY
> That's me.

Sally is in the bed next to Betty Lou. Midge jokes with them.

> MIDGE
> Hey guys, you're all in the wrong bed.

Then her smile fades and she shakes her head in disbelief.

> MIDGE
> No. Everybody's chart is on the wrong bed.

She goes to the rumpled bed, and lays her hand on it.

> MIDGE
> Then Jane Doe isn't dead. She slept here...in this bed. Where is she?

> BETTY LOU
> Probably in the bathroom counting her freckles.

"Freckles" does it. Midge heads for the door, but...

> SALLY
> Uh uh. She's gone. Bailed in the middle of the night. Totally freaked. Mumbling and shaking. (flashes a pinkie ring) Traded this for my bus ticket.

EXT. GREYHOUND BUS TERMINAL—SCOTT'S CAR—DAY

Scott sits behind the wheel staring at Red's ring. Midge comes out of the building and runs up to the car carrying a bus schedule. She gets in.

> MIDGE
> It left for Pittsburg at six a.m. But it stops everywhere. The clerk said we can catch it in Harrisburg. He also said a girl with her head wrapped-up waited all night for it.

MONTAGE

EXT. VIRGINIA HIGHWAY—VW—DAY—MOS

The VW speeds by. Midge has her head back, sunning. He's sipping a Coke. A HIGHWAY SIGN reads: BALTIMORE.

EXT. ANOTHER HIGHWAY—DAY—MOS
Midge looks over at him. He looks back. A SIGN READS: LANCASTER, PA.—20 MILES. She checks her map.

EXT. ANOTHER HIGHWAY—DAY—MOS

She's driving now. He's eating a hot dog.

EXT. ANOTHER HIGHWAY—OFF RAMP—DAY—MOS

The VW turns off, passes a SIGN: WELCOME TO HARRISBURG.

EXT. CENTRAL HARRISBURG—DAY—MOS

Midge is still behind the wheel at a stoplight. Scott asks for directions. The PEDESTRIAN points straight ahead.

EXT. GREYHOUND BUS TERMINAL—HARRIS-BURG—DAY

The VW pulls up and Scott and Midge hop out and run in.

INT. BUS TERMINAL—DAY—MOS

Scott and Midge talk to A SUPERVISOR.

EXT. BUS TERMINAL—DAY—MOS

THE BUS from Washington pulls in. The Supervisor leads Scott and Midge over to it. The door swings open and the Supervisor gets on and talks to the DRIVER.

END OF MONTAGE.

EXT. THE BUS—DAY

The Supervisor steps down, clearing the way for Scott.

> SUPERVISOR
> Take a look.

Scott's stomach tightens. Midge gives him a nudge.

INT. BUS—DAY

Close on Scott's face as he comes up into the bus. He looks and squints confused.

EXT. BUS—DAY—CONTINUOUS

Midge waits nervously, trying to see what's going on. After a minute Scott comes down the steps very upset.

SCOTT

The guy said her head was bandaged, right?

MIDGE

Yeah. Why? What?

He storms away. She jumps up into the bus.

INT. BUS—DAY

Midge comes in and sees what he saw.

HER POV

Every seat is occupied with a Sikh, dressed in a pure white robe and matching white turban.

EXT. PARKING LOT—VW—DAY

Scott is pacing in vicious circles. Midge chases after him. He is totally frustrated and takes it out on her.

SCOTT

This is ridiculous. I must be out of my mind.

MIDGE

Do me a favor and get out of your mind and into hers. The doctor said she was amnesic, remember. She's disoriented. She's wandering. If she got off at another stop we'll work our way back.

> **The Tent Pole Scene starts its build.**
> This fight leads them to the "tent pole" scene, and to their deeper trust in each other. Let them go at each other. Don't hold back any punches.

SCOTT

All we've been doing is going backwards!

MIDGE

Maybe she saw something familiar... maybe she...

SCOTT

Maybe she wasn't on the bus!

MIDGE

She was on the bus! I know it!

SCOTT

Now you're a psychic.

MIDGE

We didn't get this far on your intuition.

SCOTT

You call this getting far?

MIDGE

Hey, I don't need this! She's your sister. If you don't care about her.

SCOTT

Ah! The "little sister" drill again.

MIDGE

What's that supposed to mean?

SCOTT

All you do is lecture me about the importance of "little sisters." Well I don't like it. I don't like the implication that I failed my sister. If you've got a bitch with your brother about that, settle it with him, not me.

                    MIDGE
You don't know what you're talking about!
You don't know anything about my brother.

                    SCOTT
Let me guess. His name is Lonnie. And
Lonnie got into some kind of trouble. And
you tried to stop him. *(she's shocked)* Your
nightmare last night. You kept screaming,
Lonnie, Lonnie, like somebody was beating him up.

She covers her ears with her hands to shut out the
memory.

                    SCOTT
Probably because of, what was it you called
it, "testosterone bullshit?"

                    MIDGE
STOP IT! Just shut up!

                    SCOTT
You were hitting me like you were trying
to break it up. To stop it.

He sees her wounded hand again and slowly makes
a connection.

                    SCOTT
Your hand...that's how you got hurt.

                    MIDGE
I couldn't stop him.

INT. ER—FLASHBACK—MOS

Lonnie's gurney is wheeled in. Midge is carried in.

> SCOTT
>
> Was that you? In emergency the other
> night? It was, wasn't it?

EXT. BUS STATION—REALITY—DAY

She doesn't want to hear this.

> SCOTT
>
> And that was him. The guy who was
> stabbed.

> MIDGE
>
> Nooo...

INT. BROOKLYN APARTMENT—FLASHBACK

A crowd swarms around Midge who is sprawled
across Lonnie's bloody body, screaming at him to
wake up.

> MIDGE
>
> .....noooooo.

> SCOTT
>
> They couldn't save him.

INT. ER—FLASHBACK—MOS

Scott and Nurse Jamie strap Midge down. She
screams at Scott and spits in his face.

> SCOTT
>
> Is that why you're angry at him? For get-
> ting killed?

EXT. BUS STATION—REALITY—DAY

Midge rushes toward the station. He chases after her.

> SCOTT
>
> For changing you from a little sister to "a nothing."

INT. BUS STATION—REALITY—DAY

They burst through the doors, Scott hot on her heels.

> SCOTT
>
> But he didn't change you when he died. You're the one who thinks there's nothing left of you.

> MIDGE
>
> Just leave me alone.

> SCOTT
>
> You want to run away like a kid. Hide out in the subways.

Midge bolts into the LADIES ROOM.

> SCOTT
>
> But Grand Central isn't Neverland, and you're not a kid anymore. Can't you see that?

INT. LADIES ROOM—CONTINUOUS

She leans against the sink, crying.

> SCOTT
>
> You're a woman, Midge. A very beautiful, very smart, very aggravating woman.

The Turning Point.

Scott is not picking a fight any longer. He has had the epiphany he needs to understand her. With this understanding comes compassion. He says what he says for her benefit, not his own. He puts her well-being above his own. This emotional generosity is always the first sign of true love.

And this signals the beginning of the end to the mystery story and the beginning of the beginning of their love story.

She looks into the mirror, but can't see the person he's talking about. She can only see a broken girl.

> SCOTT
> Why does that scare you so much? What are you so afraid of?

> MIDGE
> I'm not afraid of anything.

The door slowly opens and Scott comes in, calmer.

> SCOTT
> Yeah. You are. You're afraid to forgive him for dying.

> MIDGE
> You're crazy.

> SCOTT
> You stay mad at him. That way you keep him alive.

Scott handles the situation correctly, finally, and gets more than the truth, he gets to fall in love with her. Once Midge can let go of Lonnie, she can live her life with hope instead of pain.

INT. MORGUE—FLASHBACK— NIGHT—MOS

Lonnie's body lies in front of her.

> SCOTT
> It doesn't work that way. It just doesn't. Lonnie is dead.

INT. LADIES ROOM—REALITY—CONTINUOUS

She shakes her head in denial; in pain. He goes to her. It is the moment of truth, and he's careful with it.

> SCOTT
>
> Let him rest in peace. So you can love him
> again.

She bursts. He holds her as she sobs inconsolably.
Letting go of her anger. Letting go of Lonnie.

EXT. WAL-MART TRUCK—PENNSYLVANIA HIGH-
WAY—DAY

Roaring down the road. A noisy, vulgar monster cutting through the heart of peace on earth. Painted on
the driver's door in flashy script is the owner's name
Mr. Lucky.

INT. WAL-MART TRUCK—PENNSYLVANIA HIGH-
WAY—DAY

Red sits next to Mr. Lucky. She checks things out in
the cab. Mr. Lucky sings along to a country song on
the radio.

> MR. LUCKY
> Josie, hunh? That's a
> pretty name. Where're you
> headed, Josie?

> RED
> Harrisburg. That's the
> next big city, right?

> MR. LUCKY
> You run away from home?

Now remind everyone that the protagonist will not be able to rest.

Risky behavior on Red's part and a reminder that her time is running out. This reminds the audience of that, and Midge is about to let the audience know that she hasn't forgotten either.

> RED
> I'm not running away *from* anything. I'm
> running *to*.

> MR. LUCKY
> I see. *To* what?

> RED
> To what ran away from me.

> MR. LUCKY
> If you say so, honey.

> MIDGE
> She's close. I know it, Scott. I can feel it.

EXT. BUS STATION—PARKING LOT—DAY

Scott and Midge walk side-by-side to his VW.

> SCOTT
> Those your instincts again?

> MIDGE
> (defensive)
> Yeah.

He holds up his hands to calm her down.

> SCOTT
> That's a good thing. They got us this far.

> MIDGE
> You call this far?

He looks over to the station, then back to her.

> SCOTT
> From here to there... Yeah, I call that far.

An epiphany now for Midge and a moment of great courage to admit her deep fear.

Notice the difference in the attitude now. The dialog can be just as lovely without being sarcastic or dishonest. The clarity of their feelings helps them face the truth without hurting each other. This is an expressed loving. And they take turns expressing how they feel.

She shakes her head, and looks deeply into his eyes without disguising her vulnerability.

> SCOTT
> What?

> MIDGE
> I don't know. I think I'm more lost than your sister.

This is a tremendous admission for her. Scott knows.

> SCOTT
> This morning, when I woke and you weren't in bed, and I looked outside and saw you sitting on the car with your cigarette and coffee...all alone...I hated what the world had done to you. And I wanted to fight back for you.

She starts to say something, but he goes on, taking her sweet face in his hands.

> SCOTT
> And later, when we were in the morgue waiting for that stupid man to lift the sheet, and I was scared to death to look down, I hated what the world had done to Red. And I wanted to fight back for her, too. And when he raised that sheet, I got that chance. And I made a promise. I promised myself, no matter what it takes, no matter how far I have to go, I will find my sister and bring her safely home. *(beat)* And I promise you, no matter what it takes, no matter how far we have to go, we can find you, too.

> This is the turning point in their story, and the completion of their tent pole scene.

Get them close to the kiss and milk the moment.

Slow time down here and let what has just happened and what has just been revealed to them to sink in. It's subconscious savoring for them and for your audience.

But save the actual kiss for later. This is a tease, but a legitimate one because it promises the audience there is more to come. We want the audience to want them to make love, so that when they do it will be more than a sex scene, it will be a promise of love fulfilled.

She leans in to him longingly.

MIDGE
You know, they don't sell maps for this kind of trip.

And he leans in toward her. Ever closer.

SCOTT
So I've been told.

She brushes her lips against his.

MIDGE
Scott...

SCOTT
Midge...

MIDGE
I've got some questions for that bus driver.

He freezes. The moment has passed. They look to where the bus was parked, but is no longer. Then they see it down the road, swinging onto the highway.

SMASH CUT TO:

And it is at this point that they can trust one another. The turning point in their story takes them from a plot searching for his sister to a story searching for their identity and their relationship. This search changes the film's direction. It is no longer simply an action adventure. It is a love story, and a story about love and how far we have to run to find it. You will notice the tone of the second half of your second act will change, too. The dialog you write will be denser and more earnest in its search for global truths. Decisions your characters make will be based on a higher purpose. This is the beginning of their quest for the person they always wanted to be but were afraid to seek. Every action you give your protagonist and co-protagonist in the second half of the second act must deal with this subtext. It is there, trust me, you just have to find it. The entire purpose of the second half of the second act is to search for and find the goodness within. All the strength that is needed for the climax at the beginning of Act Three is developed in this pursuit.

20

Writing the Script—Act Two, Part Two

Act Two
Part Two: The Direction Inward

Part one of Act Two pushes the protagonist and co-protagonist toward the true memories where the basis for their problems lies. Midge needed to acknowledge true memory by accepting what happened to her brother Lonnie, and she needed to accept that what happened was something she could not have changed. Her brother's fate was her brother's fate. She cannot adopt it as her own. Her own fate awaits her. Her future can only be realized by facing the past. This action is what clears the way for her.

Scott has seen this in her, in fact he facilitated the experience, but he has not dealt with his own past yet. In *Witness*, Book admitted before Rachel could that they couldn't make love without a deeper commitment. She gained much from this. Not so much that what he said was the truth, because she already knew that and she was probably already willing to go with him, but that he told her the truth. She learned from him that he would not lie to her to get what he wanted. This gave her the strength to make love to him later without the need for commitment because she had his truth in its stead. And certainly in a way "truth" is the greatest commitment there can be. First he brings the truth to her then she brings a new, stronger experience to him based on that truth.

It is usually better to have the protagonist and the co-protagonist face the past to unlock the future at different times during the story. Make it a one-two punch. They cannot both have the same epiphany at the same time. It just so happens in my script that the co-protagonist faces her past first. It can go either way. The idea is that she is strengthened by her enlightenment now and uses that strength later to help him face his.

If the second half of the second act takes this further it will show that after facing the true past and finding self-forgiveness, that the forgiveness of others will follow. All of this has to be put to the test, of course. And that is the reason we even have a second half of the second act. We put our protagonist and co-protagonist to the test. Big time. This is the part of the script where you will be at your most inventive in terms of plot. You will raise the stakes for everyone. And you will be pointing the way to a climax. But the course they must take will be through the gut.

It is not enough at the midpoint of the act, that is the "tent pole" point, for the protagonist to merely promise to do great things. Now he has to do them. There is no turning back. And no matter how hard he thought the trip would be, it is your job to make sure it is twice as hard. He is ill-equipped to meet the tasks you are to place at his feet. In most instances during the next twenty to thirty pages he will have to rely on his instincts more than his intellect. Eventually the reliance on intuition is the greatest freedom a man can have, because it stems from faith and offers hope. To get to this point, though, your protagonist has to go through the four Stages of Mastery.

THE FOUR STAGES OF MASTERY:

1. *Unconscious incompetence*
2. *Conscious incompetence*
3. *Conscious competence*
4. *Unconscious competence*

If we look at your protagonist at the beginning of your script and follow him to the end of your script we should be able to see him at all stages of mastery. He starts out as someone who is incompetent for the journey he is about to take, and he doesn't believe he is anything but competent. This is the first stage: unconscious incompetence. He's incompetent and he doesn't know it. At the end of Act One and into the first half of Act Two he gradually becomes aware of his incompetence. This is the second stage: conscious incompetence. In the second half of Act Two he will seek competence in order to reach his goal and he will be aware when he reaches the level of competence needed to defeat his enemy. This is the third stage: conscious competence. At the end of Act Two and all the way into Act Three what he learned and used to defeat the enemy is absorbed through that experience. He is not consciously forcing anything. He has become unconsciously competent, which is the fourth stage of mastery. The change has been complete because it is no longer merely change, it is now growth. Change is the victory and growth is the reward.

REMEMBER—In the first half of your script the plot is driving the story. The nature of the emotional structure and internal character disclosure is reactive. Now in the second half of your script the story will drive the plot and the emotional structure and internal character development will become more active. This is a result of your characters coming out of their denial and taking responsibility for their lives. It is change in action. Watch that your characters do this.

We rejoin Midge and Scott now where we left them at the Greyhound bus station about to kiss. Then Midge realizes the urgency of the moment. The logic of the next section is to relieve the deeper, more complex emotional scenes for a couple of minutes and return to the action plot. But notice how the story is forcing the plot now.

Indirection—continued—
Act Two—Part Two

                    MIDGE
        Scott...

                    SCOTT
        Midge...

                    MIDGE
        I've got some questions for that bus driver.

He freezes. The moment has passed. They look to where the bus was parked, but is no longer. Then they see it down the road, swinging onto the highway.

                                    SMASH CUT TO:

EXT. HIGHWAY—DAY

The VW pulls into the traffic. The bus is far ahead. Scott puts the pedal to the metal.

He weaves from lane to lane, cutting people off in his attempt to make up the distance.

INT. GREYHOUND BUS—CONTINUOUS

The Bus Driver hauls along, above the speed limit, relaxed. The rows of Sikhs are calm and quiet. Almost meditative.

EXT. HIGHWAY—DAY—CONTINUOUS

Two trucks block Scott's VW from getting any closer to the bus. He flashes his lights. Nothing.

INT. SCOTT'S VW—CONTINUOUS

He's looking for his options. They aren't good. He swerves onto the outer emergency lane and guns it, kicking up gravel.

> SCOTT
> Your questions better be good.

> MIDGE
> Don't start.

EXT. HIGHWAY—DAY—CONTINUOUS

The VW roars past the trucks as one drifts danger-ously close to Scott, just to bust his balls. Scott stays with it.

INT. SCOTT'S VW—CONTINUOUS

They pull alongside the truck. Midge looks up to the Truck Driver, smiles, and flips him off.

The truck comes EVEN CLOSER, as the Truck Driver flips Midge off. Scott can't believe it. He punches it.

> SCOTT
> Jesus! This is just a thought, but have you ever considered restraining yourself?

EXT. HIGHWAY—DAY—CONTINUOUS

The VW barely slips by the trucks, scraping the center divider, sparks fly. Scott swerves back onto the fast lane and guns it. Other cars get out of his way.

INT. SCOTT'S VW—CONTINUOUS

They can see the Greyhound bus ahead of them. Scott maneuvers into another lane and pushes it dangerously.

INT. BUS—DAY—CONTINUOUS

The Sikhs are in their zone. The Bus Driver cruises. Checks his side view mirror, and sees the VW coming up on him fast.

EXT. HIGHWAY—DAY—CONTINUOUS

The VW closes the gap, swooping past a slower car, within reach of the bus.

                    SCOTT
          Now to get him to pull over.

                    MIDGE
          That's easy. There's a universal signal for it.

                    SCOTT
          Well I certainly hope it works better than
          the universal signal you gave that truck
          driver.

EXT. HIGHWAY—DAY—CONTINUOUS

The VW speeds alongside the Greyhound bus now. The Sikhs are staring at them curiously.

INT. BUS—DAY—CONTINUOUS

The Bus Driver sees the VW is trying to get his attention.

INT. Scott's VW—CONTINUOUS

Scott's tense at the wheel. He inches closer.

> MIDGE
> Good. Just stay even with him.

EXT. HIGHWAY—DAY

They pull up next to the Bus Driver and Midge smiles at him. He smiles back.

INT. VW—HIGHWAY—CONTINUOUS

Scott can't see what's happening.

> SCOTT
> What's going on? He see you?

> MIDGE
> Oh, yeah.

INT. GREYHOUND BUS—CONTINUOUS

The Driver looks down, mesmerized by Midge's beautiful smile. Then, slowly but surely, she lifts up her blouse, exposing her breasts to him, fully and completely.

EXT. GREYHOUND BUS—CONTINUOUS

Sikhs are smashed against the windows, mouths agape.

INT. SCOTT'S VW—CONTINUOUS

Scott sees what she's doing, but not what she's showing.

> SCOTT
> I gotta tell you, I like the other signal better.

EXT. GREYHOUND BUS—DAY

The Driver leers at her breasts, then winks at Midge and makes one of those disgusting tongue-licking gestures.

EXT. VW—CONTINUOUS

Midge smiles and nods and gestures for him to pull over.

INT. VW—CONTINUOUS

Midge pulls down her shirt and faces forward. Her smile fades. She takes out her picture of Red.

> MIDGE
> Get in front of him and pull over. He'll follow.

Scott glares at her, but she won't look back.

EXT. HIGHWAY—DAY

Scott pulls in front of the bus, over to the side of the road. The bus follows, just as she said it would, and stops.

INT. VW—HIGHWAY EMERGENCY LANE—CONTINUOUS

He reaches to turn off the engine. She puts her hand on his.

> MIDGE
>
> Keep it running. I won't be long.

> SCOTT
>
> I don't think so. I don't like this.

> MIDGE
>
> You don't have to like it. That wasn't part of our deal.

This is considerably different in tone than their scene earlier in Act Two at the train station when they didn't care about one another. Now he cares that she would bare her breasts so casually. He's been intimate with them/her and it matters to him now. And he worries about her safety, and she acknowledges it.

> SCOTT
>
> That signal wasn't part of the deal, either. You doing this all by yourself wasn't part of the deal.

> MIDGE
>
> You don't like what I'm doing?

> SCOTT
>
> I don't like how I feel when I see what you're doing. And I don't like you going back there all alone.

Eye to eye. A long beat. Then she turns and goes.

> MIDGE
>
> One minute. If I'm not back by then..

> SCOTT
> (calls out)
>
> Keep your freaking shirt on!

EXT. HIGHWAY—BUS—DAY—CONTINUOUS

Midge runs up to the bus as the door swings open.

INT. GREYHOUND BUS—CONTINUOUS

Midge bounds up the steps to the Bus Driver. The Sikhs mob forward, staring anxiously at Midge and her breasts. She holds up a picture of Red for everyone to see. She's wired.

> BUS DRIVER
> I get the feeling this has nothing to do with your titties.

> MIDGE
> This girl got on your bus in D.C. and off again before you reached Harrisburg.

> BUS DRIVER
> And?

> MIDGE
> She'll die if I don't find her.

> BUS DRIVER
> And?

> MIDGE
> You may be the last one to have seen her. You may be her last hope.

> BUS DRIVER
> I may be her last hope?

> MIDGE
> I don't believe I said that.

> SIKH ONE
> Wal-mart.

Midge and the Bus Driver look at Sikh One, not understanding.

                    SIKH ONE
        With her hand.

                    BUS DRIVER
        Wal-mart with her hand?

Sikh One looks at her friends. They all stick out their thumbs as if they're hitchhiking.

                                        SMASH CUT TO:

EXT. TIGHT ON THE FACES OF SCOTT AND MIDGE—DAY

Their jaws have dropped. They can't believe what they see.

EXT. WAL-MART DISTRIBUTION CENTER—CRANE SHOT—DAY

The camera rises to reveal hundreds of Wal-mart trucks in precise patterns, loading and unloading and circling the biggest fucking warehouse they have ever seen. The trucks pass in front of them, this way and that, as if playing some twisted version of a shell game. They watch this truck. They watch that truck. This truck. That truck.

EXT. ROAD—WAL-MART TRUCK—DAY

Mr. Lucky's Wal-mart Truck pulls over to the side of the road.

INT. WAL-MART TRUCK—DAY

Mr. Lucky unbuckles his seat belt and stretches.

> The juxtaposition of the number of trucks and the one with Red is compelling. **Look for these kinds of intercuts whenever you can to heighten the danger.**

> RED
>
> What are we doing?

> MR. LUCKY
>
> Federal safety regulations says I gotta take
> a break every four hours. I take a little nap.
> You might as well, too.

He gets out of the truck, sits on the running board,
pulls off his shoes and wiggles his toes. She gets out
her door and climbs down.

> RED
>
> How far are we from Harrisburg?

> MR. LUCKY
>
> Hour maybe. My feet hurt from driving.
> Imagine if I had to walk? You leaving?

> RED
>
> I don't know, maybe take a walk, check
> things out.

She walks along her side of the truck toward the back.
She looks around. Nothing but miles of farmland.
Suddenly Mr. Lucky comes around his side of the
truck, surprising her.

> MR. LUCKY
>
> Maybe I'll take that walk with you.

> RED
>
> That's okay. Take your nap.

> MR. LUCKY
>
> Young girl all alone. I'd worry.

                    RED
          I like being on my own. It's nice.

                    MR. LUCKY
          Nice, yeah. That's what I like about driv-
          ing a truck. Freedom. No accounting to no-
          body. *(beat)* For a young girl it's danger-
          ous, though.

                    RED
          I can handle it.

                    MR. LUCKY
          I'm sure you can.

                    RED
          Besides, look around. There's noth-
          ing dangerous here.

                    MR. LUCKY
          You never know.

He takes a hold of her. She freezes.

INT. WAL-MART DISTRIBUTION CENTER—DIS-
PATCHING -DAY

Scott and Midge stand in the middle of the most sophisticated dispatching facility in the country. A huge,
liquid digital map of the Middle Atlantic States covers one wall. Technicians man monitors on ever desk,
barking into their headsets. The facility manager,
Alan Mendes, joins them.

                    MENDES
          We notified every truck in the region. So
          far no one's seen her.

> **Keep the danger real in your plot.**
> This is the ticking clock Scott and Midge are fighting against.

MIDGE
You know where every truck is at all times?

MENDES
Barring catastrophe.

Mendes mans a computer and punches up a map of
the area. We see Eastern Pennsylvania, New Jersey,
New York. Scott and Midge move closer.

SCOTT
So you'd know which trucks were in the
area at the time she was seen getting a ride.

He keeps punching the keys. A tighter map comes
up.

MENDES
If someone gave her a ride—against company regulations—it would have been one
of eleven trucks.

We see ELEVEN LITTLE DOTS appear on the map.
Then he types in the time of the incident 11:45 a.m.

MENDES
And, if your information is accurate, that
she was headed East out of York just before twelve hundred hours, that cuts it to
six eastbound trucks. We already talked to
four of those six, and they haven't seen her.
We haven't reached the other two yet.

MIDGE
Why not?

MENDES
Well, 8895 should be eating lunch. And

5932's been on the road since five so it's his nap time.

                    MIDGE
Lunch and naps.

                    MENDES
Federal regs. You've got to take your breaks.

                    SCOTT
I wish we could get a fucking break.

> This is the kind of twist you have to look for in your plot and story.
>
> The idea is to use her frustrated emotions regarding her brother's murder to go back to her "old ways" of deceit. She will learn her old ways don't work anymore. And it's a costly lesson.

Midge studies the map *intently*. We see what she sees: PHILADEL-PHIA, PA. She CLOSES HER EYES and see the YELLOW NOTE with the message: Rico. HABANA TOWN. SO. PHILLY.

MIDGE
Where are we now?

MENDES
                    (points to map)
                Here.

                    MIDGE
And those two trucks. Where are they headed?

                    MENDES
Jersey. 8895's got Newark. 5932's got the boardwalk. Atlantic City

                    MIDGE
                (grabs Scott)
Let's go.

                    SCOTT
Go where?

                    MENDES
You don't know which truck it is.

                    MIDGE
Doesn't matter. One of them's our truck,
and it's hours ahead of us. We can make
up some of that time if we go now.

She draws an imaginary line on the screen with her
fingertip toward Philadelphia.

                    MIDGE
We head as far east as we can before we
have to decide between going north to Newark or south to the Shore. Then we call
these guys and they let us know which way
we should go.

It makes sense to Mendes. Scott hesitates.

                    MIDGE
Come on! We can't just sit here and wait
when we could be gaining on them.

Mendes hands Scott his business card.

                    MENDES
My phone number. Go.

EXT. COUNTRY LANE—LATE AFTERNOON

The quiet road cuts through the amber countryside
buzzing with moths and hoppers. The cows graze
contentedly. A HORSE DRAWN BUGGY clops along
over the rise. A MAN and his SON sit side by side on

the buckboard. They are dressed simply in black wool pants, long-sleeved, collarless shirts, and straw hats. This is Amish Country. As peaceful and as pretty as it gets.

EXT. ROADSIDE CORN FIELD—CONTINUOUS

As the Buggy passes by, the camera cranes down through the tall stalks of corn. Lower and lower, until we discover the body of Red, left in a heap for the crows.

EXT. ROWS OF CORN—CONTINUOUS

Her clothes are torn. Her face is dirty and swollen from crying. Her eyes flutter open; gradually coming-to. She grimaces, wipes her mouth, and tries to stand.

LOW ANGLE—CONTINUOUS

It takes great effort, but finally she stands. And weaves. Then her legs give out and she falls back down onto her knees. She takes a deep, shivering breath and heaves violently. Puking her guts out. Puking her heart out. When there's nothing more to vomit, she lies back down and cries.

EXT. HIGHWAY 30—EASTERN PENNSYLVANIA— LATE AFTERNOON

A sign reads STRASBURG 15 MILES; PHILADELPHIA 30 MILES. Traffic shuffles along at commuter speeds. The sun is low.

INT. SCOTT'S VW—HIGHWAY 30—CONTINUOUS
Scott drives, but his mind isn't on the road. He comes

up on the car in front of him too fast. Midge practically puts her feet through the floor.

>   MIDGE
> HeyJesusBrake!

Scott brakes in time, but not before shaking them both up.

>   SCOTT
> Sorry.

>   MIDGE
> Maybe I should drive. You're a million miles away.

>   SCOTT
>   (looks at her)
> I'm sorry.

>   MIDGE
> Okayokay.

>   SCOTT
> For what I said at the bus station. About you and Lonnie. Him dying. I was angry about my own shit and I took it out on you. Losing Lonnie... it must have been so awful for you. *(beat)* I was thinking... if anything like that happened to Red.

>   MIDGE
> Don't...

>   SCOTT
> I'd never forgive myself.

>   MIDGE
> Don't blame yourself for something she did.

SCOTT

I should have seen this coming. Parents who were hardly ever there. Always criticizing us.

> Whenever you can, "tip" in information that keeps the audience on its toes.
>
> Something's really eating at Scott that he's having trouble getting out. This is the tip off. It will find its way out in a later scene when he admits the truth.

MIDGE

Sounds normal to me.

SCOTT

I figured she'd... She's strong, you know? She's... I never thought she'd run away.

MIDGE

Like you told me, my brother's fate was his fate, not mine. And your sister's fate is her fate, not yours.

SCOTT

Thing is, her fate is my fate.

She gives up.

EXTREME CLOSE-UP—BEARDED MAN

Old. Wrinkled. Wise. He stares oddly at the camera.

EXTREME CLOSE-UP OF RED

Seeing the Bearded Man's face inches from her, she screams.

EXT. CORN FIELD—DUSK
The Bearded Man jumps back as Red crabs away on her hands and knees. He waves his hands to calm her. His name is Joseph.

> JOSEPH

Wait, don't run away.

Red scrambles to her feet and runs into ANOTHER
MAN dressed like Joseph. Black wool pants. Collarless, white shirt. Suspenders. She changes direction
and runs, and A THIRD MAN stands in her way. She
spins. A FOURTH MAN, and a FIFTH, and a SIXTH.
She's surrounded by a gang of SCARECROWS.

> JOSEPH

> Don't be afraid. You've been hurt. We live
> here. These are our farms. Let our wives
> and daughters comfort you and feed you.

She stares at them, her whole body is clenched like a
fist.

> JOSEPH

> Let us help you.

She turns in a circle looking into their faces.

> RED

> You can't help me. You don't know who I
> am.

> JOSEPH

> It doesn't matter who you are.

> RED

> Of course it matters who you are. It has to
> matter. If I knew who I was I could tell
> you, don't you see? I could show you. That
> it matters. Who I am. Then everything
> would be just fine. And I would go home.
> Don't you see?

They "see" all right. They see she needs help. They close in on her, nodding and smiling.

EXT. SOUTH PHILADELPHIA—CITYSCAPE— EVENING

A very old city, on very tired legs.

EXT. SOUTH PHILLY—CITY STREETS—EVENING

A mist in the air. A shine on the streets. Shops are open as people go about the usual end-of-the-day chores: pick up the cleaning, pick up dinner, pick up something to wash dinner and the damn day down. Not an especially happy town.

Midge and Scott in a phone booth. He holds the phone, flicking the Walmart business card in his hand nervously. She's staring at him. A long time passes.

> SCOTT
> They're patching me through to Mendes' house.
> *(beat)*
> What? Something's eating you.

> MIDGE
> You ever tell your parents?
> *(off his look)*
> How you felt? The way they treated you.

> SCOTT
> They didn't take criticism too well.

She doesn't push it. Then.

> SCOTT
> You ever tell yours?

                    MIDGE
Yeah.

                    SCOTT
Yeah? Do any good?
    (she shrugs)
I'd be wasting my breath on
mine. Nothing I say would
change them.

                    MIDGE
No, but it'd change you.

> Create these little pauses in the action as a chance for your protagonist and co-protagonist to get closer.
>
> Just a little bit at a time; peeling the onion. Always try to impart a word of wisdom in here somewhere. These moments are worth their weight in gold.

                    SCOTT
Is there something wrong with the way I
am?

                    MIDGE
Seriously?

                    SCOTT
    (suddenly)
Yeah! Mendes? Scott Peck. Yeah.
    (beat)
What? What?
    (beat)
I don't understand. How could that be? But
they saw her get a ride. Someone must've
picked her up.

Midge grabs the phone from him fast.

                    MIDGE
Mr. Mendes, you have to cooperate here or
that little girl is going to die. I need more
information on those six drivers headed
east this morning. Their names and social
security numbers.
    (losing it)

The co-protagonist makes a commitment to her protagonist. She is going to use all her tools until they fail her. This is an important point in your story.

The protagonist hasn't given up his own pride, and because of that he will continue to fight her. He is stuck emotionally until he can trust her.

It is not against the law, Mr. Mendes, but here's what is: you covering up a kidnapping. Now I don't have the fucking time to debate with you, so listen up.

She looks across the street at an old lady of a hotel. It's called "The Majestic" and it definitely is not.

MIDGE
You've got half an hour to call us back at the Majestic Hotel on State Street, South Philadelphia. Half hour. Got it? Or the next call you get will be from the FBI. Right. M A J E S T I C. Goodbye.

He is showing that he can't trust her to be as good at this as he might be. And she is arguing back. This is a slip into old behavior on both their parts and it doesn't help anything until one of them breaks. It's Scott's turn to break soon.

She hangs up. Scott glares at her as she heads for the hotel.

SCOTT
Social security numbers? What are you taking a census? Jesus, we lost her. I don't even know where we are.

MIDGE
You haven't known where you are for years, so don't blame me.

EXT. THE MAJESTIC HOTEL—EVENING—CONTINUOUS

They come to the entrance. Midge pushes her way through the revolving doors, temporarily shutting his bellyaching off.

INT. THE MAJESTIC HOTEL—LOBBY—EVENING—
CONTINUOUS

Though the hotel has seen better days, it is merely
old and tattered, as distinguished from rundown and
smelly. Midge crosses to the registration desk. Scott
behind her.

>   DESK CLERK
> Good evening. Checking in?

>   MIDGE
> Yes.

>   DESK CLERK
> You have reservations?

>   MIDGE
>   *(re:Scott)*
> Have I ever.

>   DESK CLERK
>   *(amused)*
> One room or two?

>   MIDGE
> One. High up.

>   DESK CLERK
> One high up.

He checks his list while Scott and Midge glare at each
other.

>   DESK CLERK
> Here we go. Fourteenth floor. Two doubles
> okay?
>   *(she nods)*

Are there bags you need help with?

MIDGE
He's the guy with the baggage. But he won't
let you help.

She takes the key and heads for the elevator. The
Desk Clerk holds out his hand. Scott reaches for his
wallet.

INT. FARMHOUSE—LAUNDRY ROOM—NIGHT

Katherine, the Amish farmer Joseph's wife, hand
washes Red's dirty clothes in a basin. She holds up
the blouse and shakes her head and scrubs some
more.

INT. FARMHOUSE—UPSTAIRS—BEDROOM—NIGHT

An oil lamp glows in the Spartan room. Red sits on a
bed in a white, cotton dress; hair tied back with a
ribbon. She has been cleaned and bandaged. She
hardly seems fifteen anymore.

Willam, a doctor, sits on a Windsor chair facing her as
he drops bandages and a stethoscope back into his medi-
cal bag. His stethoscope catches Red's eye. Something
about it triggers a memory fragment.

MEMORY—FLASH CUT—RED AND SCOTT MEMORY

Red sits on Scott's lap singing into his stethoscope.
The action freezes into the photo Scott is carrying
with him.

INT. FARMHOUSE—UPSTAIRS—BEDROOM—
NIGHT—REALITY

Just as quickly, Red loses the memory. Willam sees this. They stare at each other is silent speculation.

CLOSE-UP—NYPD DETECTIVE DEVLIN'S BUSINESS CARD

Midge is holding it in her hand.

INT. THE MAJESTIC HOTEL—FOURTEENTH FLOOR ROOM—NIGHT

Midge studies the detective's card from the morgue. Scott comes in with a bucket of ice, soda, bags of chips, and candy bars. He throws it all on the dresser.

> SCOTT
> Dinner is on the freaking table.

The phone rings and they both jump for it. Midge wins.

> MIDGE
> Yeah.
> *(beat)*
> Yeah. Good for you, Mendes. Good for you.
> Hold on.
> *(grabs pen and paper)*
> Go ahead. Yeah.. Yeah..

Scott opens a soda and a bag of chips. He is loud and pissy.

> SCOTT
> Maybe you should get their shoe sizes.

He stuffs his face and crosses to the window. Midge takes down the names and numbers, and hangs up, and dials Devlin.

SCOTT

Now what are you doing?

MIDGE

Detective Devlin? Midge Delisa. Remember me?

Scott's chip-filled mouth drops open.

> Scott is reaching the breaking point. His co-protagonist has taken control and his loss of control freaks him out. He doesn't trust her or anyone else.
>
> **This is his flaw. He wants control because he believes he caused this to happen and he has to fix it.**

MIDGE

That's right... right, Rico. Listen, I thought it over. I want to make a deal. I'll help you if you help me.
  (she listens)
I will, I swear. Jesus, I swear. I got some names. I need to know if any of them has a record.
  (re: Scott)
My friend, he's really in trouble. Somebody could die. I won't bail on you, trust me.
  (beat)
Okay, here we go.

She reads the list of names. Then the hotel number.

MIDGE

Majestic Hotel 229.338.3838.
  (checks her watch)
Can't they do it faster? OK OK OK. Right. Thanks.
  (she hangs up)
We'll find out if one of the drivers got in trouble before. If so, we go after him, because he's the one lying.

> SCOTT

If they ever got in trouble before? You mean convictions?

She moves to him, all business.

> MIDGE

A busload of people saw Red get in that truck. One of those drivers picked her up. If he had nothing to hide, if he just gave her a lift and dropped her off, he would have told Mendes off the record. Happens all the time, company policy or not.

> SCOTT

If he had something to hide?

> MIDGE

Maybe he's on the run. Maybe he's not supposed to be driving interstate. Maybe he's keeping quiet because Red asked him to keep quiet.

> SCOTT

Or maybe he's hurt her.

She doesn't answer that directly.

> MIDGE

In a few hours we'll know what we're dealing with.

> SCOTT

A few hours? Jesus, we don't have a few hours. We can't just sit here.

> MIDGE

You want to run around in circles?
> (beat; tough)

This is the hard part.

SCOTT
Fuck the hard part.

MIDGE
This from the man who said, no matter
what it takes he's going to find his sister.
Well, this is what it takes.

SCOTT
I can't sit around and do nothing! Don't
you see? This is what I should have done a
long time ago. I should have saved her. I
should have known.

MIDGE
Known what? That she would run away?
You couldn't know that.

SCOTT
She always looked up to me. She wanted to
be just like me. Jesus.

Midge senses something. Puts two and two together.

MIDGE
To *be* like you? *(moves closer)* Or *do* like
you? Is that it? What you did? When it got
too tough for you? When nothing you said
could change them? You left home. And
you left Red.

They are nose-to-nose, and the volume is rising fast.

SCOTT
Fuck you.

MIDGE

You knew what her life was like at home. Nothing changed after you split. It was the same for her now as it was for you then. You knew she was lonely and desperate because that's the way it was for you. What did you think? That you could run away, and she wouldn't? You've been living in denial. That's what's really getting to you.

SCOTT

No, you're what's getting to me. You're the one who stole my sister's wallet and put her life in danger.

MIDGE

Right. I'm the one you didn't want your sister to be anything like. Well, have a little irony with your Fritos. She wound up to be just like you, instead. Running away from home, following in your footsteps.

SCOTT

You weren't there!

MIDGE

The hell I wasn't. I was there for the beatings. I was there for the shame. I was there for all the assholes who tried to crawl into my bed after my mother passed out. I was

It's the protagonist's turn to have a meltdown and for the co-protagonist to bring him around to acceptance.

All high emotions have what I call a "vulnerability quotient." Laughing, weeping, screaming in anger, all create an opening to a soft spot, paradoxically, where nurturing is acceptable. Nurturing by the co-protagonist is the only effective response. It allows the protagonist to self-determine with dignity.

In this case Midge does the nurturing. But she has to drop her old attitude to get there.

Her epiphany is not about what he did; it's about what she can do for him with her new emotional strength.

there to clean her up in the morning, and wash the puke out of her hair, and make her breakfast. And I was there to watch it start all over again the next night. Trust me, I have been there.

> She needs to hear herself say this as much as he needs to hear it. If she can forgive herself, she can forgive him.

Their faces are so close they can feel the heat in each other's words... see the tears in each other's eyes.

                    MIDGE
          I hung in and I fought back and gave them
          as much shit as they gave me because I
          wasn't going to let them win. So they threw
          me out on my ass. An eighth grade virgin.

His anger and fear dissolve, and he trembles into shame, hoping to be understood if not forgiven.

                    SCOTT
          I didn't know what else to do.

                    MIDGE
          Me either.

                    SCOTT
          I was fifteen and scared shitless.

                    MIDGE
          Me, too.

                    SCOTT
          I didn't know she'd do what I did. I didn't
          know I did anything wrong.

                    MIDGE
          What you did was the best thing you could
          have done. It saved your life.

She touches his face.

MIDGE

And Red ran away to save her life.

SCOTT

God...

She kisses his cheek.

MIDGE

Because you showed her how.

She kisses his eyes.

MIDGE

What you did was nothing to be ashamed of.

> This is the protagonist/co-protagonist emotional union.
>
> They have allowed each other "in" which is the basis for their intimacy.
>
> Remember: Intimacy is "me being me and letting you see me."

She kisses his lips.

MIDGE

Nothing to be afraid of anymore.

She kisses him again and he kisses her back. They fall back gently onto the bed, where they embrace. And not surprisingly, their first real kiss, so full and soft, is neither tentative nor compromised by lust, but welcomed as their long overdue unlocking.

EXT. FARM—NIGHT—MOS

Currier and Ives. The farmhouse. The barns. The pastures. All painted in moonlight. The murmur of voices from within.

INT. FARMHOUSE—DINING ROOM—NIGHT—MOS

Joseph, Katherine, their seven children, and Dr. Willam, sit around a huge table eating quietly, eyes on Red.

INT. MAJESTIC HOTEL—FOURTEENTH FLOOR ROOM—MOS

Scott and Midge have managed to take off their clothes. They make love. Gentle, delicate, thorough love.

INT. FARMHOUSE—DINING ROOM—NIGHT—MOS

Amanda, a young girl Red's age, pours milk for Red. Becka, an older sister, plops a huge pile of potatoes onto Red's plate. Red digs into them.

INT. MAJESTIC HOTEL—FOURTEENTH FLOOR ROOM—MOS

There's no holding back. No telling who is hotter, or happier, or more amazed.

INT. FARMHOUSE—DINING ROOM—NIGHT—MOS

Amanda brings a fresh-baked blueberry pie from the kitchen. Everyone oohs and aahs. But Red. Suddenly very somber, overcome by her confusion and sadness. Her eyes well.

The Doctor, Willam, reaches for her hand. She squeezes her eyes shut trying to make sense of an empty memory.

> WILLAM
> Did you just remember something? Is something coming back to you?

She shakes her head "no" in total frustration.

> RED
>
> I think and think and think. And I can't think of anything.

> WILLAM
>
> It takes time. It's best not to try to force it.

> RED
>
> What do I do in the meantime?

INT. MAJESTIC HOTEL—FOURTEENTH FLOOR ROOM—NIGHT

Scott is sound asleep. Midge stands next to the bed, dressed in her old street clothes. She bends down and carefully places A NOTE on the night table next to him. She studies him; wanting him; then heads for the door.

At the door she hesitates, turns back to him, wishing he would wake and stop her from what she's about to do. After another moment, she turns and leaves.

EXT. FARMHOUSE—FRONT PORCH—NIGHT

Joseph and Katherine bid goodnight to the Doctor Willam.

> WILLAM
>
> I'll notify the police in the morning. Somebody must be looking for her.

> KATHERINE
>
> Do you believe what she tells us?

> WILLAM
>
> I believe what her body tells me. She's been beaten and molested.

JOSEPH
And she can't remember a thing.

WILLAM
The police won't be able to do much for her until they can identify her.

KATHERINE
And in the meantime?

WILLAM
They will turn her over to Health and Human Services, which is usually a dead end.

KATHERINE
What she doesn't need now is another dead end. She needs hope. She needs to feel safe.

WILLAM
What else am I to do?

KATHERINE
Your own advice... try not to force it.

JOSEPH
She's safe here, for as long as she wants.

WILLAM
Long it could be. With amnesia sometimes the memory comes back quickly. Sometimes slowly. Sometimes never at all.

JOSEPH
For as long as she wants.

Willam nods and goes. Joseph puts his arm around Katherine.

This is the point at which you must invent a gripping series of scenes in your plot to test your protagonist and co-protagonist's commitment to their common goal, and to each other. But old fears and old habits die hard.

INT. THE IMPERIAL HOTEL—FOURTEENTH FLOOR
ROOM—NIGHT

Scott wakes up and looks around the room, jumps
out of bed.

> SCOTT
>
> Midge?

He sees the note on the bed stand and reads it.

CLOSE ON NOTE

"Gone for some air. Wait for Devlin's call. Won't be
long."

ON SCOTT

Standing in his birthday suit. Looks around, decides
to shower and get dressed.

EXT. ARMY/NAVY STORE—NIGHT

A BUM stares at the stuff in the window. After a
minute, Midge comes out wearing Dickies, sweatshirt,
jacket, and cap. She looks like she
belongs. Which is her point. The
Bum checks her out and winks.
She winks back and heads down
the street. She doesn't get twenty
feet before a street boy named
Slim steps in her way.

> SLIM
>
> All dressed up and no-
> where to go.

> **You must test your pro-
> tagonist and co-protagonist
> each step of the way.**
>
> Like an addiction, Midge
> goes back to her old ways in
> order to settle a score. She is
> risking her new relationship
> and she is risking Red's life.
> Not to mention her own.

>   MIDGE
> Sad ain't it?

>   SLIM
> I know a party. Make a sad girl happy.

>   MIDGE
> Is it a party with hard drugs and harder
> Cubans?

Slim smiles and offers his arm. She hooks hers around
his and off they go down the old brick road.

INT. MAJESTIC HOTEL—BATHROOM—NIGHT

Scott dries off, checks his face in the mirror. Something catches his eye. He turns and sees Midge's
YELLOW NOTE on the floor, picks it up, reads it.

INT. HABANA TOWN WAREHOUSE—A HUGE
PARTY—NIGHT

The shitty part of a shitty town. It would be an insult
to ravers everywhere to call this a rave. It's more of
a rant. Midge and Slim fight their way through the
mobs of young people high on xtc, groping and sweating and tempting death to the beat of an overwhelm-
ingly bad band.

Midge winces at the acrid stench of industrial rot
and body odor that identifies parties like this, and
that reminds her of the hovel she left behind underground in New York.

>   SLIM
> Good, huh?

>   MIDGE
> Just like home.

She scans the crowd. Slim screams over the din, pointing to the drugs being bought and sold in the corner.

> SLIM
>
> There we go, Sad Girl.

As they make their way to the corner, Midge catches a tall, good-looking girl, Natalia, watching her closely. Natalia, backpack over one shoulder, smiles alluringly signaling Midge to join her. Midge splits off from Slim before he can notice.

> NATALIA
>
> You don't want to be with him, Chica.

> MIDGE
>
> Who do I want to be with?

EXT. ALLEY—NIGHT—CONTINUOUS

A metal door swings open and Natalia and Midge step out into the alley. Suddenly headlights snap on as an old sedan screams to life and speeds down the alley toward them. Midge tries to push Natalia out of harm's way, but instead, Natalia pulls Midge directly into the car's oncoming path.

IN THE HEADLIGHTS

Midge's life flashes in front of her. Then, inexplicably, the sedan BRAKES AND SKIDS to a stop a foot from them.

> NATALIA
>
> God I love doing that.

She leads Midge to the door, opens it, and nudges her in.

INT. OLD SEDAN—NIGHT—CONTINUOUS

Midge and Natalia flop in the back seat. Natalia passes her backpack up to the front seat where Carmen counts stacks of cash and Camilla, her identical twin, drives.

                    CAMILLA
        You crazy fuck. Next time I don't stop.

                    NATALIA
                (to Midge)
        One more collection, then we party.

                    CARMEN
        Jesus, tell the world. You know this bitch?
        You check her out?

                    NATALIA
        My favorite thing.

She frisks Midge *thoroughly*. Midge hates it, but knows it's got to be done if she wants to get where she wants to go.

> Midge knows she's entering a dangerous world and she's scared. She's quickly reaching a point where there will be no turning back.
>
> **Make your protagonist or co-protagonist regret the** choice they make to go back to old habits. The regret is recognition that they are cheating.

NATALIA
No weapons. No wires. Great tits.

INT. MAJESTIC HOTEL—FOURTEENTH FLOOR ROOM—NIGHT

The phone is ringing. Scott crosses to it anxiously.

SCOTT
Yeah.

                    DEVLIN
        Gimme Midge.

                         SCOTT
          Is this Devlin?

INTERCUT WITH:
INT. NEW YORK CITY POLICE STATION—NIGHT

Devlin sits at his crappy desk in the middle of his
crappy precinct, tired and short-tempered.

                         DEVLIN
          You the guy she's helping?

                         SCOTT
          I'm the guy. Midge went out. You get any
          information?

                         DEVLIN
          All the names came up
          clean, except for one: a
          George Lewis Riff.

He writes the name on the back of
the YELLOW NOTE.

> This information is meant to scare the hell out of Scott and push him into a higher gear. It's complicated by the fact that he has to rescue Midge before he can go after his sister. His emotions are conflicting and on fire.

                         SCOTT
          George Lewis Riff... What'd
          he do?

                         DEVLIN
          He fucked a ten-year-old. Served his time
          in Raliegh State. Released last August. Then
          split. Probation officer hasn't heard from
          him since.

                         SCOTT
          Jesusgod.

                         DEVLIN
          Listen. I need to talk to Midge.

SCOTT
So do I. But first I have to find her and her
friend Rico.

DEVLIN
Rico?

SCOTT
(reads note)
Rico. Habana Town. South
Philly. She had it written down
on a piece of paper.

DEVLIN
Oh, shit, man, you've got to
find her and get her as far
away from him as possible.

SCOTT
Hey, you know what? If there's
something personal going on here between
her and...

DEVLIN
It's personal all right, Rico killed her
brother. You have to find her before he kills
her, too.

> There is a danger in separating your protagonist and co-protagonist for any length of time. When they are apart you have to connect them visually and emotionally. Timing your intercuts and matching their pacing or intensity are good ways to achieve this.

SCOTT
You've got to be kidding!

DEVLIN
Do I sound like I'm kidding?! Get out of
there and find her!

INT. RUNDOWN APARTMENT—NIGHT

Dark and stinky and filled with stoned boys and girls.
Midge and Natalia cross through the room. For Midge,

she could just as well be back in the Bronx. Just as well be watching Lonnie dance.

                    NATALIA
          Stay close.

INT. BEDROOM—NIGHT—CONTINUOUS

No bed. People flopped on the floor, too wasted to stand and leave. Across the room is the bathroom. Its door has been replaced with a heavy-gauge steel mesh cage. This is the drug store and the bank.

Natalia goes directly to it and nods to a Scuzzy Guy with very few teeth.

> Construct visual connections to your character's past to tie these story experiences together. This creates an emotional cumulative effect and relates what's happening today to what has to be cleared up from yesterday.

                    NATALIA
          She here?

                    SCUZZY GUY
          She's still counting.
               (to girl o.s.)
          Your ride's here.

He grins stupidly at Midge.

                    SCUZZY GUY
          Want something?

From out of nowhere Natalia produces a 9mm and aims it between his beady eyes. He backs off. Natalia puts the gun away and smiles at Midge. Then a blonde steps up from the back of the room.

                    NATALIA
          Ready?

The blonde nods as she sees Midge and tries to place her as she comes out of the cage. Midge tries not to overreact.

INT. NEW YORK WALK-UP APART-MENT—BLACK & WHITE—FLASHBACK

> This is Midge's point-of-no-return. Deep trouble is ahead.

Yvonne, the very same blonde, chews Lonnie's face, devouring him as they dance the dance of death.

INT. BEDROOM—REALITY—NIGHT

Midge clutches her crippled hand as Yvonne joins them and they head out.

> NATALIA
> It's time to party.

INT. THE MAJESTIC HOTEL—LOBBY—NIGHT

Scott gets directions from the Desk Clerk to Habana Town. He charges out.

EXT. THE MAJESTIC HOTEL—NIGHT

Scott runs to his car, gets in and fires it up, and speeds off.

INT. ELEVATOR—NIGHT

Packed with hopped-up, happy-and-about-to-be-happier night people jukin' and jivin' around Midge, Natalia, Carmen, Camilla, and Yvonne. Yvonne studies Midge. Midge doesn't flinch. The elevator stops with a "bing" and a cheer.

INT. FUNKY PENTHOUSE—NIGHT—CONTINUOUS

The crowd pours out of the private elevator into the huge, white salon of an overwrought penthouse. The place is packed with cheap hoods wearing cheap cologne, all emulating Enrique Iglesias. Midge has seen her share of parties, but none quite like this. She and Natalia follow Yvonne, who now holds all the money. Midge senses she's getting closer to Rico.

> NATALIA
>
> What'd I tell you. Just like Miami.

Yvonne heads off and disappears through a pair of doors. Midge follows, but Natalia steers her away.

> NATALIA
>
> Uh-uh. That's the office. (into the fray) This is the office party.

EXT. FUNKY PENTHOUSE TERRACE—NIGHT—CONTINUOUS

Not really a penthouse terrace...more a tarpaper and gravel roof. But, in South Philly at least, it's the top of the world. Potted palms. Salsa. The local mid-level thugs enjoy their employee benefits. Getting high. Getting lucky.

> MIDGE
>
> All the worker bees.

> NATALIA
>
> It's payday. They all feel rich. Me, I feel naughty. Let's party.

She kisses Midge on the mouth, smiles wickedly and heads off. Midge wipes her mouth as she watches her go, then looks toward The Office.

EXT. HABANA TOWN STREETS—NIGHT

Scott cruises slowly through a particularly frightening neighborhood. He slows at a corner where A
BUNCH OF GUYS stand. He rolls down his window
to ask them a question. They take one look at him,
presume he's a cop, and take off.
He cruises further down the road and spots THREE
BAD LOOKING LADIES tapping to an inner beat. He
pulls over and rolls down the window again. They
approach him.

> SCOTT
> I'm looking for a very special person here
> in Habana Town?

> FIRST BAD LOOKING LADY
> You just found her, Sugar.

> SCOTT
> His name's Rico.

They laugh. He tries to find them amusing, but can't.

> SCOTT
> No shit, I need to find him.

> SECOND BAD LOOKING LADY
> You have any idea how many Ricos there
> are in Habana Town?

> SCOTT
> This is like a big guy.

> THIRD BAD LOOKING LADY
> Honey, they all think they're big.

> SCOTT
> "Important" big.

>   FIRST BAD LOOKING LADY
> That, too.

>   SCOTT
>   (frustrated)
> Do they all kill people? Because this son-
> of-a-bitch kills people!

They look at him for a beat, then at each other and
nod.

>   FIRST BAD LOOKING LADY
> That Rico.

He opens his wallet. First Bad Looking Lady moves
in.

>   SCOTT
> Just point me in the right di-
> rection.

>   FIRST BAD LOOK-
>   ING LADY
> I can point you in Rico's direc-
> tion, Sugar, but I wouldn't call
> it the right direction. It's about
> as wrong as it gets.

> Ending scenes on
> tense notes is a good
> dramatic technique.
> Look for ways to end
> your scenes this way
> when you can.

INT. FUNKY PENTHOUSE—NIGHT

Midge works her way through the party, her anxiety
building, checking everyone out. Her past clouds her
vision.

INT. BROOKLYN APARTMENT—BLACK & WHITE—
QUICK CUTS

The party from the opening. A different time and place, but the same party in so many ways. Reckless. Deadly. Midge walks amid the danger, tough and confident.

INT. FUNKY PENTHOUSE—NIGHT—REALITY

TWO GUYS salsa up to Midge and sandwich her. One kisses her face, the other licks her neck. She smiles, lets them play for a minute, then squirms free and points down the hall.

> MIDGE
> Ladies room. Hold that thought.

INT. POWDER ROOM—NIGHT

Midge goes to the basins where TWO GIRLS fix a syringe. Already high, they eye the heroin with more desperation than anticipation: more needing than wanting. One girl ties the other's arm off, spanks the vein, and shoots her up. She puts the paraphernalia down as her girlfriend swoons, and lowers her onto a couch. Midge eyes the syringe.

EXT. FUNKY BUILDING—NIGHT

Scott pulls up across the street. First Bad Looking Lady is with him. The lobby is guarded by a couple of tough looking BODY GUARDS. They keep an eye on all the people coming and going. A lot of people.

> FIRST BAD LOOKING LADY
> This is where I say goodnight.

> SCOTT
> Everybody's just going right in.

> FIRST BAD LOOKING LADY
> You ain't everybody, handsome.

> SCOTT
> I would be everybody if you came with me?

> FIRST BAD LOOKING LADY
> You're shittin' me, right?

He takes out his wallet again.

INT. FUNKY PENTHOUSE—NIGHT

The party's in full swing. The "office" doors open and a lot of very heavy dudes file out, followed by their minions holding their cuts. The men have finished their business and mingle at the fringe of the party as a courtesy. But they are on guard, and stay near the private elevator. Midge sees the group and heads toward it. And then her heart stops.

ON THE GROUP

Preening among them is Rico.

INT. BROOKLYN APARTMENT—BLACK & WHITE—QUICK CUTS

The same face. It is Rico, Lonnie's murderer.

INT. FUNKY PENTHOUSE—NIGHT

The moment Midge has been waiting for has her frozen in fear.

INT. FUNKY DOWNSTAIRS LOBBY—NIGHT

Scott and First Bad Looking Lady wait for the elevator with an antsy group of druggies. Scott tries to fit in. He drifts to the back of the crowd as everyone stares at the floor indicator above the elevator door.

> DRUGGIE
> What's with this thing?

Scott slips away and heads up the stairs.

INT. FUNKY PENTHOUSE—NIGHT

Rico and the others say their goodbyes and move to the elevator. Rico blows Yvonne a kiss goodbye. She blows one back, then her face tightens.

YVONNE'S—NEAR THE ELEVATOR—CONTINUOUS

People crowd on. But something's not right. Trying to record what she just saw. She looks around anxiously and sees Natalia.

AT THE PRIVATE ELEVATOR—CONTINUOUS

Rico and the others get into the elevator. The doors close.

INT. STAIRCASE—CONTINUOUS

Scott races up the stairs. As he passes the third floor he sees that the elevator is coming down. He punches the "down" button anxiously and waits.

INT. FUNKY DOWNSTAIRS LOBBY—NIGHT

The group sees the descending numbers light up above the elevator door—12; 11; 10—and let out a collective sigh. First Bad Looking Lady looks around for Scott.

INT. ELEVATOR—NIGHT

Descending, packed to the rafters with money and drugs and cheap cologne. The men are quiet. A sign of their nervousness. They will not relax until they get home. They watch each other, trying not to be obvious.

INT. THIRD FLOOR—ELEVATOR—CONTINUOUS
Scott waits. Jumping out of his skin. Five, four, three. Ding. He holds his breath. The doors open. He's staring right into faces of every bad ass in Philly. One of them holds out his hand.

                    BAD ASS
          Next car.

Scott spots Midge. She's shocked to see him, and tries not to let on. Rico sees Scott's reaction and looks to his left. Right at Midge. He freezes. Instantly, he knows something's wrong. The elevator doors close.

Scott races down the stairs.

INT. ELEVATOR—NIGHT—CONTINUOUS

Rico stares at Midge. She stares back and holds up her mangled hand.

                    MIDGE
          Hi, Rico. Remember me?

Before Rico can say a word, he feels a hot pin prick in his groin. He looks down. He turns white.

                    MIDGE
          That's your femoral artery. And that's air
          in the syringe.

Everyone in the elevator reaches for his gun.

> MIDGE
>
> Don't.

> A BODYGUARD
>
> Who the fuck are you?

> RICO
>
> Jesushelpme.

The elevator comes to a slow stop. The doors hiss open.

> MIDGE
>
> Everybody out. This is personal.

No argument. The men scramble back out into the lobby.

INT. FUNKY DOWNSTAIRS LOBBY AND ELEVATOR—
NIGHT

The waiting druggie crowd is crushed backwards by the panicked men with their guns trying to scramble off. Scott charges down the stairs into the chaos when suddenly the beautiful Natalia stumbles onto the scene, dazed and confused, and bleeding from a pistol whipping.

> NATALIA
>
> Chica? What...

Yvonne jumps into the fray brandishing a huge automatic. She shoves Natalia into the car and reaches for Rico.

> YVONNE
>
> Rico!

Rico makes his move, but when he does, Midge BREAKS OFF THE HYPODERMIC NEEDLE in his leg viciously. Rico screams in agony and tumbles out the elevator. Yvonne fires wildly into the car. The sound is deafening. The slugs ricochet savagely. Natalia's face lights up as several direct hits slam into her, pounding her into Midge. They crash against the back wall and then slide to the floor.

As suddenly as it exploded, the lobby is deafeningly quiet. Scott, Midge, and Yvonne are paralyzed in the echo of death.

The elevator doors, trying to shut, stubbornly bang against Natalia's beautiful, long legs. Midge squirms out from under her and tries to stand, but slips in a pool of blood and falls down. Hands and knees, shaking uncontrollably, she throws her head back in rage and failure.

> MIDGE
> Noooo.....

Scott tries to find Natalia's pulse, but there is none. He crawls to Midge, gathers her in his arms, but there is no consoling her. He lifts her and carries her out.

This is the end of the action sequence in which Midge's deepest fears were tested. She failed to commit a murderous act of revenge—which keeps our co-protagonist from becoming every bit as bad as the bad guy—but she has not failed taking care of her primal need. She needed to show her brother somehow that she would die for him. She needed to try this, or she would have lived the rest of her life wondering if she could have or should have. The act of trying was enough. In the sequence coming up in their hotel room Scott will accept what she tried to do, and they bond permanently.

It is a good practice to come off of an action sequence with a quieter more reflective scene or two in order to allow the audience and the protagonist a chance to absorb what has just happened. It's my belief that in the quiet moments, or the "emotional transitions" as I think of them, the change the protagonist has made becomes growth. It is an internal and permanent absorption of a new strength and a new truth, and it is the signal that your protagonist has reached the Fourth Stage of Mastery: he becomes unconsciously competent in the matter. His belief is part of him now. This will happen to Scott in the hotel scene upcoming. The change can be shown physically in the final plot action sequence when he acts out of bravery rather than out of panic or anxiety. There is an unspoken confidence and a spiritual knowing that guides him to a higher purpose. It is from this new emotional posture that he will draw the strength he needs for victory. We shall see.

We left Scott carrying Midge to safety. Now we go to Red's plot and bring Scott and Midge to her in the final plot climax. We start with some of those quiet moments between action that I spoke about.

FIREFLIES WEAVING IN THE FOG

A tender ballad on HARMONICA, soft as angel's breath. The fireflies become clearer. They are not fireflies at all.

A ROW OF BOBBING LANTERNS—LONG LENS

Moving across an open field, the lanterns, held by half a dozen children, swing in slow arcs to the sway of the ballad.

EXT. FARM FIELD—PRE-DAWN

The Lantern Children head to the barn silhouetted on the brim of the rise by the promise of daybreak. They hum the ballad surely warming the waiting Guernseys.

INT. MILKING BARN—CONTINUOUS

The door swings open and the children file in and turn on the lights. The cows sway to receive them. Red steps in, holding a lantern. She takes in the sights and smells and sounds and is comforted and awed.

INT. THE MAJESTIC HOTEL—FOURTEENTH FLOOR ROOM—DAWN

Scott stands at the window with neither comfort nor awe. He stares at daybreak with bloodshot eyes, blinded by the residue of fear that clouds his comprehension.

INT. THE MAJESTIC HOTEL—BATHROOM—DAWN

Midge is a statue under the spray. Eyes shut. Heart broken. Hopes dashed. She sucks in a fractured breath, and tears and snot work their way out of her eyes and nose.

The shower curtain slowly draws back and Scott stands there. She doesn't know what to expect. He joins her face-to-face. He takes her in his arms and she succumbs limply into the safety of his embrace. He runs his fingers through her hair, washing away the blood and grime of the night.

For a long time they say nothing, asking the water to soothe them, but there is only so much water can do; for there is cleaning, and there is coming clean, and they know it.

> MIDGE
> I'm sorry I screwed you up. I'm sorry I made it worse. Please don't be mad at me.

> SCOTT

I'm not.

> MIDGE

Please.

> SCOTT

Really, I'm not.

He wipes the snot from her face.

> MIDGE

He was like you, you know. Lonnie. He was such a good guy. He was fucking perfect.

> SCOTT

I know. I know.

> MIDGE

Rico killed him a thousand times. People don't understand. They don't know that every time I think about Lonnie—every minute of every day that I miss him—is one more time Rico kills him.
> *(more tears)*
All I could think about was getting even. I wanted to kill him harder. I had to kill him enough. I had to kill my pain.

> SCOTT

I tried to kill my pain by running away from home. I lived on the streets like you. And I found more pain. I never told Red that part. I did shameful things to survive, because going back wasn't an option. The more ashamed I got, the angrier I got. I blamed everybody else but myself. I hated the world. Man, I was so sick. I was dying inside. I used

everything I could; drugs, alcohol, sex... but
I never could kill my pain.
> (beat)

I almost killed myself, though. Someone
dropped me off at the er. Someone else helped
me detox. Someone else helped me get a job.
Someone else helped me get my place. There
was always someone else once I gave up trying to do it alone.
> (into her eyes)

We aren't meant to do it alone, Midge.

> MIDGE

I just want the pain to go away.

> SCOTT

Let me be your someone else.

This is their emotional story climax.

We can now go back to the plot and to our heroes' final quest to
save the runaway sister, Red. Success in the *plot climax* will be attainable
only because they have had this *emotional climax* first.

We quickly wrap up the plot with a gripping action-filled lead-up
to the climax. Here we go.

EXT. AMISH FARM—HILLSIDE—DAY

A perfect day. A living quilt. Crows soar over the corn
fields. Workers till the land with horse and plow. To
the south, the cows graze near a pond. To the north,
Red and two of the other girls hang wash on the lines.
Rows of blouses and dancing grey dresses. Red looks
at the clean clothes and the blue sky above and she
closes her eyes and inhales deeply, sucking in the
beautiful air.

EXT. FARM HOUSE—CONTINUOUS

Katherine carries platters of food to a huge picnic table where the rest of the meal is set. Amanda runs to the iron triangle hanging nearby, and clangs it with a poker. The triangle's ring carries over the countryside, and in the distance the workers drop their tools and head in.

EXT. TRUCK STOP AND DINER—DAY

Lots of trucks out front. Mr. Lucky comes out and walks to his truck, hitching his belt, picking his teeth.

EXT. FARM HOUSE—DAY

Red eats with the family, fitting in a bit more easily.

INT. WAL-MART TRUCK—DAY

Mr. Lucky climbs up and into his truck; straps his seat belt; and belches loud and clear.

EXT. FARM HOUSE—DAY

Red laughs at something Amanda tells her. A good, deep laugh.

INT. WAL-MART TRUCK—PENNSYLVANIA HIGH-WAY—DAY

Mr. Lucky pulls out onto the highway and adjusts his rearview mirror. And jumps when he sees Midge in it. She pokes her head out of his sleeping compartment.

> MIDGE
> I was wondering if you're the kind of guy who would give a girl a ride?

MR. LUCKY
Sweetie, I can give you the ride of your life.

MIDGE
I'll be the judge of that.

She smiles seductively, starts taking off her jacket, and ducks back into the sleeper. That's all he needs to see.

EXT. HIGHWAY—SIDE OF THE ROAD—WAL-MART TRUCK—DAY

It pulls over and stops. Scott's VW slides in behind it.

INT. WAL-MART TRUCK—DAY

Mr. Lucky turns the ignition off, unsnaps his seat belt, all smiles. Suddenly his door swings open and Scott reaches in and yanks him out of the cab and down onto the ground. He pins him there with a tire iron across his throat. Midge jumps down and joins him. Mr. Lucky can hardly breathe.

MR. LUCKY
I'll give you everything I've got. You don't need to hurt me.

SCOTT
You're wrong. I need to hurt you.

Midge holds the picture of Red and Scott in Mr. Lucky's face.

SCOTT
Because I'm the guy in the picture with the girl you picked up yesterday.

He sees the picture; the color drains from his face.

                    MIDGE
          Your parole officer misses you. He's got a
          cell waiting for you.

                    SCOTT
          No cell. Not yet.

Scott presses the tire iron harder into his throat. Mr.
Lucky tries to talk and cry at the same time. He's
petrified.

                    SCOTT
          I got something I want to do first. I want
          to make sure you never talk to a kid again.
          One hard push on the voice box and you're
          a mute.

He pushes harder still.

                    SCOTT
          Two hard pushes, and you go to hell.

Tears stream down Mr. Lucky's face. He gags. Midge
leans into his ear.

                    MIDGE
          Maybe if you tell us where his sister is,
          you'll get to go to heaven.

EXT. MAIN STREET—STRASBURG, PA.—DAY

Pennsylvania Dutch. Shops from another era. Midge
and Scott at the VW look around. She goes to a pay
phone.

                    SCOTT
          I should have killed him. I should go back.

Just because he said he dropped her off here, doesn't mean he did.

MIDGE
(dials 911)
I want to report a rapist on the prowl.

INT. WAL-MART TRUCK—DAY

Mr. Lucky, his hands tied behind his back, squirms and kicks at the car door handle.

MIDGE
That's right. A child molester.

EXT. WALMART TRUCK—DAY

The kicking continues. Suddenly the driver's door springs open. Mr. Lucky slides out feet first, hands still tied.

MIDGE
Parked in his truck on highway 209 just outside of Strasburg.

Mr. Lucky leans into the truck and desperately pulls at his jeans jacket on the floor behind the driver's seat. He clamps it in his teeth like a dog with a chew toy.

MIDGE
He's been picking up little girls.

Jacket in mouth, he runs into the weedy field and drops to his knees. He unbuttons a jacket pocket and spills out a small, plastic device. He presses a button on it, eyes wide.

                    MIDGE
         I know because I'm a little girl, and I just
         left him there.
He hears a BEEP in the distance and scrambles toward it.

EXT. WEEDY FIELD—DAY—CONTINUOUS

Mr. Lucky stumbles through the field, following the
sound of the beep. Until he comes upon its source.
He crouches and picks up his KEY RING, and smiles
as it beeps away.

INT. BARBER SHOP—STRASBURG, PA.—DAY—MOS

Scott shows Red's picture to THE BARBER and HIS
CUSTOMER in the chair. They study it. Study him.
Shake their heads.

EXT. WAL-MART TRUCK—DAY

Mr. Lucky stands next to his truck, engine running.
He presses the rope binding his hands against the
vertical exhaust pipe. And the rope starts to burn.

INT. FABRIC STORE—STRASBURG, PA.—DAY—MOS

Midge shows Red's picture to TWO LADIES cutting
patterns from a bolt of material. Midge runs her fingers gently over some flannel. They watch her, then
shake their heads.

EXT. ROAD—WAL-MART TRUCK—DAY

Prowling slowly into the farmland. Mr. Lucky at the
wheel.

INT. BARN—HAY LOFT—DAY—MOS

A bale of hay swings through the high loft doors on a rope and pulley. Red, covered with sweat and straw, grabs the bale with Amanda, pulls it to the floor, unhooks it, and tumbles backwards into a heap. Tired and dirty, Red looks up at Amanda, who extends her hand and pulls Red to her feet.

EXT. COUNTRY LANE—DAY—MOS

The Wal-mart truck rolls along very slowly. The monster sniffing out its quarry.

INT. LIBRARY—STRASBURG, PA.—DAY—MOS

The LIBRARIAN hands the picture back to Midge. Midge looks around at all the books. All the mystery and glory and adventure they hold. A sense of loss sweeps over her.

INT. FARM SUPPLIES AND FEED STORE—DAY—MOS

SEVERAL FARMERS pass Red's picture around as Scott takes in the store, touches the tools. None of them has seen her. He thanks them, puts down a pitchfork.

INT. BARN—HAY LOFT—DAY—MOS

Another pitchfork leans against a mountain of hay bales. Red and Amanda atop them, take a well-deserved break. Amanda chews on a piece of straw. Red imitates her. Sun streaks in through the big open loft doors.

EXT. COUNTRY LANE—CORN FIELDS—DAY—MOS

The Wal-mart truck pulls over and stops. Mr. Lucky

gets out. Looks around. Walks to the rows of corn. Searching.

INT. ICE CREAM PARLOR—STRASBURG, PA.—DAY—MOS

The SODA JERK gives Scott back the picture, shaking his head. Scott turns to go, looks at all the ice cream, stops.

INT. DOCTOR'S OFFICE—STRASBURG, PA.—DAY—MOS

Midge and a NURSE are looking at the picture. A DOCTOR comes out of an office. It's Willam, the doctor we met at the farm. He sees Midge. He sees the picture.

EXT. MAIN STREET—STRASBURG, PA.—DAY

Scott waits by the car with an ice cream cone in each hand. Midge approaches with Willam. The sense of Red having been found registers on his face.

INT. BARN—HAY LOFT—DAY

Red stretches and goes to the loft doors and looks out across the farm fields. And her heart stops.

RED'S POV

She sees the Wal-mart truck parked far off in the distance.

INT. BARN—HAY LOFT—CONTINUOUS

Red begins to hyperventilate. She spins, confused and

frightened. She runs past Amanda. Amanda chases after her.

At the far end of the corn field a SHERIFF'S PATROL CAR pulls up behind the Wal-mart truck, with its lights flashing.

EXT. FARM—CONTINUOUS

Red runs out of the barn and away into the fields.

EXT. EDGE OF CORNFIELD—WAL-MART TRUCK

Two SHERIFF'S DEPUTIES check the truck for the driver. Not finding him, they draw their weapons and head into the field.

EXT. CORN FIELD—DAY

Red runs for her life, bursting up one row and down another, getting cut by the stalks, getting more lost by the minute.

EXT. COUNTRY LANE—CORN FIELDS—DAY

Scott's VW tears down the road and skids to a stop by the Wal-mart truck and the Sheriff's patrol car. Scott, Midge, and Willam pile out and look around anxiously. Scott panics.

> SCOTT
> Jesus! Where is he? Red!

He runs into the field desperate to find his sister. Midge and Willam chase after him.

EXT. CORN FIELD—DAY

Red runs from one row of corn to another. She hears Scott call but doesn't know who he is, which scares her more.

The Sheriff's Deputies charge through the corn. They hear Scott, too, and wonder if he's the guy they're looking for.

Scott crashes from one row to the next, calling Red's name.

Red makes a quick turn and comes to a sudden, complete stop. She is face-to-face with Mr. Lucky.

> MR. LUCKY
> We gotta talk.

Red backs away from him, shaking in fear. He keeps on coming.

> MR. LUCKY
> Do what I say and I won't hurt you. Just do what I say.

He reaches for her. A loud noise behind them startles them. Mr. Lucky spins, and winds up facing an insanely angry Scott coming at him.

> SCOTT
> You stupid fucking man.

Mr. Lucky steps back. Red looks at Scott, scared to death.

> SCOTT
> It's okay, honey. It's okay.

Another CRUNCH startles them. They turn.

> SHERIFF DEPUTY ONE
> (aims at Scott)
> It's okay, if you hold it right there, son.

Deputy Two steps out from another angle, with deadly aim.

> SHERIFF DEPUTY TWO
> Back off very, very slowly.

Scott hesitates. Then, suddenly crunching sounds pop all around them. They freeze as a dozen farmers step out from the corn, armed with pitchforks.

> JOSEPH
> Leave the girl alone. All of you. Take your guns and leave my land.

Mr. Lucky takes advantage of the distraction, and runs for it. The Deputies give chase, firing their weapons as they do, and all hell breaks loose.

The farmers protect Red and hit the ground for cover. Bullets and bodies fly.

Mr. Lucky doesn't get far. The wild hail of the Deputies' shots scream around him, cutting down the stalks. He is hit from behind. His legs go out from under him, and he falls, screaming in pain. The Deputies rush in and pin him down.

Scott pushes past the farmers to Red. He scoops her up in his arms.

> SCOTT
> You're safe. You're safe now.

Suddenly the cornstalks crash behind the Deputies. They spin and raise their guns. Scott covers Red.

Midge stumbles through the stalks, out of breath. She scans the scene frantically, finally seeing Scott and Red.

> MIDGE
> Thank God.

She takes another step and buckles in pain. She grabs her side, blood oozing from a gun wound, and looks to Scott and smiles weakly. And collapses.

This Is the End of Act Two.
They caught the bad guy. They found Red.

In Act Three our protagonist and co-protagonist will have to face the difficult question: What now? Now that they have fallen in love, what do they do? Do they go back to their lives as they were? Is that even possible? The answers to these emotional questions are in the film's resolution.

21

Writing the Script—Act Three

Act Three:
A New Beginning

A friend and writer who mentored me when I was a youngster in the business was fond of saying "the final act writes itself." I thought he was crazy. I always found the final act difficult and far from writing itself. Now I am older and a wee bit wiser, and I understand today what I couldn't then. He knew his characters and he knew what issues they had to resolve. Knowing that meant he knew what his ending had to be. No, the ending didn't write itself literally. But it wasn't a big puzzle, either. He knew that in his last fifteen or so pages he was going to need a handful of scenes to wrap everything up and he had a very good idea what those scenes would be.

We are now in that same position. We have known our ending from the start. And now we have arrived at the moment of truth.

This is where we will endeavor to create what William Goldman calls "the inevitable surprise."

In our plot we will bring our protagonist and antagonist together in a final confrontation; with the encouragement of our co-protagonist our hero will win the battle. He will save the day, catch the bad guy, rescue the damsel in distress. He may or may not survive, but his purpose will.

These scenes of the final confrontation will embody the climax to the plot.

And we know that in the aftermath of the *plot* we will need a few scenes to clear up the story. They will involve the forecast of the hero's future, or the future he has endowed as a result of his heroic actions.

> **These scenes, dealing with the emotional fallout of everything that has happened along the way, will embody the script's resolution. Your climax answers the question, Who will win?**

In the finale of *The Thomas Crown Affair* the scenes that formed the climax dealt with the confrontation between the thief and the police. Would Thomas Crown get away with the theft of another masterpiece right under the noses of a massive security force? Or would he get caught in the trap set up by his co-protagonist, who drifted back into co-antagonist mode because she could not trust her ability to live with his love at any cost? This is a classic plot climax and it would be worth your while to watch it now and then for inspiration. It has a great energy, and the combination of mystery and emotional anxiety creates terrific tension.

> **Your resolution answers the question, Now what?**

Immediately after the climax in *The Thomas Crown Affair* the co-protagonist, who knew she did the right thing legally and ethically, now had to deal with the consequences of her choice; her emotional pain. These scenes created the film's resolution.

In *Wonder Boys* the climax arrives on the heels of one disastrous event after another when Michael Douglas, with nothing left to lose really, *finally* makes a choice. He takes the great leap of faith required in all climaxes and publicly declares his love for Frances McDormand even though he is completely uncertain of the fallout. He gets himself "unstuck." The fallout of course will be his resolution and will answer the question, What will happen to him? Here the writer can choose the ending that pleases him most. Happy ending or sad? Michael Douglas' Grady Tripp finally chose, now the writer must.

Think of your final fifteen to twenty pages framed in these references. Look to other great films you have admired. Films that made you feel good. Films that moved you and inspired you. Keep foremost in your thinking that goal for your ending. Move and inspire your audience.

We have seen how many films end back where they began. The valid point in doing this is to demonstrate the resolution in action. Your hero has returned home a different man or woman than when he or she left. How does this difference now affect everything else in his or her life? What will happen now? What does the future look like? Was this trip worth it? The answers to these metaphysical and emotional questions all add up to the point of your film and the reason you wanted to write it in the first place. However, I must warn you not to confuse a resolution with a summary. You cannot wait until this point in your film to explain what it's about. That has to have been made clear throughout. The ending is not a summary. The ending is the beginning anew.

Like the sign says, wash your hands.

The most important occurrence between the protagonist and the co-protagonist in the film up to this point has been what I call the "cleansing scene." This is where they "come clean" with each other. If they don't do this they will not be able to go to the next stage in their relationship. If you don't have a "cleansing scene" you have to go back and find out where it should have happened and write it. This is critical. It removes any improper motive from the table. It purifies the hero's intent. It raises his reasoning and his reason for being above the physical and material boundaries in which he finds himself entangled. He will now act according to the calling of his higher purpose. This is not grandiose. This is the moment when his life is given new meaning. Sometimes it is the first time the hero has found any meaning at all. Don't underestimate the dramatic power this shift will give you and your hero.

In my script of *Indirection* the cleansing literally takes place in the shower of the hotel room after Scott brings Midge home from her near fatal run-in with Rico. She confesses all, giving up in the process her will to revenge her brother's murder. Rather than be furious with her for derailing their effort to rescue his runaway sister, Scott comforts Midge. He knows exactly what she's going through and he knows intuitively that it's more important for him to acknowledge that and assuage her fears than it is to vent his own anger. In fact he is not angry at all. And this is a classic sign that he has reached the fringes of stage four of the Four Stages of Mastery. He is acting unconsciously competent in the matter because he senses the higher purpose of the moment. This enables him to disclose to her feelings about the nature of their hearts' dilemma passionately and selflessly. His only concern in the "cleansing scene" is her welfare, not his own. No hidden agenda, no motive other than the obvious.

This mutual exposure to the most intimate source of fear creates a bond that will last forever if they choose to honor it. For the immediate future it will certainly be more than enough for them to face the antagonist. For the antagonist in their story isn't the bad guy, it's their own fearful behavior, which is the behavior of their histories. Now that behavior must be left in the new past as they go forward.

The strength of the new bond will be most in evidence in the resolution. It is the strength of knowing what is right. You might recall that earlier we said that we might not always know what is right, but we always know what is wrong. Well, now, in the newness of their ways they will know intuitively what is right, as well. This is the true sign that change has turned to growth. The sign of growth is the foundation of your resolution. Is your protagonist about to show his growth? Double check now, then start your Act Three.

My Act Three picks up right after Midge collapsed from her gunshot wound in the cornfield. Time has passed and she is being tended to in the house. I've given myself nine or ten pages to finish up my story. I want to express three resolutions. First, I want to resolve Red and Scott's situation. Did she feel abandoned by him? Did she blame him for anything? Could he make it up to her now if she did feel abandoned? Second, I want to resolve Midge and Red's situation. Midge owes Red a big apology. And Red has the right to let her have it. And finally I want to resolve the relationship between Midge and Scott. What will they do now?

Indirection – Act Three

INT. FARM HOUSE—BEDROOM—DAY

Willam and Scott finish cleaning and bandaging Midge's wound.

> WILLAM
> I appreciate your help, Scott. I don't treat many gunshot wounds.

> SCOTT
> That must be nice.

> WILLAM
> Fortunately it's just a flesh wound. But you're going to have a nice scar.

> SCOTT
> How's the pain?

> MIDGE
> Not bad. How's your sister?

Scott looks out the window toward the pond where Red and some of the other children are sitting.

> WILLAM
> Scars of a different kind.

> MIDGE
> Go see her. I'm in good hands.

This is the start of Red and Scott's resolution. I will break it up with another scene at one point just so it doesn't seem like it goes on forever.

EXT. FARM HOUSE—DAY

The Deputies put Mr. Lucky in the squad car. The

family watches with a mixture of fear and fascination. Joseph and Katherine look toward the pond.

EXT. FARM—BY THE POND—DAY

Scott and Red walk along the pond's edge as she studies the frayed picture of her and Scott.

> RED
> We sure look alike.
> (struggling)
> I'm... trying. But I can't..

> SCOTT
> It's okay. It'll get better, Red. It'll all come back once we get home.

> RED
> Red? And all this time I've been trying to come up with a name.

> SCOTT
> Eileen. Eileen Elizabeth Peck. You're fifteen. You live with Mom in Muncie, Indiana.

> RED
> With Mom. No Dad? Or you?

> SCOTT
> Dad left us a long time ago. I live in New York. I drive an ambulance. You visit me sometimes. We goof off.

> RED
> Do I visit New York a lot?

> SCOTT
> Every couple of months.

                    RED
To see you?

                   SCOTT
I'd like to think so.

                    RED
You'd *like* to think so? Or you *do* think so?

                   SCOTT
                 (the truth)
It can get hard for you at home with Mom.
Coming to see me helps, but obviously not
enough to fix things. So this week, instead
of coming to see me, you hit the road with
what you called "a one-way ticket to independence."

                    RED
Good grief. I ran away.

                   SCOTT
Sooner or later, it's what we all do.

                    RED
Sooner or later, do we all go home?

The million dollar question.

INT. FARM HOUSE—BEDROOM—DAY

Midge sits on the bed looking out the window at Red
and Scott. There's a gentle knock on the door.

                  AMANDA
Dr. Willam says lots of liquids.

Amanda joins her, offering her a glass of juice. She carries a simple white blouse with her.

> AMANDA
>
> And here's a clean blouse for you.

> MIDGE
>
> Thank you.

Amanda studies Midge as she sips the juice.

> AMANDA
>
> Is he your boyfriend?

> MIDGE
>
> No. I was just helping him out.

> AMANDA
>
> That's very nice.

Amanda crosses to the window and watches Red and Scott.

> AMANDA
>
> She seems very nice, too. I like her. She's brave.

> MIDGE
>
> Brave.

> AMANDA
>
> Because it must be very scary.

> MIDGE
>
> To have no memory?

> AMANDA
>
> To have to run away.

This is an innocent observation made by Amanda to Midge. It is my way of letting her speak for me. Midge needs to be reminded that running away is not a good option anymore.

Midge nods knowingly.

EXT. FARM—BY THE POND—DAY

Red turns to Scott and gives him back the picture.

> RED
>
> I know how hard it must have been for you to find me. And I'm really grateful. But, I'm going to pass.

> SCOTT
>
> Pass? On what?

> RED
>
> On your invitation to go with you.

> SCOTT
>
> My invitation?

> RED
>
> Look at me. It's like I'm two days old. I mean, that's all I remember. And in those two days I've been smacked on the head, assaulted, molested, and left for dead in a corn field.

> SCOTT
>
> Yeah, but...

> RED
>
> ...but, for whatever reason, Fate made sure I was left in this corn field, with this family, who have cared for me and given me hope.
> (pointedly) Things any girl would run away for.

This is the conclusion to their reconciliation and resolution. These can be tricky waters to sail, so take your time and don't be surprised if you feel you need to re-work it a number of times to get it just right.

                    SCOTT
You can't mean what you're saying.

                    RED
If I hated it enough to leave in the first
place...

                    SCOTT
Hate's a bit strong. You didn't hate anything, you were angry.

                    RED
Still...angry enough to run away. Why go
back?

                    SCOTT
Because you live there.

                    RED
That's not a very good reason.

                    SCOTT
You're serious.

                    RED
I need more time to figure things out.
There's no rush to go back. As far as I'm
concerned, there's no rush to remember.
Maybe not remembering is good.

Scott knows this includes him as well. It stings.

                    SCOTT
Red, you're not making sense.

                    RED
Yes, I am. You know I am. It's just not the

answer you came for. *(beat)* I have to make sure of the answers I've come for.

SCOTT
Once you're home, the answers will come easier.

RED
"Home?" Apparently I've been "home" all my life and there is no "home" there. And there are no answers there. I need time away from the past, because I need to know who I am, not who I was. Why does that bother you?

SCOTT
It bothers me because I should have been a big part of who you were, and I wasn't. And now I want to make up for that and be a big part of who'll you'll be.

RED
You can start by letting me go.

SCOTT
I can't let you go.

RED
Can't or won't?

SCOTT
You're my baby sister.

RED
That will never change.

He eases.

> SCOTT
> I'm going to have to do it in stages.

She takes his hand and walks him back to the house.

> SCOTT
> I'll call you every week. Just to see if you need anything.

> RED
> Does it look like I'm going to need anything here? I'm going to be fine.

> SCOTT
> I'm calling anyway.

> RED
> Let's go see how your girlfriend's doing.

> SCOTT
> She's not my girlfriend.

> RED
> Who is she then?

> SCOTT
> Someone I met along the way. And even though I hate to admit it, I couldn't have found you without her.

> RED
> Why is that something you hate to admit?

He thinks about that.

INT. FARM HOUSE—BEDROOM—DAY

Midge buttons the clean blouse as Red and Scott enter.

> RED
>
> How are you feeling?

> MIDGE
>
> Good. It looks a lot worse than it is. The real question is, How are you?

> RED
>
> I look a lot worse than I am, too.

> MIDGE
>
> I'll be ready in a minute. You must be dying to get home.

Red and Scott share a look.

> SCOTT
>
> Take your time.

Midge looks at each of them, realizing something's up.

> MIDGE
>
> What?

There is an awkward silence. Scott moves to the door.

> SCOTT
>
> You know, if I'm going to call you every week, I'm going to need their phone number. See you downstairs.

> MIDGE
>
> Call you every week?

> RED
>
> I told him he didn't have to.

MIDGE
You're staying?

RED
That he didn't have to worry about me here.

MIDGE
You're kidding.

Now I have the chance to resolve the issues between Red and Midge... and add a few surprises to give the ending more fun.

Remember that your ending should be uplifting. We don't want to bum the audience out. We want them to be happy they paid to see your film. Make them wish they were friends with your characters.

RED
But he's a little stubborn.

MIDGE
It must run in the family.

Midge drifts over to the window and Red follows.

RED
He said he wouldn't have found me without your help.

MIDGE
He wouldn't have needed to find you in the first place if it weren't for me either.

She turns to face Red, and to face the truth.

MIDGE
You may not remember it, but I started all your troubles.

RED
Memory or no memory, I seriously doubt that you started all my troubles. I have a feeling they were around long before you.

                    MIDGE
In New York, while you were waiting for
your train in Grand Central, I picked your
pocket and stole all your money. What should
have been a good trip for you turned into a
nightmare, and it almost cost you your life.
I never meant for that to happen.

                    RED
Whatever happened, it all worked out in the
end.

                    MIDGE
But what you went through to get here...

                    RED
Is what we all go through to get here. A lot
of us never get here at all.

                    MIDGE
I really am sorry.

Red studies her for a beat, then gestures out the window at the beautiful, surrounding countryside.

                    RED
If I'm safe and sound because of something
you did, you hardly owe me an apology. Look
around. I'm in the best place in my life.

Midge looks around at the countryside and nods.

                    MIDGE
It is amazing here. It's like heaven on earth.

                    RED
It sure as hell beats Disney World.

Midge is STUNNED. She starts to say something but Red raises her hands to still her. She smiles at Midge.

> Surprise!

                    RED
If you had a choice to live with a family that wants to take care of you, or go back to where there is no family at all, what would you do?

                  MIDGE
This isn't about what I would do.

                    RED
You're avoiding the question.

                  MIDGE
No I'm not.

                    RED
Would you go back?

                  MIDGE
You have a brother.

> The smart-ass attitudes are gone, replaced with generosity. This is honesty in action. And this particular honesty is about to create a valuable trust on the next page.

                    RED
Yes or no, would you go back?

Midge tries to find an argument.

                  MIDGE
                 (finally)
No.

                    RED
                 (gently)
Then why are you?

MIDGE

For starters, you have a family taking care
of you. I don't.

RED

That depends on your definition of family.

Red glances out the window at Scott standing by the
car chatting with the Joseph and Katherine.

RED

It's funny. It's easy for me to
stay here. The hard part is
watching him go. I know he
hasn't always worried about
me. But, I have always worried about him.

> How far these girls
> have come. They were al-
> ways smart. Now they are
> wise.
>
> You *must* express their
> wisdom in their final
> scenes for the audience to
> see and appreciate.
>
> It is unconscious com-
> petence in action.
>
> **This is not just
> change. This is growth.**

MIDGE

I can see why.

After a long beat Midge turns to Red.

MIDGE

We could make a deal. Forgive
me for what I did, and I'll keep
an eye on your brother for you.
I mean you don't want this guy running
around alone anyway. He's sort of a danger
to society, you know?

Red smiles gratefully.

RED

Deal.

EXT. FARM—DAY

Red, Joseph, Katherine, Dr. Willam, and all the boys and girls say goodbye to Scott and Midge.

Scott helps Midge into the car, then goes around to the driver's side and gets in.

The family waves as the VW heads down the long drive to the county road.

After a long beat the family slowly turns and goes inside.

All except Red, who doesn't budge. She stands alone. Watching. Remembering.

> Now the third resolution. In my heart there was only one way to go with Scott and Midge. Short and sweet and full of hope.

EXT. NEW YORK CITY—AERIAL SHOT—DAY

Manhattan glistens under low clouds and a fine mist.

EXT. NEW YORK CITY STREETS—DAY

From Times Square to Broadway, from The Plaza to McSorley's, the city is on the move.

INT. NEW YORK CITY POLICE STATION—DAY

Devlin sits at his crappy desk in the middle of his crappy precinct. He's on the phone. Nodding. Taking notes. Satisfied, he hangs up, pulls on his jacket, and moves out.

EXT. GRAND CENTRAL STATION—DAY

Midge hangs up the phone in the phone booth. Looks around the great room with its thousands of lost souls, and heads for the exit.

INT. PECK HOUSE—KITCHEN—DAY

Mary Anne, Red and Scott's mother, sits at the table, the phone to her ear. Relief comes to her face. Then tears. She hangs up and looks over to Warren who paints a doorjamb.

INT. SCOTT PECK'S SUB-STREET LEVEL APART-MENT—DAY

Scott hangs up the phone. He tries to slide the picture of Red and him back into the picture frame, but it's a disaster. He leans it against the frame, instead.

He crosses to his closet and opens it. There are very few things hanging on hangers. He shoves them all to one side, leaving empty hangers hanging on the other side.

He goes to his small bureau and takes his things out of the top drawer and jams them into the bottom drawer.

He looks around. Takes a deep breath.

MIDGE (V.O.)
I see now that we need each other.

EXT. CEMETERY—DAY

Midge sits at Lonnie's grave site. There is no perma-nent headstone yet, just a small, temporary plaque with Lonnie's name on it. Midge has flowers in her lap. She is saying a prayer. And she is crying.

MIDGE

Because no matter where I go, I can't go without you. No matter what happens to me, you are a part of it. No matter who else I love, I will never love you less. No matter what it takes, I'll do better so you'll be proud of me. I'll change what I have to change. I'll even grow up. But you'll always know it's me.

> I discovered that I had one more resolution to deal with. This mirrors Scott's scene with Red. I like how it feels.

She sees Scott's ambulance pull up and park. She lays the flowers next to Lonnie's nameplate and gets up.

MIDGE

I'm scared, you know? But it's a happy scared if that makes any sense. I don't know, maybe it doesn't. Maybe life isn't supposed to make sense. Maybe I should just live it instead of trying to figure it out. Maybe the best way to do that is not alone anymore.

She turns and walks toward the ambulance. A breeze shudders the flower pedals. And the mist closes in.

FADE OUT.

THE END

You can see that it doesn't take a huge page count to cover a lot of ground. All of my stories were resolved in about ten pages. You should be able to do the same. I say that with confidence because you already know what you have to resolve. You won't be wasting any time wandering around in unnecessary scenes desperately searching for a way to say goodnight. You should be ready and eager to get to the ending you've been working toward, and you can be confident that they will be satisfying scenes to write and they will be entertaining and memorable for your audience.

The resolution scenes do more than wrap up your story, they demonstrate that the end is really the beginning for your characters. They give you the chance to express your personal view, emotionally and artistically, regarding this issue. That for all of us, when we have the courage to face our ghosts we can move on with confidence to a better life.

Always remember that the ending is about the future, not about what happened in the ninety pages. Don't go back over old ground if you can help it. Focus on what will come next in the lives of your wonderful characters. Everyone in your audience wants to know what's going to happen, because they want to be reassured that life can get better. In particular, they want to know that their lives can get better. Let them know it can.

Know when enough is enough. When your point has been made, stop.

Grace and directness, without pomp and sanctity, reflect your certitude that what you've told us is worth our attention. If you have done this, you have done enough. Let the script go. It has a life of its own now.

The Fish Never Knows the Water

Zen Ko'an

Men wander. From the Garden of Eden to the Garden at Madison Square we have wandered through millennia with questionable consequence. We wander without meaningful awareness of direction or distance, drawn to the horizon of promise, imagining in its glow an assumption of glory. We cross the landscape without a knowing. We rush in the direction chosen at dawn that rarely brings us to the night we expect. If the fish does not know the water, then what do we know?

We know the pain our wandering causes.

When we grow tired of the pain we cause ourselves, and become weary of the effort and wary of its promise, then we have reached a crossroads of another kind. It is the crossroads of accountability. There we stand unique among all earth's creatures, because we have a choice. Elephants have no choice. My German Shepherd has no choice. Butterflies, bunny rabbits, and Bambi have no choice.

They keep going. They keep wandering. Our choice is to keep going, too, but not to wander. It *sounds* so simple. As writers we have already learned that choice is no simple matter. Choice is everything. If you are a writer who is tired of wandering and chooses to stop, you *start* something else. Something more meaningful. You start searching. Every serious writer will reach this point sooner or later.

Within the particular time frame of writing your script, your life had its own "wandering fatigue" set in. From fade in to fade out you told the story of the meaningful change in your hero during his journey from one of wandering to one of searching. Did you know that you were changing, too? You became aware that wandering is outward, and that searching is inward. That wandering is earthbound, and that searching has no bounds. That your writing had to be more searching if it was to have real meaning.

As you changed, so has your writing.

I hope you felt your writing shift from wandering to searching. I hope your writing got you under your skin. Because you would be surprised to learn how many screenwriters have never made the journey. Have never felt what you've felt. And I hope you agree with me now that there is no point in writing at all if you're not going to go where you're afraid to go.

Structure is calculable. Emotional structure is incalculable.

You have nurtured your three-sentence idea into a three-page pitch. You have expanded the thoughts in the pitch by using a couple of hundred handy-dandy note cards. You shuffled those cards time and time again until they became the basis for your two-line outline, which you then explored and deepened into a full-blown outline. And finally, using the outline as a guide, you wrote your screenplay. Calculable, yes, but your screenplay has had its solid emotional structure built into it from the very beginning. And that difference is incalculable.

Each step along the way you also clarified, expanded, and strengthened your idea. In a series of artistic choices you brought a vitality and an importance to a story you might not have otherwise known existed. By going deep, you became deep. It took hard work and it took guts, and you owe it to yourself to acknowledge that.

So now what?

Go fish.

You may have heard this before. It's good advice. Put the script in a drawer and leave it alone. Don't look at it again for at least a week. Two weeks is better. Treat yourself to some serious spa time, or whatever else relaxes your mind. A sunny beach? Vegas? I try to get away to my friend's cabin in the middle of a forest where I daydream and do some flyfishing.

You deserve it. And your script deserves it.

When you do get back to your script make absolutely sure you will be alone and uninterrupted. You must read your work from beginning to end without stopping. Straight through without any pen or pencil within reach. No editing or re-reading. No folding corners to mark pages you think need something done to them. Just read.

Focus on what the script says. See your film. This is a very important process, and it is not an editing process. You are trying to put yourself in the shoes of a person who will be seeing this for the first time without any knowledge of its content. In order to get the most out of it you mustn't pause to celebrate or weep. Focus. Read.

Author Deena Metzger notes that Zen masters try to achieve a state they call sho-shim, or "beginner's mind," believing that such a mind remains open to many possibilities while the expert's mind opens to fewer and fewer. It would be very wise of us as writers to keep this open mind, a "beginner's mind," as we read our work. It is extremely challenging, but remain as open as you can.

Your spiritual reflex

My writer friend Jack B. Soward says that writing is more than an occupation, it is a calling. And he's right. Just as it is hard to remain open with a beginner's mind, so it is very hard to remember your calling. Especially as you struggle with your screenplay. It can be very frustrating and at times disappointing. If you are not a full-time screenwriter yet, and 98 percent of screenwriters are not, and you are holding down a day job while you write, these frustrations can be especially devastating. More than ever, take it easy on yourself. The disappointments are not an indication that you lack talent. Disappointments come with the territory. Sometimes we set pretty high goals. Our expectations are often our enemy, because too often expectations are based in comparisons. Don't compare your work to anyone else's. Stay within yourself. You will know when your work is good. You will know when your script is finished and ready to go to market. You will know this because as a writer you have a gift that is uncommon in others. I call it your spiritual reflex. This spiritual reflex points writers in the direction of purposeful expression. Your spiritual reflex is your very own emotional depth finder. It is unique in all creation. Trust it.

Earlier you wrote a page describing how you were like your mother and on the back of the page how you were different. The purpose of that assignment wasn't to judge who was better or brighter or stronger. The purpose was to see if you could appreciate the similarities and differences *without* judging. Observing without judgment is the writer's duty. It is the most important talent a writer can cultivate. No matter how close to home the writing comes, objectivity and grace—a spiritual generosity—are necessary. I hope you found, in writing about your mother, two wonderful people. Your mother, and you. I hope that as you grow as a writer and as a person your spiritual reflex will refine your mercy, and expand your heart.

I hope you learn that appreciating every thing for what it is, and every person for who he is, will develop your writer's soul.

The world needs good writers.

Be one.

25 Films Every Screenwriter Should Study

This list is not a list of the most popular films or the most honored, necessarily. It is, rather, a list of films whose Emotional Structures I have found particularly helpful to study. They range from oldies-but-goodies to brand spanking new; they vary from shades of gray to glorious color; they run the gamut of genres, and they speak in many languages. Some of them are the best of their kind; others, while not exactly the best, are pretty damn good. This is a list of films for writers, in honor of writers. And even more important it is a list to encourage writers to go beyond the obvious in their work. To take the high road of storytelling—the one called truth. To use all the senses. To write what you know better than anyone else can. To write with conviction and compassion. To illuminate.

This list is not constructed in any particular order. Every one of these films deserves to be recognized without the burden of numbering them as other lists insist upon. I encourage you to add your favorites to this list, and in doing so, honor those screenwriters who have gone before us and shown us the way.

Shakespeare in Love
Screenplay by Marc Norman and Tom Stoppard

This script is a great example of how plot and story can be seamlessly interwoven to create the purest form of epigenetic development. The character of Shakespeare writes an utterly romantic stage play inspired by a woman who in turn gives life to the romance through a performance inspired by his gift of words. She inspires his words (plot) as he inspires her flowering (story).

Children of a Lesser God
Screenplay by Hesper Anderson and
Mark Medoff, based on a play by Mark Medoff

A prime example of Emotional Structure in every way. Watch for the peeling away of the four emotional levels of the protagonist. How fascinating to show rather than tell how the heart feels by using visual language—sign language—to emphasize the emotions. These are not empty words, clearly. Notice, too, how at the turning point of the film the teacher becomes the student. Great work all around by the director Randa Haines, and the lead actors Marlee Matlin and William Hurt.

Sideways
Screenplay by Alexander Payne and
Jim Taylor, based on Rex Pickett's novel

If Emotional Structure teaches us anything, it teaches us that we are all afraid to open up—to be vulnerable. Here is the story of four terrific characters each suffering from that hopeless modern malady of exposure to truth. The antagonist in the piece is vulnerability itself. Each of us only wants to be safe. And each of us needs to be heard. And that is the crux of the matter in *Sideways*—being heard begins the healing. Such a simple plot structure that holds at its side a complex and intelligent story.

L.A. Confidential
Screenplay by Brian Helgeland and
Curtis Hanson, based on the novel by James Ellroy

James Ellroy writes pure emotion whether in his fiction or non-fiction work. It is a testament to his talent and to Brian Helgeland's that nothing was lost in the translation from book to film. The sprawling plot and the large cast do nothing to diminish the intimate power of human exposure. Everyone in the film faces a difficult transition, and the Emotional Structure weaves all of those individual transitions into an epigenetic sequence that produces a flawless and increasingly powerful story. This is L.A. Noir at its best and is in many ways more accomplished than Robert Towne's *Chinatown*.

Network
Screenplay by Paddy Chayefsky

This is the granddaddy of films about the media's insidious hold on us, and I include *Citizen Kane* in that. Paddy Chayefsky won just about every award imaginable for his original screenplay, and deservedly so. This is a prime example of making a social statement with your script. The antagonist in *Network* is *not* the network. The antagonist is our complacency. It is a monumental task to take such a concept and embody it so convincingly. The absurdities of his suggestions about a future culture become entirely believable because of his ability to ground the plot and story with a spectacular Emotional Structure—an Emotional Structure teeming with riveting personal, emotional journeys. It's all about human nature, and in particular human denial. When you reduce your plot and story to human nature—with all its frailties—you, too, will create a great film.

Good Night, and Good Luck
Written by George Clooney and Grant Heslov

While we're looking at the power of the press, this film emphasizes the paradox that threatens it. With the influence it possesses comes the allegiance to an unblinking truth. And we know that truth will not tolerate fear. So, in this case, the enemy of the press is the enemy of the truth, which is fear. Once again we have the protagonist representing truth and the antagonist representing fear. This is a film that delivers an important history lesson for screenwriters—never embellish the facts for fear your story won't be interesting. Make the facts interesting. That is your job. Do not fudge the facts. That is fear's job.

Broadcast News
Screenplay by James L. Brooks

I include this film here because it takes a completely different tack on the theme of truth in broadcasting. Writer and director James L. Brooks reduces his theme to a very personal story between three people who must wrestle with their personal ethical standards. This is a film about personal choice, and is a good example of how some characters can grow and change in your story while others may not. The protagonist, Holly Hunter, represents Truth—no matter how painful, while the antagonist, William Hurt, represents Truth's compromise. Here's the interesting thing: While compromise's hallmark is change, it is never about growth. Remember: change is inevitable, growth is optional. Brooks has a lot of fun with this timely and relevant topic, but never compromises its importance.

The African Queen
Screenplay by James Agee and John Huston,
based on the novel by C. S. Forester

We've talked about this wonderful film in the text of the book, but maybe not enough. Settle in for a long look at its very clear and powerful use of the structure we've studied. Our deepest fears create our outer beings and none are more profound creations than Humphrey Bogart's Charlie or Katharine Hepburn's Rose. The wars they fight against the Germans and against the treacherous environment are nothing compared to the war they fight against the stuff they've stuffed down all their lives. The events of the plot force the revelations of the story. Little by little, as they change so do they grow. A wonderful human story against a larger-than-life plot.

The Lion in Winter
Screenplay by James Goldman

A perfect example of a film that takes on the complexities of global history through the hearts of personal history. A film of monumental achievement in its application of Emotional Structure. James Goldman's screenplay illuminates the universality of humankind across the centuries, and shows us that fear does not have an expiration date. Fear does not live outside of us. Breathtaking performances all around. But they would not be breathtaking without the power of Goldman's extraordinary intelligence and wit. This is a film all screenwriters should watch at least once a year.

The Cider House Rules
Screenplay by John Irving, based on his novel

John Irving won an Oscar for this screenplay adaptation of his novel, and it is probably one of the finest screen adaptations of all time. The language of film and the language of novel are so completely different, yet Irving is a master at both. Knowing when to let the picture tell the story, and not to "over-write" dialog, is the hallmark of this film. The use of the correspondence between the protagonist and his mentor is an exquisite transformation of the first-person novel narrative to first-person film dialog. Using this technique allows the author to make jumps in the plot and the story seamlessly, while he compresses the sheer volume of the work into a manageable screenplay length. The use of the correspondence also keeps the epigenetic structure of the plot and the story vibrant. A great Emotional Structure to study time and again.

The Quiet American
Screenplay by Christopher Hampton and
Robert Schenkkan, based on the novel by Graham Greene

Just consider the pedigree of the writing for a minute. These guys seriously know what they're doing. Greene's ability to create characters of enormous emotional complexity and depth is on full display. Playwrights and screenwriters Hampton and Schenkkan (a Pulitzer Prize dramatist himself) handle the adaptation from novel to screen with such precision and compassion that it takes one's breath away. All the troubles of the world seem to be carved onto the face and into the heart of Michael Caine's journalist, Fowler, who is stuck in the heartbreak of his own disappointing life. The Emotional Structure is subtle and layered and gorgeous. I have watched this film many times when I'm "stuck" myself. Enjoy and learn.

Besieged
Screenplay by Clare Peploe and
Bernardo Bertolucci, based on a story by James Lasdun

Il Maestro is in rare form here. This is a two-character play starring Thandie Newton in a career defining performance, and the always-understated David Thewlis, who are worlds apart in birthright yet living desperately similar lives of loneliness and fear. Each must learn from the other how to cope and how to hope. This is a great illustration of the lessons we have studied regarding the things that bind us not being the things we have, but rather the things we have lost. It is this kind of loss that makes compassion and vulnerability possible. Because the writers bind the plot and story with inextricable epigenetic composition, the film is as emotionally elegant as film can be. Study the push and pull of protagonist and antagonist, and of plot against story.

This Is My Father
Written and directed by Paul Quinn

This is a case study in the power of personal history and the frequently unresolved connection to it. Who is to blame for that disconnect? Powering the historical plot in this film, as the antagonist against which the innocent young men and women are forbidden to battle, is the oppression of organized religion. The Emotional Structure never stops building upon itself, until our hearts are broken in the end.

Eve's Bayou
Written and directed by Kasi Lemmons

Just as in *This Is My Father*, Kasi Lemmons' emotional reconstruction of her personal history in *Eve's Bayou* brings a family, an era, a place, a race, and an infidelity together in an extraordinary drama. This is a solid film on every level because the Emotional Structure is so vibrant and vital. This is a story of nuance and grace—of dignity and fortitude—that gives more than voice to history. It gives it value. As writers, we must never underestimate the power of our own personal history.

About a Boy
Screenplay by Peter Hedges, Chris Weitz and
Paul Weitz, based on the novel by Nick Hornby

The Emotional Structure built into Nick Hornby's clever story depends on the details in each character's behavior being absolutely honest at all times... even when characters are lying. Very much like *Witness*, this plot continues to force the protagonist into a world where his tools of survival are inadequate. As he learns new ones, he must succumb to the emotions attached to them...Remember: Everything (and every little boy) comes with strings attached. Look for the midpoint that turns to plot into service of the story, and notice how "character" is the key to all things.

Talk to Her
Written and directed by Pedro Almodovar

When we talk about the power of personal history in drama, we must not only consider ancient history. Sometimes history was just last year, or last month, or yesterday. Here, in Pedro Almodovar's riveting drama of missteps and the misery that accompanies them, we see that personal history can also be a living history, and one that can still be affected. *Talk to Her* is a story of intimate courage in all its beautiful and painful glory. Observe how little an incident can be to still cause a great emotional upheaval. In my estimation, this is Almodovar's finest screenplay.

The Motorcycle Diaries

Screenplay by Jose Rivera, based on the books
The Motorcycle Diaries by Ernesto "Che" Guevara and
Traveling with Che Guevara by Alberto Granado

The intertwining of plot and story in this film is masterful. There isn't a false beat in the movie, really, and there isn't a moment when it doesn't open your heart. If we were all to pay attention to the things that matter in this world, and to the things that matter to us, and embrace those things in our stories, we, too, might create our own *Motorcycle Diaries*. Each incident the two close friends face brings with it an emotional and ethical component with which they must contend. Remember the passage we studied from Thomas Merton's *Seeds of Contemplation* telling us that everything and every moment in our lives plants something in our soul. This biographical film captures that phenomena so exquisitely it hurts. If you are contemplating writing a biographic film then you should make a commitment to study *The Motorcycle Diaries* in depth.

Out of Africa

Screenplay by Kurt Luedtke, based on
the novel *Out of Africa* by Isak Dinesen

So much can be said about this film that I have just said about *The Motorcycle Diaries*. The care and the wisdom used by Kurt Luedtke and the director Sydney Pollack while distilling the mounds of autobiographical material into a cohesive and passionate portrait is incomparable in modern filmmaking. Each and every time I watch this film it is as if it were the first time. I am always surprised by some detail I hadn't noticed before, and I am always moved by the emotions of each character. My goal as a writer will always be to reach your emotions with mine. *Out of Africa* teaches me time and again how powerful the results can be.

Nowhere in Africa
Screenplay by Caroline Link, based on the novel by Stephanie Zweig

I can't help pairing this film with the one above. Though they are completely different in nature and tone, they are equal in personal and emotional power. This story is also one of a family relocating to Africa, and the struggle to adapt to a new life while holding onto a semblance of the past. Its Emotional Structure is as clear as a bell, which makes this wonderful film a great study tool. Look for the emotional act breaks as you go along, and especially look for the tent pole scene that turns the whole story in an entirely different direction. For me, films like this, based on fact and the facts of life, are always more powerful than fiction.

Under the Tuscan Sun
Screen story and screenplay by Audrey Wells, based
on the book *Under the Tuscan Sun* by Frances Mayes

I can't remember a film with simpler plot and story structure in recent years. What makes it work, however, is an exacting Emotional Structure. Emotional Structure is not confined solely to works of great seriousness or depth. Commercial films can be good films, and are no exception to the Emotional Structure paradigm. *Under the Tuscan Sun* is a fine and fun example of a romantic comedy shored up with solid emotional architecture. If you are working on a light-hearted romantic comedy, you would do well to study the ease and clarity in this film's Emotional Structure. Once it's in place, all the fun can begin.

Picnic
Screenplay by Daniel Taradash, based
upon the play *Picnic* by William Inge

The play's the thing. Inge won the Pulitzer Prize for his play in 1953. Add the director Joshua Logan of *Mr. Roberts* and *South Pacific* fame, and Daniel Taradash who won the 1953 Oscar for *From Here to*

Eternity, and you've got what's known in film circles as *pedigree. Picnic* is a simple, and classic, story. It is reminiscent of so many old Westerns in that the plot centers around a stranger coming to town and stirring things up. In this case, William Holden's Hal Carter rides into town on a freight train, and nothing in Kansas will ever be the same. What he stirs up are all the secrets and fears the rest of the characters shield. It's a classic, and it should be honored by your presence. Jot down the act ends and the tent pole scene as you watch it. There is elegance in simplicity.

To Kill A Mockingbird
Screenplay by Horton Foote, based on the novel by Harper Lee

And speaking of pedigree, this project had it all. Surprisingly, it took a long time to get this film made (some things never change in Hollywood), but when it was made, it was made to perfection. The dual plots of the children's anxiety about a mysterious and tortured neighbor, Boo, and the adults' hatred of a black man, drive the interwoven story of the fear of the unknown. Each plot pushes the fear further into the open where prejudice and lies are exposed. Though by contemporary standards the film may feel stilted and overly simplistic, it is nonetheless, by any standard, a classic example of building an emotional story within a plot about the fear of emotion.

Touchez pas au Grisbi
Screenplay by Jacques Becker, Albert Simonin,
and Maurice Griffe, based on the novel by Albert Simonin

Film noir at its finest. The Emotional Structure even works in French. I can't implore you enough to take the time to find this film and to buy it and watch it every three months. Its act structure and Emotional Structure are crystal clear and cannily clever. There is drama and comedy all in one, and a protagonist everyone will love. If you haven't seen this yet, treat yourself. You deserve this wonderful experience, and as you make note of the act ends and tent pole scene, you will thank me.

Night and the City
Screenplay by Jo Eisinger, based on the novel by Gerald Kersh

Another classic. A down-and-out hustler played by Richard Widmark desperately tries to pull off an easy money scheme. He should have known better. The plot is simple, with nice curves and roadblocks, but the emotional story is as rich as it gets. The emotional build, brought on by a series of fractures in a plan that teeters on collapse, is wonderful. This is another film you will thank me for mentioning. It is a story of compromise, and every man, down-and-out or up-and-coming understands the risks involved. A great tent pole scene.

A Face in the Crowd
Story and screenplay by Budd Schulberg

An uncompromising look at fame and its potential to corrupt anything and anyone. Schulberg and director Elia Kazan, who collaborated as well on the Academy Award-winning *On the Waterfront*, push their plot and story in your face. The style is slick and the writing is sly, and the cumulative effect of one surprise after another is chilling. This film has a fine Emotional Structure and is a good example of weaving plot and story imperceptively. I think everyone who sees it is surprised at his or her sympathy for the protagonist's recklessness and greed. Probably a sign that we all could have easily made the same decisions he did. If anything, let's hope when we make our films we make the same decisions Schulberg and Kazan made. Notice how spare dialog can carry such weight.

Remember, too, those films we mentioned many times in the text of this book, among them, *Witness, The Thomas Crown Affair, Lost in Translation, Wonder Boys, The Fabulous Baker Boys, Casablanca, Manhattan*, and *The Professional*.

The day may well come when your film will be on this list. For now though, it is a good idea for you to add the films that have moved you and made you think. Try to watch them again, as well. Keep them around. They are good friends. Goodness knows every writer needs good friends.

Index

Peter Dunne

P eter Dunne, Emmy and Peabody Award-winning producer, writer, and teacher, has written and/or produced, among others, "Sybil," "CSI," "Jag," "Dallas," "Knots Landing," "Savanah," "Nowhere Man," and "Dr. Quinn: Medicine Woman." He divides his time between Topanga, California and the West of Ireland.

Please visit:
PDunne.com

101 Best Beginnings Ever Written
A Romp through Literary Openings for Writers and Readers
—by Barnaby Conrad

For writers and readers, the first part of every story is the most important. Bestselling author Barnaby Conrad identifies the twelve types of beginnings, teaching writers how to start their stories with forceful, compelling prose that hooks their readers from page one.

❝ A book as wise and companionable as its author, and a superb resource for writer, student and literary bystander alike. Bravo! Ole! ❞
—Christopher Buckley, author of *Thank You for Smoking*

$15.95 ($15.95 *Canada*)

• ISBN 978-1884956-86-7

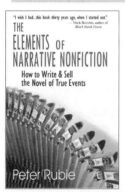

The Elements of Narrative Nonfiction
How to Write & Sell the Novel of True Events
—by Peter Rubie

Author and literary agent Peter Rubie, a former BBC Radio and Fleet Street journalist, provides guidance and practical advice on how best to meld careful journalistic research with narrative writing techniques. Filled with insights and interviews with authors, agents, and editors such as Mark Bowden, Jon Krakauer, Jonathan Galassi, Peter Gethers, George Gibson, and Jack Hart, this is the essential guide to writing this hot new genre.

❝ I wish I had … this book thirty years ago when I started out. ❞
—Mark Bowden, author of *Black Hawk Down*

$15.95 ($15.95 *Canada*)

• ISBN 978-1884956-91-1

The Author's Guide to Building an Online Platform
—by Stephanie Chandler

With more than 175,000 titles published each year, publishers want to sign authors who can market their books through an established online platform. Small business expert Stephanie Chandler shows how even the ordinary guy can successfully build an online marketing platform right from your kitchen table—even if your kitchen table is in Manhattan … Kansas.

$14.95 ($14.95 *Canada*)

• ISBN 978-1884956-82-9

Available at better brick and mortar bookstores, online bookstores, at
QuillDriverBooks.com or by calling toll-free 1-800-345-4447

$14.95 ($19.95 *Canada*)

• ISBN 978-1884956-56-0

101 Best Scenes Ever Written

A Romp through Literature for Writers and Readers

—*by Barnaby Conrad*

Here in one volume you will find beloved scenes you read in the past, or perhaps great scenes you had forgotten, or totally new scenes to be discovered and savored. Any reader will enjoy browsing Barnaby Conrad's choices of the greatest scenes ever written, but the real benefactors of this book will be the countless fledgling writers who will benefit enormously by sampling and studying these gems from the masters of the written word.

❝ A superb book! Indispensible! Get it! ❞
—Ray Bradbury, author of *The Martian Chronicles*

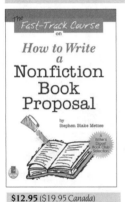

$12.95 ($19.95 *Canada*)

• ISBN 978-1884956-22-X

The Fast-Track Course on How to Write a Nonfiction Book Proposal

—*by Stephen Blake Mettee*

A Writer's Digest Book Club Selection

Mettee, a seasoned book editor and publisher, cuts to the chase and provides simple, detailed instruction that allows anyone to write a professional book proposal and hear an editor say "Yes!"

❝ ...essential, succinct guideline. This is a must have reference book for writers ...sets the industry standard. ❞
—Bob Spear, *Heartland Reviews*

$14.95 ($19.95 *Canada*)

• ISBN 978-1884956-55-6

Damn! Why Didn't I Write That?

How Ordinary People are Raking in $100,000.00 ...Or More Writing Nonfiction Books & How You Can Too!

—*by Marc McCutcheon*

A Book-of-the-Month Club, Quality Paperback Book-Club and Writer's Digest Book Club Selection!

More nonfiction books are breaking the 100,000-copy sales barrier than ever before. Amateur writers, housewives, and even high school dropouts have cashed in with astonishingly simple best-sellers. This guide, by best-selling author Marc McCutcheon, shows the reader how to get in on the action.

❝Comprehensive and engaging this book will save you time, energy, and frustration.❞
—Michael Larsen, literary agent, author